W9-CQB-020

DATE DUE

MAR 26 JAN 18 2000		
DEC 10 75		
DEC 14 77		
FEB 1 79		
JAN 30 80		
OCT 22 80		
MAR 25 81		
FEB 23 83		
DEC 5 84		
FEB 24 '88		
JAN 04 '95		

JAN 3 79

LENDING POLICY
IF YOU DAMAGE OR LOSE LIBRARY
MATERIALS, THEN YOU WILL BE
CHARGED FOR REPLACEMENT. FAIL-
URE TO PAY AFFECTS LIBRARY
PRIVILEGES, GRADES, TRANSCRIPTS,
DIPLOMAS, AND REGISTRATION
PRIVILEGES OR ANY COMBINATION
THEREOF.

Che Guevara

To live is to verify . . .

ALBERT CAMUS

CHE GUEVARA
The Failure of
a Revolutionary

by
LÉO SAUVAGE

Translated from the French by Raoul Frémont

PRENTICE-HALL, Inc., Englewood Cliffs, New Jersey

Also in English by LÉO SAUVAGE

THE OSWALD AFFAIR

Le Cas Guevara copyright by *Editions de la Table Ronde* 1971

Che Guevara: The Failure of a Revolutionary by Léo Sauvage
Translated from the French by Raoul Frémont

Copyright © 1973 by Léo Sauvage

Printed in the United States of America
Prentice-Hall International, Inc., London
Prentice-Hall of Australia, Pty. Ltd., North Sydney
Prentice-Hall of Canada, Ltd., Toronto
Prentice-Hall of India Private Ltd., New Delhi
Prentice-Hall of Japan, Inc., Tokyo

Library of Congress Cataloging in Publication Data
Sauvage, Léo.
 Che Guevara; the failure of a revolutionary.

 Translation of Le cas Guevara.
 Includes bibliographical references.
 1. Guevara, Ernesto, 1928–1967.
F2849.22.G85S2813   1974   980′.03′0924   [B]
ISBN 0–13–128330–8   73–9516

10 9 8 7 6 5 4 3 2 1

Contents

Above all, always be capable of feeling deep inside any injustice committed against anyone anywhere in the world. It is the finest quality of a revolutionary.

CHE GUEVARA
(*Letter to his children*)

The peasant base still is not developing, although it seems that by means of systematic terror we will obtain the neutrality of most of them; support will come later.

CHE GUEVARA
(*Bolivian Diary*)

I

Vallegrande

Remember the photographs? Fidel Castro held them before the Cuban television cameras on Sunday, October 15, 1967, to announce that these pictures published on October 11, plus the news stories of October 9, had convinced him that "this news—that is, news related to the death of Major Ernesto Guevara—is unfortunately true." In Washington, State Department spokesman Robert McCloskey had declared on October 11: "We are inclined to consider these reports as authentic." On the following day Secretary of State Dean Rusk himself said he saw no reason to doubt that "it was indeed Che Guevara." Mr. Rusk did not hold up any photos, but they were in all the newspapers.

The most striking of these showed a dead man on a stretcher. The stretcher had been placed on a huge cement sink, in a slightly forward position because of the faucet. The improvised morgue—there were two other bodies on the ground, at the foot of the sink—was the laundry shed of the Señor de Malta hospital in Vallegrande, a large village in southeastern Bolivia. In other photos, the laundry shed is seen from outside: a small tile-roofed structure, open in front, atop a slope behind the hospital.

About thirty journalists and photographers—including a Frenchman, an Englishman, and a Swede—were there on

October 10, invited by the military authorities to inspect the
corpse. No one had bothered, or had been permitted, to
close the eyes. The hair was abundant, shoulder-length; a
thick mustache, above the open mouth, joined the beard.
On the cheeks, near the long and bushy sideburns, there
were two familiar light spots. The body was clad only in
olive green military pants, rolled up to the calves.

Without proof to the contrary, the body appeared to be
that of an anonymous guerrilla leader who had called
himself Ramón or Fernando.

For the Swedish journalist Bjorn Kumm of the Stockholm
Aftonbladet, there was no doubt: "It was Che," he later
wrote in the *New Republic*. "Much slimmer than he used to
be in the old photographs, smiling at Punta del Este, cutting
cane in Cuba. But that seemed to be a normal consequence
of half a year in the Bolivian jungle."

The French journalist was Marc Hutten of Agence
France Presse. He cabled his Paris office that "at first
glance" there were certain features in common between
"the face of Ramón and that of Guevara as it was known by
his photos." But he had been struck by "an appearance of
extreme youth," which might raise doubts as to the
"presumed Ramón-Guevara identity." Ramón, he said,
seemed to have "hardly passed thirty." Guevara was nearly
forty.

Richard Gott of the Manchester *Guardian* had met
Guevara at a British Embassy reception in Havana in 1963.
The body now seemed to him "smaller and thinner," but,
like his Swedish colleague, he added that this was not
surprising after months in the jungle. Finally, he concluded,
"there is no doubt in my mind that it was the body of Che."

Jailed in Camiri, Régis Debray also had no doubts. On
October 11 he gave his lawyer, Raúl Novillo, a five-page
statement addressed to *Señores Oficiales* of the Court
Martial. It began: "After the heroic death of the man whom

the future and all peoples of the world will place among the great liberators of America. . . ."

The Debray statement was published in Havana on October 14 by *Granma*, the official newspaper of the Cuban Communist Party, across the front page but without comment. A sentence above the headline even identified it as one of the "international reports reproduced for the information of the people." It was under this heading, and with this objectivity unique in the history of the Castro press, that all of the dispatches from the "bourgeois" or indeed "imperialist" press agencies concerning Che's death were published until October 16, the day after Castro's speech.

On October 16, from Vallegrande to Camiri and from Havana to Washington, the conclusion was unanimous: Che was dead, and if the body displayed in the laundry shed of the Señor de Malta hospital had now disappeared, there was no doubt that it had been Che's.

The British art critic John Berger, author of *Success and Failure of Picasso*, was particularly struck by a Vallegrande photo taken by a United Press International photographer. It shows two Bolivian officers describing Che's wounds to the journalists. In an article published in the leftist periodical *The Minority of One* (now defunct), Berger recalls two famous paintings. First, Rembrandt's "Anatomy Lesson":

> There is a resemblance between the photograph and Rembrandt's painting of "The Anatomy Lesson of Professor Tulp." The immaculately dressed Bolivian colonel has taken the Professor's place. Figures on his right stare at the cadaver with the same intense but impersonal interest as the doctors on the Professor's right. There are as many figures in the Rembrandt as in the stable [laundry shed] at Vallegrande. The placing of the corpse in relation to the figures above it, and in the

corpse the sense of global stillness—these, too, are very similar.

The other painting Berger recalled was Mantegna's "Dead Christ."

> The body is seen from the same height. The hands are in identical positions, the fingers curving in the same gesture. The drapery above the lower part of the body is creased and formed in the same manner as the blood-sodden, unbuttoned, olive green trousers on Guevara. The head is raised at the same angle. The mouth is slack of expression, in the same way. Christ's eyes have been shut, for there are two mourners beside him. Guevara's eyes are open, for there are no mourners: only the colonel, a U.S. intelligence agent, a number of Bolivian soldiers, and thirty journalists. . . .

The art critic's conclusion about this photograph is that "we must either dismiss it or complete its meaning for ourselves." And he emphasizes: "It is an image which, as much as any mute image ever can, calls for decision." I don't agree. I believe it calls for the will to understand what happened, and for that kind of courage Camus called "the courage of what one knows."

As for Fidel Castro, in his amazing speech of October 15, 1967, he appeared anxious above all to prove that the image corresponded to reality. Waving the pictures on the television screen, he explained why he was convinced of their authenticity, but not why he had waited so long to state his conviction.°

"In this case it was not a matter of photographs

° All quotations from this speech are taken from the official translation published in the English-language weekly edition of *Granma* (October 22, 1967).

distributed by the government," he said. "It was a matter of photographs that had been taken by numerous newsmen right there in Bolivia, in the very place where the body was. And those newsmen took those pictures and retransmitted them. That means that there was no possibility of a fabricated photograph. The thesis of a fabricated photograph could not be accepted. Other hypotheses: The hypothesis . . . , well, of fabricating a wax figure. It is scarcely probable, nor easy. . . ."

According to the Agence France Presse dispatch that day from Havana, Castro had mentioned still another hypothesis: "It might be considered possible," he is reported to have said before dismissing this and the other hypotheses, "to find or create a double."

I searched in vain for this sentence in the official Spanish and English texts of the speech, and also in a private French version published by Eric Losfeld in Paris in 1968. Perhaps AFP reporter Michel Tourguy's notes were mixed up? It is strange, anyhow, that in addition to the unlikely hypotheses offered only to be quickly discarded, there was one which seemed somewhat less improbable but which was either omitted by Castro or edited out of the printed version.

It certainly is difficult to imagine how photos taken by different photographers could have been faked. The idea of a wax dummy did not stand up any better, and I believe that except for Castro, no one ever bothered to discuss it. The notion of a double, however, was not so farfetched. To begin with, Che Guevara in fact *had* a double among his companions, or at least someone who tried to become one.

Little has been told about the Cuban known among the guerrillas of Nancahuazú by the name of Tuma. Havana eventually confirmed that this was Lieutenant Carlos Coello, son of a peasant, who had joined Castro's men in the Sierra Maestra in 1957, at the age of seventeen. He could neither read nor write, but Che, under whose command he fought in the campaign of Las Villas, promoted him to sergeant, and after the victory sent him to school so that he could become an officer.

In Bolivia, Tuma was not only the personal bodyguard of the commander, but also to some extent his orderly—performing routine chores for Che, carrying his bags, helping him as much as he could during Che's constant asthma attacks.

We owe to Tuma one of the few notes in Guevara's *Bolivian Diary*° in which Che as friend prevails over Che as commander. Tuma was slain on June 26, 1967, in an ambush during which the guerrillas killed four soldiers and captured two prisoners, including a lieutenant of the *carabineros*. In spite of the fact that the ambush was a success, Guevara sums up the day as follows:

> A black day for me. . . . Tuma's wound tore his liver and produced intestinal perforations. He died during the operation. I have lost with him the inseparable companion of all these last years, unfailing in his loyalty, and his absence now strikes me as if he had been my son. . . .

Whether by a sort of affectionate imitation, or more probably as the result of a joint decision aimed at future diversions, Tuma had been working at becoming the physical double of Che. There was little natural resemblance between the two men. Tuma had a rounder face and was darker (in fact he was mulatto). But when Guevara arrived in La Paz on November 3, 1966, with two Uruguayan passports bearing different names but the same photos, Tuma, who was waiting to serve as his chauffeur,

° *El Diario del Che en Bolivia* (Mexico City: Siglo XXI Editores, 1968).

put on the same cap and the same horn-rimmed glasses. In a photo which appeared in every picture magazine in the world, showing a group of guerrillas before a campfire in the woods, Tuma is seated at Guevara's left, the same cap on his head, hands crossed in a similar way, the pipe at the same corner of the mouth. It is impossible not to be struck by the presence, in this picture, of a *double* of Che.

Tuma died on June 26, 1967, and thus could not have been the corpse in Vallegrande. But if the guerrillas, thanks to Tuma, had a man who could eventually pass for Guevara, and make people believe that Guevara was in a place where he was not, why couldn't the Bolivian military, if they thought it useful, have their own double of Che? After all, they had some friends at the CIA who were well equipped to help them.

What appeared most disturbing to me about the Vallegrande photos was not an insufficient resemblance to the face of Che as I remembered it, but on the contrary, a too detailed similarity to the best-known photos of the past.

On November 3, 1966, at La Paz, when Ernesto Guevara de la Serna was known as either Ramón Benítez Fernández or Adolfo Mena González (depending on which passport he pulled from his pocket), the top of his head was shaved clean with only some grey hair left at the back. The *Bolivian Diary*, true enough, tells us that Che was hoping soon to regain his old appearance. Five days after his arrival, on November 12, 1966, he notes with satisfaction that his hair is "growing, even though very sparsely." And the grey is wearing off. "A few more months and I shall be myself again," he rejoices. But wasn't Che too optimistic, even concerning his hair?

According to my New York barber at the time, it would take much longer than eleven months for a completely bald head to grow the shoulder-length hair of the Vallegrande photos. My barber could be wrong, of course; he was a

Cuban refugee, firmly convinced (as they were in Havana when he escaped from there less than two years earlier) that Che had been dead for some time. The hair, however, had not only grown back but now looked exactly the same as in older photos which had not been taken eleven months after total baldness.

Thus it was not impossible that makeup had been applied to the head, and that the makeup artist betrayed himself by following too closely the photos he copied. Since the body had been treated with chemical preservative, the traces of makeup might not have attracted attention. Fidel Castro, after all, went so far as to suggest the theory of a "wax figure," at least long enough to reject it.

The reason given by Castro for rejecting the dubious hypothesis he had conjured up equally applies, I admit, to the more believable hypothesis of a dead man made up to look like Che Guevara.

"From a technical standpoint," Castro said, "they [the Bolivians] would need resources and experience to a degree that doesn't exist there." Castro in the past had credited the CIA with feats requiring resources and experience well beyond that needed to find a good makeup artist. The argument is nonetheless valid, and furthermore it is hard to see at what point the transformation could have been carried out.

There remains one bizarre aspect of the Vallegrande story for which no explanation has ever been given. All the journalists who saw the body mentioned a scar on the back of the left hand, since the Bolivian officer in charge of the "demonstration" had taken care to draw their attention to it. According to him, this was one more proof that it was Che's body: the scar, he said, was the mark of a wound received during the fighting in the Sierra Maestra.

I met Che several times in January 1959, well after that

fighting. I never noticed such a scar. Moreover, no one ever mentioned it to me, although I often heard of a scar on his neck—a souvenir of the disaster of Alegría de Pío on December 5, 1956, when Batista troops surprised the eighty-two men of the Granma three days after they came ashore, decimated and dispersed them, and finally reduced the force to twelve or fifteen. Guevara also had been wounded on the left foot a year later, on December 8, 1957, in a skirmish.

Now in his speech of October 15, 1967, in which he certainly did not try to cast doubt on the "bitter truth," Castro confirmed that nobody around him remembered a scar on Che's left hand. He recalled that Guevara had scars on the neck and on a leg (a foot?) and also disclosed, for the first time to my knowledge, that "once, an accidental shot left a scar on his face."

Could the scar on the left hand have been so recent as to be unknown to Castro and his friends and, in fact, to everybody? That appears rather improbable, and in any case it would then be quite the opposite of an identification mark. In their effort to prove that the body was Che's, why didn't the officers point out to the newsmen the two known scars as well as the third one mentioned by Castro? Left by the CIA to their own ignorance, did they believe the left-hand scar was more telling? But there is also the medical report signed on October 10, 1967, at the Señor de Malta hospital by Drs. Moisés Abraham Baptista and José Martínez Caso. This report specifically refers to "a scar covering almost the entire back of the left hand"; no other scar is mentioned.

Thus, if there is no longer today anything unexplained about La Higuera, where Che Guevara was put to death, it is still possible, and necessary, to talk about the mystery of Vallegrande, where the body was shown. True, at La

Higuera even more than at Vallegrande, the Bolivian
authorities were constantly contradicting themselves; at La
Higuera, at least, it is easy to understand why.

Che did not die of the wounds he suffered in the fighting
of the Quebrada del Yuro. He was killed by a burst of
machine gun fire while held prisoner in the small school of
La Higuera, where he lay wounded. The series of lies
concerning the time of his death or the nature of his
wounds, the changing versions on the individual role of
various participants, are not difficult to explain. The two
generals in charge at La Paz did not wish to admit that two
wounded prisoners had been finished off on their orders (the
Bolivian Willy, captured with Ramón, died in the same
way). The officers in charge at La Higuera had no desire—
perhaps some credit should be given to them for it—to
assume the responsibility. There was evidently neither
enough time nor intelligence, not even Central Intelligence,
to establish a coordinated version and adapt the "facts" and
"eyewitness accounts" to that version.

To understand what happened at Vallegrande is quite a
different matter. Once we admit—together with Castro, the
State Department and the rest of the world—that the body
in the laundry shed was Guevara's, there is no logical
explanation whatsoever for the way the identification was
handled, or mishandled. It is already hard to believe that
the officers leading the campaign against the guerrillas had
not been provided with a detailed description of the
guerrillas' suspected leader, including the number and
location of his scars. It is utterly impossible to fathom the
sheer stupidity with which the authorities managed to make
the usually unquestionable proof by fingerprints seem so
unconvincing.

To begin with, the Bolivian military appear to have
actually believed that their word would be accepted as the
truth. On this same day, October 10, 1967, which had begun

with the exhibition of the corpse, General Ovando, commander-in-chief of the armed forces, told journalists in
Vallegrande that the dead man's identity had been definitively established through comparison of his fingerprints
with those of Guevara, "received from Argentina." The
future President of Bolivia added that the journalists could
make the comparison themselves if they so desired.

Argentina, in fact, was not alone in having the fingerprints of Che. The immigration service in Caracas had taken
his prints in July 1952, when Ernesto Guevara de la Serna,
coming from Bogotá, arrived in Venezuela with his friend
Alberto Granados. As to the government in Washington, it
never said where it obtained the prints, but it had them, as
the State Department spokesman confirmed on October 17,
1967.

The statement by Robert McCloskey was quite matter-of-
fact:

> The Bolivian government has furnished us with a
> series of fingerprints taken from the body of one of the
> guerrillas which it identified as Ernesto Che Guevara.
> These fingerprints have been compared with a series of
> prints in the possession of the United States govern-
> ment for several years. They are identical.

McCloskey added that there would be no further comment. The State Department reporters were curious to
know how the American government had come to possess
the fingerprints in its files. The government was anxious,
above all, to avoid any question as to when it had received
the Bolivian prints.

There can be no doubt that the fingerprints of Ramón had
been sent to Washington from Vallegrande at least as
quickly as Guevara's prints had been sent to Vallegrande
from Buenos Aires. Why was the statement of October 17

not issued as early as October 11? And why did the State
Department, during the entire week, seek to give the
impression that it was only "inclined" to believe the reports
from Vallegrande, when it already had the material proof in
its hands?

The answer is obvious today: Washington was playing cat
and mouse with Havana. *Messieurs les Cubains, tirez les
premiers!* It was not a question of manners but of Machia-
vellianism. By October 17 Washington had no more to do
than to confirm, in a rare but subtle accord between the two
capitals, the announcement made by Castro in Havana two
days earlier.

Meanwhile, back in La Paz, the Bolivian military had
piled blunder upon blunder, contradiction upon contradiction, making a mess of the whole affair.

On Thursday morning, October 12, Argentine lawyer
Roberto Guevara de la Serna, Ernesto's younger brother,
had landed at Santa Cruz in a small chartered plane. He
asked Colonel Joaquín Zenteno Anaya, commander of the
military region covering Vallegrande, for permission to see
his brother's body. Zenteno answered that the order had to
come from headquarters in La Paz, and Roberto Guevara
went back to his plane. That night in La Paz he was
received by General Ovando, who gave him the authorization. But when he landed at Vallegrande the next day
(October 13), it was only to learn that the body he now had
permission to see was not there anymore because it had
been cremated.

The cremation had been announced to the press in La
Paz the night before, while Roberto Guevara was in
seclusion in his hotel room after having left General
Ovando. The man who gave the information to the news-
men was Ovando's aide-de-camp, Lieutenant Commander
Oscar Pano Rodríguez.

Until that moment, that is all through the day of October

12, General Ovando as well as President Barrientos maintained that Che's body had been secretly buried in the Vallegrande region. They referred to the state of the corpse and to the fact that the formaldehyde had not sufficed to prevent decomposition; one general invoked his "respect for the dead," the other his desire to avoid "exhibitionism with a corpse." Shortly before Roberto Guevara's visit to Ovando, President Barrientos had told the press, clearly intending his words for Roberto Guevara, that the body would not be exhumed.

But on the morning of October 13, without further explanation, President Barrientos had reversed himself. He too now spoke of cremation, and this became the only official version that day. It was to be muddied again, however, by some more false notes later on when General Ovando made a trip to Brazil. On two occasions, at the end of November and the beginning of December 1967, the commander of the armed forces rejected the new version which the President of Bolivia had been led to adopt by statements emanating from the military authorities, including Ovando's own aide-de-camp.

"Guevara was not cremated, he was buried in a place whose whereabouts are a State secret," Ovando now was telling the Brazilian journalists. In La Paz, General Juan José Tórrez hastened to explain to Bolivian newsmen that their Brazilian colleagues had misunderstood Ovando, since he was speaking in Spanish and not in Portuguese.

General Tórrez was to become commander of the armed forces when Ovando took over as President, and then he took over from Ovando as President. In October 1967 he was chief of staff. Barrientos, rallying to the cremation story on October 13, specifically declared that Tórrez had been in charge of the cremation.

It was only on December 9, 1967, in Montevideo, where General Ovando was continuing his travels, that the "mis-

understanding" was cleared up, if one may say so since this
"clearing up" gave birth to a third version. It now seems
General Ovando had wished to say only that the *ashes* of
Che had been buried, after the body had been cremated.

In his biography of Che Guevara, Daniel James,° to
whom we also owe the first complete English version of the
Bolivian Diary, offers an explanation of General Ovando's
Brazilian statements about Che's body. He believes that the
general, having announced that he would be a candidate for
President in 1970 (he was not to wait that long), was seeking
to pacify Catholics offended by the report of cremation.
James recalls on this subject the critical attitude of the
newspaper *Presencia*, which is close to the Catholic hierarchy.

When I myself sought the answers from La Paz, Alfredo
Ovando Candia was President of the "Revolutionary Government" set up after the *pronunciamiento* of September
26, 1969, and Alberto Bailey Gutiérrez, co-director of
Presencia in October 1967, was his Minister of Information.

The people of the "left" dodged my questions. They
supported "the anti-imperialist attitude" of the Ovando
government and clearly preferred not to speak about Che,
his body, or his ashes. Most others were sure that there
never had been any cremation, for the simple reason that it
was technically impossible. There was no crematorium in
Bolivia, and certainly not at Vallegrande. It appeared
equally doubtful that the authorities could have improvised
one without anyone knowing—and talking—about it. The
story of the cremation, it was explained to me, had been
invented first to get Roberto Guevara out of the way. The
authorities then stuck to that story to keep people from
trying to locate, or even remove, the remains of Guevara.

In any case, the operation could not fail to provoke some

° *Ché Guevara, A Biography* (New York: Stein and Day, 1969).

suspicions, as was foreseen in the editorial in *Presencia* mentioned by James. This editorial denounced "the serious error consisting in the hasty and secret cremation of the corpse" and added that such an error "could lead to the belief that there was something to hide."

True, President René Barrientos Ortuño did retain a secret weapon. But the bewildering ineptness in the use of this weapon only introduced an Elizabethan touch into the already macabre spectacle of Vallegrande without making things more believable.

In his press conference on the afternoon of October 12, Barrientos had referred in rather obscure terms to new information he expected to receive shortly from the Argentine government which would complete, he said, the "official confirmation" of Che's death. It was soon learned that two federal fingerprint experts and a graphologist from Argentina had just arrived in Bolivia at the request of the La Paz government. But it was also made known that the visiting experts, like Roberto Guevara, had been informed at Vallegrande by General Juan José Tórrez that the body had been cremated.

If in La Paz the Argentine experts now were going to receive a series of fingerprints marked "Ramón" in order to compare them with those of Argentine citizen Ernesto Guevara de la Serna, on file in Buenos Aires, the disappearance of the corpse became logical, as part of a rather naive attempt at trickery.

According to Ovando's remarks in his press conference of October 10, the Bolivian authorities had the Argentine prints two days before the arrival of the experts who were to make the comparisons; other prints, in any case, had been in Washington's possession for several years. There was nothing to prevent the Bolivian authorities from handing the Argentine experts a copy of Guevara's fingerprints and telling them they were those of Ramón.

And then, on Friday, October 13, a strange bit of news spread through La Paz, to be relayed to the world press: before cremating the body, the authorities had amputated and preserved the two thumbs. This was a curious report, but it was not a wanton invention. It came straight from the headquarters of the Bolivian armed forces at Miraflores and was given to journalists by qualified officers who authorized publication on condition they would not be named as the source.

That night the press service of the Casa Quemada, the Presidential palace in La Paz, distributed a statement by President Barrientos on "the fatal outcome of the interventionist adventure of Señor Guevara." The statement concluded:

> It is the decision of the armed forces, and also mine, that the remains of the usurpers and adventurers who interrupted the development of the nation and caused serious damages to the country should be left where they were buried, in that ground which they trampled with such perfidy. In the case of *Señor* Guevara, the last thing my government will do is to supply the proof through fingerprints, with the aid of the amputated finger—*con el dedo amputado*—which will be made available to experts.

One finger or two? The written statement of President Barrientos must take precedence over the reports whispered by General Ovando's colleagues; thus the official version on the night of October 13 was that only one finger had been preserved, not two. The truth, however, apparently unknown to both the President of the Republic and the chief of the armed forces, was that not *one* finger and not *two* fingers were amputated, but the *two hands* complete with all ten fingers.

This fact emerges from the report of the Argentine experts, added as an annex to the final communiqué of the Bolivian government on October 16. Also attached were the death certificate (with no estimate of the time of death) and the autopsy report (with no precise data on the nature of the different wounds and no indications as to which were mortal).

On Saturday, October 14, at 4:00 P.M., the experts, accompanied by several members of the Argentine Embassy at La Paz, had visited the Miraflores headquarters where, as they stated, they met General Ovando's aide-de-camp, Lieutenant Commander Oscar Pano Rodríguez. They also met Major Roberto Quintanilla, chief of intelligence for *Ministro de Gobierno* Antonio Arguedas Mendieta (the *Ministro de Gobierno* in many Latin American governments is the most important member of the Cabinet, in charge of both administration and police). Major Quintanilla gave them a "cylindrical metal container" which they opened. Inside were "two hands immersed in a liquid which had the odor of formaldehyde, a powerful disinfectant used to preserve such parts."

After having carried out the complicated operations necessary (because of the formaldehyde) to ink and imprint the "papillary patterns of the fingers of the amputated hands," the Argentine experts compared them with the "individual prints on the photostatic copy of the original card contained in the files of the identification section of the Argentine federal police, number 3,524,272, under the name Ernesto Guevara." The comparison, the report concludes, "irrefutably" established a "perfect identity" between the two series of fingerprints, which thus were from "one and the same person."

The horrible tale of Che's hands (according to the account given by one of the experts to Argentine journalist

Hugo Gambini,° "it was necessary to boil them for a long
time in water so that the tissues expelled the formaldehyde
and the ink could adhere") has a grotesque epilogue which
will be discussed in the proper place, in the chapter dealing
with the adventures of Señor Arguedas. Meanwhile it is
amazing to note that on December 9, 1967, nearly two
months after the Argentine experts' report had definitely
confirmed the identity of the dead guerrilla of Vallegrande,
the commander of the armed forces and future President of
the Republic did not yet seem ready to take account of this
report.

This at least is what can be deduced from the press
conference General Ovando held that day in Montevideo, in
which he explained that it was the *ashes* of Che which had
been buried, and not the body. To a question concerning
the fingerprint identification, General Ovando, according to
the reporters present, replied in these terms: "It is not true
that the hands or certain fingers were cut off for the
fingerprint identifications. These were made before cremation. . . ."

Fidel Castro, in his speech of October 15 confirming
Che's death, had sought to push aside the questions
suggested by the contradictory statements of the Bolivian
authorities concerning the corpse of Vallegrande.

This speech, in fact, does not merely announce the "bitter
truth." It is also an appeal to Cubans not to discuss the
matter: "In our opinion," said the *jefe máximo*, "the only
party to benefit from the indefinite perpetuation of doubt,
from unfounded illusions among the masses, would be
imperialism."

Castro did not deny that the question had arisen in
Havana as to "whether or not maintaining doubt concerning
the news could be useful in any way." This idea was

° *El Che Guevara* (Buenos Aires: Editorial Paidos, 1968).

rejected, Castro nobly added, because "even if doubt could have been beneficial in any way, lies, fear of the truth, complicity with false illusions, complicity with lies of any kind, have never been weapons of the revolution." However, the decision about "whether a state of uncertainty might be useful to the revolutionary movement" was made easier, he admits, by the realization that "as a matter of fact, we don't believe it to be beneficial in any way. . . ."

The theory set forth by Castro to explain how doubts about Guevara's death could benefit only "imperialism" is somewhat puzzling.

The "imperialists," he said, would like "to dispel all the impact of his conduct, his example, his staunch, heroic revolutionary life, and weaken that example, that impact, that deed, by surrounding it with mystery, with uncertainty, with illusion." They would like "five years, ten years, fifteen years, or even twenty years to pass by with his example attenuated by mystery, hovering between doubt and hope." He even cited among the benefits the "imperialists," and the "imperialists" only, could derive from a "state of uncertainty," the possibility of spreading "speculation and stories" such as "we saw him here" and "we saw him there." Such speculation and stories had not disturbed him in earlier times, when they compensated for the speculation and stories on the death of Che. But in 1967 the opposite had become desirable from Castro's point of view: henceforth the example of Che could be fruitful only if he were dead, and totally dead, that is, if no one doubted any longer that the body displayed in Vallegrande was truly his:

> We had to concern ourselves about the possibility that an illusion might arise on a false basis, with nothing in reality to contradict it. And that would only weaken, with the passage of years and surrounded by the deepest mystery, the impact of one of the most

extraordinary examples known to history of loyalty to
revolutionary principles, integrity, valor, generosity,
and selflessness.

Castro's speech of October 15 failed to explain how "the
imperialists" might have initiated the plan Castro attributes
to them, a plan his arguments are supposed to destroy.

Far from sowing doubts, the State Department seemed
quite content to confirm the news announced in Havana. It
even took special care to make sure it was not announced
first in Washington, for that indeed would not have been
convincing. From all evidence, the "imperialists" considered that the spectacular demonstration of Che's pitiable
fate served their interests infinitely better than encouraging
illusions about his possible return.

It is true that in Bolivia the military were behaving as if
they were maintaining a credibility gap on purpose, and you
never know with the CIA. . . . But Castro had already
absolved them from any responsibility: "We are not about
to believe," he stated in his speech, "that the imperialist
puppets in Bolivia, out to appear as the vanguard lackeys of
imperialism, want us to doubt their news. It cannot be
doubted that the imperialist puppets in Bolivia want the
news to be believed, because it has to do with their role,
their part, their hope, as vanguard puppets."

The Bolivian leaders, according to Castro, would not have
dared to lie in announcing that the Vallegrande body was
Che's, because to manufacture this kind of lie would be
completely pointless.

Of course, he comments, "the government of Bolivia is
characterized by its cretinism and imbecility." But "not
even the most imbecile, the most idiotic of all governments . . . , not even the biggest imbecile would have
resorted to such a senseless, stupid thing. . . ." The

senseless, stupid thing, according to Castro, would be to announce that Che was dead when it couldn't be proved, when it could even be disproved, since Che could appear alive anywhere at any moment: "Why should that regime fabricate a report that ten days, fifteen days, twenty days later would be exposed and proved false?"

Though he didn't seem to be aware of it, Castro was throwing away the only argument which could have lent some credibility to the idea he himself had suggested. His theory was that the "imperialists" sought to weaken the influence of Che by spreading doubts as to his death. In addition to being rather absurd, the theory, as we have seen, was contrary to fact. But there still remained the erratic, incoherent, suspicious behavior of the Bolivian leaders. Instead of using that behavior to prop up his theory, Castro dismisses it, the Bolivian leaders being not imbecilic, not idiotic enough: "It would be absolutely illogical for anyone to attempt to invent this kind of news. . . . There is no possible motive here. . . ."

There is, however, an easy answer to the question posed by Castro. If the Bolivian leaders wanted "to invent this kind of news," the possibility that it could be exposed and proved false would not have stopped them. Similar reports had been circulated many times in the past, and Che had not appeared ten, fifteen, or twenty days later.

Perhaps they were convinced in La Paz—as were many elsewhere, in Havana no less than in Washington—that Che Guevara had been dead for a long time. In that case, if General Barrientos considered it in his interest to add a world-shaking dimension to the elimination of a small group of guerrillas by passing one of them off as the famous *comandante*, he had no reason to fear that a man missing since the spring of 1965 would suddenly arise in the fall of 1967 to call General Barrientos a liar.

Despite all its bizarre or even troubling aspects, the mystery of Vallegrande could be disregarded if not for the earlier unexplained disappearance of Che Guevara—the mystery of Havana.

II

Havana

The Tricontinental Conference in Havana opened its afternoon session on January 7, 1966, with a minute of silence in memory of Mehdi Ben Barka. Later that afternoon the delegates stood for a minute-long ovation at the mention of Che Guevara's name; was this, too, a memorial tribute? Ben Barka, chairman of the Conference preparatory committee, had been kidnapped in Paris in October 1965, and everyone knew he was dead. Guevara had disappeared from Havana in March 1965, but Fidel Castro said he was alive.

"We are following the heroic example of *Comandante* Ernesto Che Guevara," was the cry that touched off the ovation. The speaker was *Comandante* Pedro Medina Silva, who had come to denounce the "fierce repression" of the Venezuelan guerrillas by the constitutional government in Caracas.

Why heroic? Why Guevara? This took place in 1966: the body of Vallegrande did not appear until October 1967, and it was 1968 that Castro proclaimed as *año del guerrillero heroico*. Wasn't it odd to single out, as an example for the fighting men of three continents, the former Director of the National Bank of Cuba and Minister of Industry, an economic specialist in the Cuban administration who as far as most of the delegates knew hadn't handled a gun for seven years?

Usually, when an orator evokes an emotional response in an audience by citing an heroic example, the hero is a dead man. If Pedro Medina Silva wished to name a living example, and to honor his Cuban hosts as well as the precedent set by the Sierra Maestra rebels, why not Fidel Castro? Why not the leader, the *jefe máximo*, rather than the lieutenant?

In New York, where communist intrigues are revealed with the same ease as CIA plots are exposed in Havana, some of the Cuban refugees viewed the ovations for Che as a sign of a major political maneuver.

The conflict between Moscow and Peking was at its peak, and Castro clearly had opted for Moscow. Now Peking, these "experts" said, was trying to improve its position in Latin America and to prevent a debacle at the Tricontinental by building up Che as a rival of Castro. The Chinese were orchestrating a campaign for Che while their man waited in some hideout to make a sensational reappearance.

The theory was rather farfetched. Even if such a plan were conceivable, it was very unlikely that a Guevara would let himself become its tool, and quite unbelievable that a Castro would be tricked into becoming its dupe.

The theory, moreover, did not match the facts. The Tricontinental obviously had been arranged in such a manner as to ensure a comfortable majority for the newly consolidated Moscow-Havana axis. Perhaps the arrangers did not always know the exact ideological tendencies of every guerrilla group attending along with the official delegations of Communist governments and Communist parties. Guatemala was an example: Marco Antonio Yon Sosa was the best-known Guatemalan guerrilla leader, but he was accused of being influenced by Trotskyites (he was later slain in Mexico, in May 1970, under suspicious circumstances) and therefore had been kept away from the Conference. Luis Turcios Lima, who replaced him, was considered more suitable; but when the *Saturday Evening Post* a few months later asked Turcios Lima to name the two men he admired most, he answered: Mao and Guevara. In any case, the ovations for Che at the Tricontinental neither surprised Castro nor erupted against his will. All of the eyewitness accounts leave no doubt that if the "cult of Che" was indeed orchestrated from the beginning of the Conference, the conductor was Castro himself, and the people supervising the sound system as well as the enthusiasm were Castro's men.

The "cult of the personality" had always been part of Castro's Cuba, but only one living person had ever possessed an official right to this cult: Fidel Castro Ruz, *jefe máximo y gran líder de la revolución*. His lieutenant, Camilo Cienfuegos, was included in the rites of praise along with José Martí, dead since 1895, only because in October 1959 Cienfuegos's plane had disappeared in circumstances never explained, and he was considered dead. It seemed that if Che Guevara now ranked with Camilo Cienfuegos and José Martí, it could only be due to the fact that he, too, was now a dead hero.

The Havana authorities attributed that widespread idea to the CIA, but Cubans do not need help from the CIA to notice when something is wrong, and they had begun to wonder before the CIA started looking for answers. Besides, the CIA people had trouble making up their minds about which answers to provide, since their purposes were shifting and sometimes conflicting.

From the standpoint of pure propaganda, there seemed to be a clear advantage for the United States to encourage the belief that Fidel Castro had gotten rid of his second lieutenant of the Sierra, Che Guevara, as he already had been suspected of having eliminated the first, Camilo

Cienfuegos. But there were strategic worries. Washington was finding it increasingly difficult to keep up the holy fear of Havana, which had proved so useful to the United States in holding Latin American governments on the alert, and in dependency. Perhaps there was good reason to mention rumors of Che's death in some countries, where obsessed or insatiable petty tyrants never ceased their clamor for more money and weapons. But in the capitals viewed by Washington as "insufficiently conscious of the Cuban danger," the accent was placed rather on the rumors of the continuing activities of Che, and on the menace that these activities implied.

In Mexico in 1966 nearly everyone I met believed that Che was dead. But the North Americans I encountered there were warning Mexicans against "the authenticity of this rumor."

The Mexicans, and other peoples of Latin America as well, thought the death of Che more plausible than his sudden reappearance at the head of a powerful army of guerrillas. In June 1966 a group of Mexican journalists were received in Havana by the Minister of National Education, Armando Hart Dávalos, who had become one of the secretaries of the new unified Communist Party. Without concealing their skepticism, they asked him if it was true not that Che was dead but that he was alive. His answer seemed ambiguous to several of them. "I am sure," the minister said, "that one day you will be hearing about him."

Fidel Castro, in his closing speech to the Tricontinental on January 15, 1966, vainly sought to portray what he called the departure of Che as a perfectly natural event. It was not, and the "departure" remained a disappearance.

The tributes paid to Guevara were meant to convey at least the impression that the disappearance was not the result of a disagreement. Paradoxically, they aggravated the problem, for they suggested the inevitable question: since

Che's heroic example was to inspire the uprising of three continents, why was he not here in person to pass on to the delegates his torch and his ideas?

The answer, it seemed, was that he was physically prevented from doing so, and this answer became more and more convincing as other events took place in Havana in the name of Che but still in his absence.

Those who persisted in believing that Che was alive thought he would reappear between July 28 and August 5, 1967, on the occasion of the first conference of the OLAS (*Organización Latino-Americana de Solidaridad,* Latin-American Solidarity Organization). In April the secretariat of the OSPAAAL (*Organización de Solidaridad de los Pueblos de Africa, Asia y América Latina,* Solidarity Organization of the Peoples of Africa, Asia and Latin America, otherwise known as the "Tricontinental," of which the OLAS was to become the Latin-American branch) had distributed Che's manifesto, *Crear dos, tres, muchos Vietnam, es la consigna* (Create two, three, many Vietnams is the watchword). Clearly, this was to be the main point of the Conference, and Che could not fail to personally emphasize its importance through his presence. But Che did not come, and when the Conference appointed him honorary president in his absence, it looked very much indeed like a posthumous honor.

Today we know from the *Bolivian Diary* Che's thoughts between July 28 and August 5, 1967. They were far from the Havana Conference and its heroic proclamations. They were entirely absorbed by the small daily problems of plain survival.

On July 28 he is preoccupied by the fact that the horses "sink into the sand or suffer from the stones." On August 5 he notes that "there is no more horsemeat left," that "tomorrow we will try to catch some fish," and that "the day after tomorrow we will sacrifice another animal." On

July 30, while he is having an asthma attack, his men clash
with a detachment of soldiers under unfavorable conditions.
The cost of this, he relates on July 31, is the loss of two men
and some important equipment, including medicines and
"the machine on which the messages from Manila° are
recorded." He also misses "Debray's book annotated by me,
and a book by Trotsky." And the honorary president of the
OLAS Conference concludes his notes for the day with, it
seems, as much sarcasm as sadness: "There are 22 of us,
with two wounded, Pacho and Pombo, and me with my
asthma going full blast. . . ."

But it was not because of these difficulties that Che did
not attend the OLAS Conference. The *Diary* makes it clear
that the possibility of going to Havana for any reason did
not arise at *any* time. Among the insights provided by his
notes, this conclusion is among the more striking revelations: Guevara did not intend ever to return to Havana, and
Castro had no intention ever of receiving him there. How
can one help asking why?

And how could the various Latin-American guerrillas,
who had incurred some risks in order to reach the "guerrilla
capital," understand the absence of the man who was
supposed to be their leader, not their absent honorary
president?

The honorary presidency of the OLAS Conference was
the final stage in a process of erosion which began much
earlier. The turning point had been reached when Castro,
confronted with the fact that Che's disappearance had led
to unexpected, and unpleasant, interpretations, decided to
counterattack and do away with all those questions, suggestions, and even accusations. For that, the *jefe máximo*
announced on September 26, 1965, that he would read a
message from Che on October 3, "explaining his absence

° Code name of Havana in the *Diary*.

during these recent months." The occasion was to be a conference of the unified government party, the PURSC (*Partido Unido de la Revolución Socialista Cubana*).

The PURSC was improvised in 1963 as the successor to the ORI (*Organizaciones Revolucionarias Integradas,* Integrated Revolutionary Organizations), which in turn had been formed in 1961 by what was left of the 26th of July Movement, the former student movement of Faure Chomón (*Directorio Revolucionario*), and the orthodox Communist Party of Blas Roca (*Partido Socialista Popular*). On October 2, 1965, again without previous notice, it was announced that the PURSC would become the Cuban Communist Party. In his speech on the following day, Fidel Castro offered his "explanations" of Che's disappearance at the same time that he confirmed the creation of the new Communist Party—to which Che no longer belonged. For the name of *Comandante* Guevara, who had been one of the best-known members of the national council and executive committee of the PURSC, did not appear in the rosters of any of the directing organs of the Communist Party, not even the 112-member central committee.

The change was so striking that the Paris *Figaro* headlined its dispatch from Havana: "Che Guevara officially expelled from Cuban Communist Party." This was either an exaggeration or an understatement. If the letter read by Castro on October 3, 1965, was authentic, it was a case of resignation rather than expulsion. If the letter was false, Che Guevara had been expelled not only from the Party but from the ranks of the living.

"I formally renounce my functions in the Party leadership, my post as minister, my rank of *comandante,* my Cuban citizenship," the letter said. In three sentences Che gave two reasons for the absolutely total break. "Other parts of the world are calling for my modest efforts," the first explained. "I can do what is denied to you by your responsibilities as the leader of Cuba, and the time has come for us to part," stated the second. The third repeated: "I say, once again, that I free Cuba of all responsibility, except that which stems from its example. . . ."

The letter also contained political tributes to Castro, which could have been flatteries, and sentimental tributes to the Cuban people, which should have been apologies.

The Cuban people had good reason to feel offended. If Che's concern, as stated in the letter, was to free the Cuban authorities from any responsibility for actions he planned, all he had to do was to resign as minister and as a Party leader. There was no need to renounce his rank as major, which had become an honorary title, or at most a reserve rank, since Major Guevara had not exercised any active military command for some years. Such an unnecessary renunciation on the part of the former chief of the Ciro Redondo column and winner of the battle of Santa Clara could have been taken by his former companions of the Sierra Maestra as an insult. As to his brusque rejection of the Cuban citizenship conferred on him for life, how could this be accepted as a gesture of friendship?

The legalistic rationale for this total and brutal break was so strained and disproportionate that it seemed to be only a pretext.

The Cuban government had long since abandoned any worries over obligations of international law or even about routine diplomatic niceties. There was not a statesman in Latin America whom Castro had not described by name as a "lackey of Yankee imperialism"; he once called the President of Ecuador an old drunkard. His responsibilities as the leader of Cuba had not prevented him from intervening in Venezuelan affairs, without bothering to take precautions so that he could eventually deny it.

The Cuban government, moreover, had nothing left to lose. Following its overt intervention in Venezuela in 1964,

Cuba had already been expelled from the Organization of American States (OAS). If the thought of a United Nations condemnation caused Castro any anxiety (which seems unlikely), the Soviet veto was there to protect him.

Those who nevertheless wish to take seriously the sudden legal preoccupations displayed in the letter read by Castro should remember that Bolivia did not lodge any complaint against Cuba in the United Nations. The obvious reason was that it had no interest in starting a debate which would have reminded the world of the circumstances of Che's death. But if Che really had been killed in combat, or if his execution in the schoolhouse of La Higuera had been better concealed, would the Bolivian government have refrained from going to the Security Council simply because Guevara was officially no longer a military officer or a Cuban? The idea is ridiculous, and would still be so even had there not been three majors, eight captains, and four lieutenants— none of whom renounced rank or citizenship—among the seventeen Cubans under Che's command in Bolivia.

In his speech of October 3, 1965, Castro tried to convince the world of the validity of the letter's arguments, but was so carried away by his own eloquence that he ended by virtually dismissing Che's stated reasons.

We could reply, all of us: Comrade Guevara, it is not responsibility which worries us. We bear the responsibility of the revolution. We have the responsibility to aid the revolutionary movement to the extent of our capabilities. We assume this responsibility and the consequences and the risks. This has been so for nearly seven years, and we know that as long as imperialism exists, as long as there remain exploited and colonized peoples, we will continue to run these risks and we will continue to calmly accept this responsibility.

Since we all could answer in this way to Comrade
Guevara, why didn't Comrade Castro do so? Why didn't he
return his letter, slap him on the back, and tell him to stop
kidding, take a few days off, and come back to discuss his
plans with him later?

Not until January 15, 1966, did Castro outline an answer
to the questions raised by his October speech. In his closing
address to the Tricontinental Conference, he said:

> Comrade Guevara joined us during our exile in
> México, and always, from the very first day, he clearly
> expressed the idea that when the struggle was com-
> pleted in Cuba, he would have other duties to fulfill in
> another place, and we always gave him our word that
> no State interest, no national interest, no circumstances
> would lead us to ask him to remain in our country, or
> hinder him from carrying out that wish, that desire.
> And we fully and faithfully kept that promise made to
> Comrade Guevara.

The official text of the speech as published in the English
edition of *Granma*, adds here: "[Applause]."

If Guevara had set such conditions in 1956, before joining
Castro in Mexico, and if Castro had accepted them, it would
be astonishing not only that Castro waited until 1966 to
mention his promise, but that Guevara waited until 1965 to
take advantage of it.

According to Castro, it was on April 1, 1965, that
Guevara sent him the undated letter, which remained
unknown until October 3, 1965, and unexplained until
January 15, 1966. Militarily, the "struggle" had been
finished, if not since January 1959 when Batista's army
collapsed, then at least since April 1961 with the no less
complete collapse of the CIA plot in the Bay of Pigs, or in
any case since October 1962 with the Kennedy-Khrushchev

agreement. True, Castro has gone on periodically denouncing some "imminent aggression of Yankee imperialism," but 1965 in this regard did not mark an end to such
"struggle" any more than 1964 or 1966.

There was also, of course, the economic struggle to which
the former guerrilla turned Director of the National Bank
and then Minister of Industry had devoted most of his
activity. Was the Cuban economic situation sufficiently
stabilized so that Che could have considered his task
fulfilled in the spring of 1965?

In one of his last texts published before his disappearance,
Che exhibited no such feeling; on the contrary, he recog-
nized that the Cuban economy was only beginning to
recover from certain errors. The article was titled, "Cuba:
Its Economy, Its Foreign Trade, and Its Significance in the
Contemporary World." It was written at the request of the
British journal *International Affairs*, and appeared in the
October 1964 issue. The Spanish version appeared in
December 1964 in the bulletin of the Cuban Ministry of
Industry.

Far from hinting that the moment was nearing when he
would have "other duties to fulfill in another place,"
Guevara focuses on "the problems connected with the
future development of Cuba which are at present being
studied." He writes about "the policy we shall follow in
years to come" and states that "we expect the Cuban
economy to develop along three principal lines between
now and 1970—sugar will continue to be our main earner of
foreign exchange. . . ." (The other two were nickel and
cattle raising.) The "we" and "our" evidently included Che
Guevara.

This "we" also is found in an essay completed in March
1965 during his African trip, written for the magazine
Marcha of Montevideo and issued in Havana as a pamphlet
titled *El socialismo y el hombre en Cuba*, in July 1965—that

is, three months after Castro, according to his own statement, had received Che's farewell letter to Castro and
Cuba.

Much can be said (and will be said in later chapters)
about this extraordinary text, which is revealing in more
than one way. What should be mentioned here, because of
the date of the manuscript and the state of mind attributed
to its author at that time, is that Che constantly expresses
himself in it as a Cuban. When he writes, for example, of
Fidel's insistence on the technical training of "our people,"
no one would imagine, as Castro affirms, that Che is
connected to the Cuban people only by a temporary tie
which he is about to dissolve. When he stresses the role of
youth and of the party in "our society," when he speaks of
the education given to "our students," he certainly does not
appear on the verge of renouncing his Cuban citizenship.

Even when he declares that "proletarian internationalism
is a duty, but it is also a revolutionary necessity," he hastens
to add: "That is how we educate our people."

Finally, it is utterly impossible to reconcile the terms of
Che's letter of resignation with this passage in which he
identifies himself completely with Cuba:

> We know that there are sacrifices ahead of us, and
> that we must pay a price for the heroic fact that we
> constitute a vanguard as a nation. We, the leaders,
> know that we must pay a price for having the right to
> say we are at the head of the people which is at the
> head of America.

Does this mean that the letter read by Fidel Castro on
October 3, 1965, was a forgery? Some passages fawning on
Castro seem to bear the mark of those toadying to Stalin,
which Beria and his predecessors did not need to fabricate
since Stalin's prisoners, sooner or later, were ready to write

them themselves for use in their trials. Che, however, contrary to what some intellectuals in New York or Paris wish to believe about his nonconformist mind and theirs, had shown in the past that he was quite willing to pay his tribute to the glory of the *jefe máximo,* without the help of any Beria.

"My only fault of some gravity," he now is perfectly able to confess on his own, "is not to have trusted you more from the first moments of the Sierra Maestra, and not to have realized with enough celerity your qualities as a leader and a revolutionary. . . . I am also proud to have followed you without hesitation, identifying with your way of thinking and of seeing and grasping the dangers and the principles. . . . I thank you for your teachings and your example, and I will try to be faithful to it up to the ultimate consequences of my acts."

One may well wonder how Che could have trusted Castro more since he followed him without hesitation, and the letter here certainly offers a plenitude of platitudes. But that fact, unfortunately, does not point to forgery, for it is not at all incompatible with the known style of Che Guevara.

On April 9, 1961, for example, in *Verde Olivo,* official publication of the armed forces, he discussed "this force of nature named Fidel Castro Ruz," comparing him, or it, to the "noblest historical figures of all Latin America." He saw in Castro "the characteristics of a great leader of men, which, added to his personal qualities of boldness, strength, and courage, and to his extraordinary care to always give an ear to the will of the people, have brought him to the place of honor and sacrifice which he occupies today. . . ."

In his *Socialism and Man in Cuba* we find this vision of the revolution on the march, which seems a pale reflection of bureaucratic or even Stalinist Communism rather than a beacon for rebellious youth:

> At the head of the immense column—we are neither ashamed nor afraid to say so—marches Fidel; after him, the best cadres of the party, and just behind, so close that its enormous power can be felt, come the people as a whole.

It is thus not the style of the letter but Castro's pretended interpretation of its contents that inspires doubts. What Castro wanted people to believe about the feelings of Che at the time he wrote it, about the circumstances and motivations of the letter, could not be true. Clearly, the disappearance of Che Guevara was the result of a crisis, and this crisis had led to such a profound change in his personal situation that he could no longer stay in Cuba.

After the announcement of October 3, 1965, the first to reject Castro's explanation as inadequate and unacceptable were various Trotskyite groups. As Trotskyites, they knew the Stalinist tradition of the bullet in the back of the neck. Juan Posadas, secretary of the Latin-American Bureau of the "Fourth International," had launched a campaign demanding that the Cuban government produce Guevara. There could be no question, he said, of trusting the methods of the Cuban government, because "these are the methods of bureaucrats, and perhaps of assassins."

Whatever Posadas' personal standing might be (among certain Bolivian Trotskyite groups, the epithet *Posadista* was used as an insult), the questions he had raised could not be brushed aside: "Why have they not shown Guevara? Why has he not spoken?"

Castro had first proposed in 1963 the possibility of expanding to Latin America the Organization of Solidarity of the Peoples of Africa and Asia, whose headquarters were in Cairo. Che's African voyage at the end of 1964 and the beginning of 1965 gave substance to the project. In February 1965, taking leave of President Nyerere at Dar es

Salaam to visit President Nasser in Cairo, Che confirmed that the time had come: "After having visited seven African countries,* I am convinced that it is possible to create a common front for the struggle against colonialism, imperialism, and neo-colonialism."

Less than a year later, the new Organization of Solidarity of the Peoples of Africa, Asia, and Latin America (OS-PAAAL) was set up at Havana. Everyone exchanged congratulations in the name of Che, everyone acclaimed Che, but Che himself remained invisible. Where was he?

The following month he sent from Brazzaville a letter to his eldest child, Hildita (the daughter from his first marriage to the Peruvian Hilda Gadea), who had just reached the age of 10. The letter contains a curious sentence: "Even though my role here may not be very important, it is useful." Why could Che not leave his useful but not very important role for a few days to undertake the major role which would seem to have been his at the Tricontinental Conference in Havana? The delegation from Brazzaville, present in the hall, had perhaps slept poorly en route, but it made the trip.

In spite of all these real questions, when Fidel Castro took the floor for the closing session on January 15, 1966, it was only to denounce "the campaign carried out by imperialism and its agents with regard to the departure of our comrade Ernesto Guevara." Forced to defend himself, Castro counterattacked, the classic last resort of bad faith. What then followed was a raging denunciation, in language reminiscent of the purest Stalinist tradition, of "the repugnant and nauseating thing that is Trotskyism today within the field of politics [Applause]."

Quoting various Trotskyite newspapers which had carried and supported the accusations of Posadas, Castro did not

---

* Algeria, Mali, Congo-Brazzaville, Guinea, Ghana, Dahomey, Tanzania.

reply to any of the questions asked. Instead he fumed about
Guatemala, where "Yankee imperialism has used one of the
most subtle tactics to liquidate a revolutionary movement,
that is, the infiltration of agents of the Fourth International
in it, who brought it to adopt . . . this discredited thing, this
antihistoric thing, this fraudulent thing which emanates
from individuals so known to be at the service of Yankee
imperialism, as is the program of the Fourth International."

I leave it to the pro-Cuban Trotskyites the world over to
untangle the neo-Castroist and neo-Stalinist elements in a
sentence such as this one:

> If Trotskyism represented at a certain stage an
> erroneous position, but a position within the field of
> political ideas, Trotskyism became in later years a
> vulgar instrument of imperialism and reaction.

Castro, in any case, proved wrong in thinking that the
questions would vanish once he had given his assurance that
"these are matters which in time, when circumstances allow
it, will be clarified." And the doubts, contrary to his hopes,
were not erased by his peremptory remark: "For us,
revolutionaries, these clarifications are not necessary; it is
the enemy who tries to use these circumstances in order to
scheme, to create confusion and to slander."

In the April 1966 issue of *Monthly Review*, a New York
"independent socialist" magazine with some influence in
the American "new left," editors Leo Huberman and Paul
M. Sweezy, until then dedicated Fidelists, replied to this
speech with an editorial warning:

> Fidel should be under no illusions that only imperi-
> alists and their agents are interested in Che's fate.
> More than anyone else, even more than Fidel himself,
> Che has come to symbolize all that is best, all that is

pure, all that is beloved in the Cuban revolution. . . .
If, as some charge, anything untoward has happened or
should happen to Che, those responsible (and that
would necessarily include all who knew and kept
silent) will be forever disgraced.

The *Monthly Review* editors, on the other hand, considered the possibility that Che might reappear "as a revolutionary fighter and theorist elsewhere." In this case, they
said, "if he retains his close ties to Fidel and his other
former comrades in the Sierra Maestra," the chances of a
favorable evolution inside Cuba would be "immeasurably
improved." Indignant over Castro's return to the anti-
Trotskyite accusations which "provided the rationalization
for the Soviet purge trials of the 1930s," they saw in this "a
sure sign of either ignorance or malice." Granting Castro
the benefit of ignorance, they added that "the malice comes
from advisors who never abandoned the attitudes and
methods which underlay the trials." They also expressed the
hope that "Fidel's bad example is not going to lead to a
revival of the kind of witch-hunting which so bedeviled and
stultified the world revolutionary movement in the Stalin
era."

Then the *Monthly Review* raised some questions of its
own: "Is Fidel Castro aware of the real issues at stake in the
Guevara affair? And does he realize that every day's delay in
clearing up the mystery brings anxiety and doubt to honest
revolutionaries everywhere, and joy to their enemies?"

Apparently Fidel Castro had not yet realized this at the
time of the OLAS (Organization of Latin American Solidarity) Conference in the summer of 1967, when he had Che
named as honorary president *in absentia*, a few months
after ordering, on April 16, the distribution of the manifesto
Create Two, Three, Many Vietnams together with a series of
photographs of Che, some of them in color, and one
showing him close-shaven with hair trimmed short.

The only valid argument the Cuban leaders could use to avoid producing their ex-colleague had to do with possible security considerations; they would naturally be expected to avoid putting a number of secret services on Che's trail. "Of course," Castro observed on January 15, 1966, "the imperialists would be most eager to learn, in every detail, where he is, what he has done, how he is doing it. . . ." And again later in the same speech: "Naturally, if Comrade Guevara was going to leave the country, it was logical for him to do it secretly, it was logical for him to move secretly, it was logical for him not to be in contact with journalists, it was logical for him not to give any press conferences. It was logical for him to act as he did, because of the task he proposed to undertake."

He might have added that it was logical also for Comrade Guevara not to distribute his pictures, and that it was logical, for the comrades of Comrade Guevara, not to hand them over on a silver platter to the CIA.

The first point—the photographic mania of Che and his "clandestine" group—belongs to the mystery of Nancahuazú, dealt with in the following chapter. The second point—the amazing carelessness of Castro in supplying the CIA with a picture they might not yet have filed away—adds a bizarre touch to the mystery of Havana. The photos passed out by the Tricontinental secretariat to newsmen on April 16, 1967, were dangerously precise, and the one showing Che in impeccable business attire, complete with necktie, was the most precise and dangerous of all. It was also the most compromising for Fidel Castro. The entire world visualized Che only with his unkempt beard and long hair. Combed, shaved, necktied, elegant, and furnished with false papers, Ernesto Guevara could have stepped off the plane at any airport without attracting attention, as long as no one pointed him out. Once this picture had been distributed, however, Che no longer could use that easy disguise.

Why then had the Cubans handed out the photo? The only logical explanation at this time, April 1967, was that the Cuban authorities must have known Che had no further use of that disguise or any other, because they knew Che was dead.

The same logic, based on the facts known at the time, also explained the photos of Che exhibited by the authorities of Bolivia in September 1967 as evidence of his living presence there. Rather than weakening the conviction that Che was dead, the Bolivians' photographic display merely raised the question as to which of the two secret services, the Cuban G-2 or the American CIA, had planted those photos in Bolivia. For Havana and Washington had a common interest in confirming that Che was alive: the Cuban officials to prove that they had not killed him; the Americans to prove that the menace of Cuba in Latin America had not disappeared.

The belief that Che was dead thus was perfectly reasonable—but wrong. Soon the *Bolivian Diary*, found on the body at Vallegrande, cleared up the mystery of Havana by showing that logic had very little to do with the strange and shifting relationship between Che and Castro.

Che, after all, *was* alive until October 1967, but he had authorized Castro to consider him dead. His letter read by Castro in October 1965 had been a definitive farewell—the farewell of a man who knew, as Castro knew, that he would never return. Che had retired from the world, but in his own way: fighting. And when a Che Guevara resolves to die fighting, his battle becomes more important to him than his death.

Che did not know then, and he realized too late, that he was better equipped to die than to fight.

III

Nancahuazú

The Bolivian soldiers, cautiously advancing through the tropical forest covering the jagged rocks and shadowy ravines of the Iñaú mountains, finally broke into a sheltered clearing above the gorge of Nancahuazú. It was the afternoon of April 4, 1967, and the troops had arrived at the site of the main guerrilla camp, abandoned only two days earlier.

Che had returned on March 20 from a long training and reconnaissance march with most of his band, and he was not very happy: there had been terrible difficulties, revealing a number of weaknesses among his men. The situation was not more comforting at the camp: "Everything gives the impression of a terrible chaos," he notes in the *Diary*. A messenger already had informed him that the army was in the region and had moved in on the farm which served as a front for the guerrillas. Two Bolivian recruits who had arrived during his absence had deserted, and nobody knew what to do.

Antonio (Captain Orlando Pantoja Tamayo) was responsible for the camp in Che's absence. Evidently he had not been equal to the task. But Marcos (Major Antonio Sánchez Díaz) had made things worse.

Marcos was the chief of the forward group. The first to return, he let himself be seen at the farm against Che's

orders and then went straight to the camp, putting the
troops on the trail. The soldiers, true enough, had a guide of
their own: while guarding an outpost, the Bolivian recruit
Salustio Choque Choque had been caught by the army, and
soon was drawn into its service.

On March 25 Guevara lets us know in his *Diary* that
Marcos, because of his "errors" as chief of the forward unit,
has been stripped of his command and replaced by Miguel
(Captain Manuel Hernández Osorio).

We also learn on this occasion that among the Bolivian
recruits, in addition to the two deserters and the prisoner
who had gone over to the enemy, four men are to be
considered as "discharged." They "will not eat if they do
not work," their tobacco ration is "suspended," and their
personal effects are divided "among the other comrades
who have more need of them." On this same day, March 25,
Che's guerrillas take the name of *Ejército de Liberación
Nacional de Bolivia* (ELN). An unpromising debut for the
Bolivian National Liberation Army.

In spite of the "climate of defeat" he had noted at the
camp on his arrival five days earlier, Che's major concern
for the moment was to settle the problems of his "visitors."

Led by Tania, the liaison agent in La Paz, the Frenchman
Régis Debray and the Argentine Ciro Bustos had arrived on
March 6, and had been waiting for him since then. Also
waiting at the camp was a Peruvian, Juan Pablo Chang
Navarro (El Chino). On the night of his arrival, Che had a
talk with El Chino, who seemed "very enthusiastic" to him.
The interview continued on the next day, March 21, and
then Che turned to Debray: "He comes to stay, but I have
asked him to return to organize an assistance network in
France and to stop on his way in Cuba, which coincides
with his desire to marry and to have a child with his
companion."

And the army? And the imminent occupation of the main

camp? On March 23 there is a clash with the troops, the first
guerrilla combat. Militarily, it is a great success: the army
loses seven men and the guerrillas capture fourteen prisoners including a major and a captain, as well as a large
quantity of arms and ammunition. But the base at Nancahuazú is now endangered more than ever, and Che is
aware that this unhoped for success is premature: "Obviously," he notes in his summary of the events of March, "we
are going to have to get moving earlier than I had thought."

A significant account of events preceding the capture of
the camp appears in a report prepared for the Bolivian
authorities by the Argentine Bustos (who was later sentenced, like Debray, to a thirty-year prison term). This
report has been made public in English by Jay Mallin.° To
the extent that its author has a part in the story, the Bustos
report, of course, is suspect. But Bustos had no reason to
alter the facts about life at the camp just before and after
Che's return, when they did not concern him personally.
We thus have his confirmation that Antonio, and then
Marcos, had lost their heads; that outposts had been
withdrawn or had fallen back in disorder; that equipment
was transferred from one place to another with little
method. According to Bustos, Che was in a rage—Che
himself reports on March 22 that he "exploded" against
Marcos—and he violently criticized most of his men,
especially Antonio and Marcos, whom he accused of having
planned to evacuate the camp rather than defend it.

Bustos notes that, on this latter point, Marcos rejected
Che's criticism; he adds that others, including Debray and
himself, shared Marcos' point of view "based on Che's own
premise, expressed in his books, that guerrillas should be
constantly on the move and there should be no defense of

° *"Che" Guevara on Revolution* (Coral Gables, Fla.: University
of Miami Press, 1969).

fixed positions." After the successful ambushes of March 23,
he states later, Che remained "stationary" for eleven full
days, while "we all thought, including myself, that he should
give orders to abandon the camp and move to a different
area."

The *Bolivian Diary* certifies that in the last days of
March, life at camp indeed went on in a routine way. The
only special orders given by Che concerned the building of
new underground storehouses. Not until the 29th is there an
allusion for the first time to a planned move out of the
camp, which is now "uncomfortable and too well known."
On March 31, listening to the radio, Che finds that the
military have determined his position "with absolute preci-
sion," and he expresses the fear that they might try "some
encircling movement." Finally on April 1 he announces his
decision to "evacuate everything the very next day." The
operation is completed only on April 2 at 5:00 P.M. "The
incredible quantity of things accumulated," he writes, "has
made us devote the entire day to arranging them in their
respective caves."

In his *Guerra de guerrillas* published in 1960, the same
Che had written:

> The *guerrillero* is a soldier who, like the snail, carries
> his house on his back. . . . He will carry only the
> indispensable, but he will conserve it in all circum-
> stances as something essential which cannot be lost.
> . . . Encampments must be easily dismantled, and no
> traces must be left that might betray them.

At Nancahuazú, however, in 1967, having allowed his men
to accumulate an "incredible quantity of things," he loses
an entire day in hiding them (they will be discovered
anyway), while the enemy threatens to surround him at any
minute. He finally leaves without having erased any of his

traces, losing, or rather abandoning, some of his most
essential possessions.

The first European newsman on the scene was a reporter
from the *Times* of London, Murray Sayle, whose story was
distributed throughout the world by the Associated Press.
Though Sayle admits having accepted, in addition to his
normal journalistic job, "an unofficial assignment by the
Americans, who wanted to know whether these rebels really
existed," his story also appeared in *Granma*, the Cuban
Communist Party organ.

After having described various fixtures—such as individual latrines which, he says, "would have pleased a jungle
warfare instructor at the famous British military college of
Sandhurst"—Sayle reports how he came upon a field
hospital in working order: "I found there packages of
antibiotics, surgical clothing, instruments made in Italy,
Britain, Germany, and the United States, records of patients
identified by first names, and bills from a medical supply
firm in La Paz amounting to $5,000, incurred between last
November 8 and 20 in the name of a fictitious company. . . ." He also reports having seen "a perfectly
equipped field kitchen whose oven could bake bread for a
hundred men," "a garden where vegetables were growing,"
"a butcher's stall," and "dormitories where I found more
than fifty homemade grenades."

Murray Sayle then gives us a personal interpretation:
"The camp had been abandoned in good order, about three
days earlier; no objects of value had been left and the rebels
had tried to burn the documents which they had left
behind. . . ."

Apparently the British newsman and unofficial *chargé de
mission* for "the Americans," thought that antibiotics and
surgical instruments are of no value to guerrillas. Che's
Diary suggests that Che agreed with Sayle's evaluation,
since it shows no undue haste in evacuating the camp, nor

concern as to the items left behind. But if the camp was "abandoned in good order," why had the guerrillas failed to destroy completely the documents which they had "tried to burn"? The medical supply bills, for example, made out to a fictitious firm but sent by a real company, could help the La Paz police track down the intermediaries.* In any case the discovery of the bills closed off that source of supply.

Sayle also saw a photo of Che Guevara and the Spanish translation of a speech by General Giap. He says that he found the photo and the text "among the carefully swept refuse of a dormitory," and adds: "It is impossible that these documents could have been 'planted,' since I found them myself in the garbage, and the Bolivian patrol with me had never heard of Giap."

In their book *The Great Rebel*, published in New York by Grove Press, Luis J. González and Gustavo Sánchez Salazar complicate the matter even more. Just before quoting Murray Sayle's dispatch as printed in *Granma*, they affirm that "the photographer from the Palace of Government, Fanor Ugalde, found a photograph of Che Guevara." Was this the same picture or another one? González and Sánchez Salazar neither raise the question nor answer it. According to Sayle, the photo had been taken "in a forest." So was the one found by Fanor Ugalde, if we are to believe González and Sánchez Salazar, who add that the Bolivian armed services studied the vegetation in the area and determined that the photo was taken at that spot. But if it was the same picture, did Fanor Ugalde, who seems to have been first on the scene, then place it with the garbage so that Murray Sayle would find it?

The authors of *The Great Rebel* observe that the photo was "one more piece of evidence to prove that the

---

* They did: Message No. 38 from Havana informed Che that "Doctor Rhea [is] out of circulation for bill [found] at camp."

legendary revolutionary had been with the Bolivian guerrillas."

It was rather one more proof that an effort was being made to spread that belief. It seemed unlikely that Che, even if the camp had not been evacuated in "good order" as Murray Sayle reported, could have left behind documents proving his presence. The fact that the British journalist found the photo himself, or that Bolivian soldiers with him never heard of Giap, obviously did not rule out the possibility that these documents had been planted there.

Both the French and the Cuban version of Sayle's article refer to an American diplomat who told him: "The Bolivians are pressuring us to give them more military aid." It was this diplomat who had unofficially asked Sayle to find out whether these rebels really existed. The discoveries at the camp of Nancahuazú convinced the inquiring Americans not only of the existence but of the importance of the rebels. From the remark of Murray Sayle's diplomat, that was exactly what the Bolivians wanted, as did perhaps some Americans who did not qualify as diplomats. The coincidence was at least suspicious.

But the *Bolivian Diary* has shown that what seemed probable was not true, and that the truth was what seemed most improbable: that it was Che himself who had supplied the Bolivian generals and their CIA friends with all the evidence they needed.

The first news about the Bolivian army's occupation of the abandoned camp reached Che on April 8, through three of his men sent on a scouting mission and through a report of Joaquín (Major Juan Vitalicio Acuña), chief of the rear guard. On the 10th, a detachment of soldiers who had taken part in the occupation of the camp was ambushed; some were killed and others taken prisoner. "According to the soldiers," Che notes, "they had found nothing, even though the radio talks of photos and documents found there."

Did he believe the prisoners rather than the radio reports? He does not reject the possibility that there were in fact some photos and documents to be found.

On the next day, April 11, he summarizes the outcome of the two clashes of the 10th. Despite the loss of El Rubio (Captain Jesús Suárez Gayol, former head of the sugar industry under Guevara), the guerrillas had won a notable victory: two lieutenants and eight other Bolivian soldiers killed, and thirty captured, including a major, along with a plentiful supply of weapons. But Che also has listened to the radio and he ends his April 11 notes by worrying:

> A Chilean journalist has given a detailed description of our camp and discovered there a photo of me, without beard and with a pipe. We'll have to investigate a little more to learn how this photo was obtained. There is nothing to prove that the upper cave was found, although there are some indications of that.

Perhaps it was inevitable that the army would get to the underground storage caches sooner or later and find the food and ammunition that had to be stored somewhere. But was it necessary to leave all those souvenirs, such as the photo of an unbearded Che?

Thanks to these photos and other documents strewn along the way by Che and his guerrillas, the governments at La Paz and Washington had at hand, for use at any chosen moment, all the evidence they needed to suit their purposes. The CIA had no reason to manufacture false documents since all it had to do was bend down and pick up the real ones. Never before in the history of secret wars were the coincidences so miraculous, the circumstances so unlikely, the intentions so transparent, but the documents, each time, so perfectly authentic.

The discoveries of April 1967 came just before the

conference of Latin-American presidents at Punta del Este, Uruguay. In September 1967 they would come in time for the Organization of American States conference in Washington, and would give all the desired effect to the speeches of President Johnson and Secretary of State Rusk.

The OAS meeting began on September 22, at the foreign minister level, with discussion of a Venezuelan complaint of Cuban interference in its internal affairs. But after a short speech, Ignacio Iribarren Borges, the Venezuelan minister, quickly yielded to his Bolivian colleague Walter Guevara Arze. On a screen installed in the chamber, Guevara Arze projected enlargements of a hundred discovered documents, making only brief comments during the hour-long presentation. These documents, he said, had been found in a storehouse kept by the guerrillas near their zone of operations.

On the same day, at the Palacio Quemado in La Paz, President Barrientos Ortuño and General Ovando Candia held a press conference and gave newsmen copies of some of the documents projected in Washington. The Bolivian armed forces, General Ovando said, had found 21 false passports, and had identified not only Guevara but other Cuban army officers whose names he read out.

In his speech at the OAS conference Dean Rusk took advantage of the effects of Guevara Arze's screening, inviting the countries of the hemisphere "not to remain indifferent to the violence and disorders which can result from such subversive activities."

Speaking at a luncheon in honor of the visiting ministers, President Johnson had already denounced this "virulent form of subversion directed by Havana," and called on the governments to face their "immediate responsibilities." These, according to the President, consisted of "fighting against terrorism and sabotage by resorting to a resolute use of force where that may be necessary," and remembering that "mutual assistance among neighboring countries reinforces their capacity to resist indirect aggression."

Again, the most elementary logic suggested that the "evidence" had been manufactured, even tailor-made, for a purpose: to revive the old project of an inter-American peace force.

The landing of the United States expeditionary force in Santo Domingo in 1965 had discredited this project. The strenuous *post facto* efforts to have it renamed "inter-American" had served only to crudely emphasize the role of any such "peace force" as a façade and alibi for United States intervention. But the idea was still dear to Washington, and continued to be defended publicly by General Onganía's government in Buenos Aires. The "magic lantern" show of documents had been produced, one could not help thinking, to permit Argentina's Foreign Minister Costa Méndez to take up again the need to use force: "My government," he told the OAS gathering, "considers necessary a response that is adequate, effective, coordinated, and systematic."

But logic does not apply to Nancahuazú. Who could have believed that a photo such as the one made public on September 22, 1967, was genuine? In that photo, Che Guevara displays the baldpate and spectacles of "Adolfo Mena González" and "Ramón Benítez Fernández" amid a group of guerrillas in the bush. The men are posing* for the photographer, and Che, very relaxed, smiles as though it were perfectly natural for the leader of a secret guerrilla band to pose for a cameraman.

---

* In one of the many books glorifying Che Guevara, the French writer Philippe Gaví (*Che Guevara* [Paris, Editions Universitaires, 1970].) claims that "an agent of the Barrientos government infiltrated the guerrillas in January 1967," and attributes to this agent "photographs taken with a tiny camera." All of the photos were obviously taken with the consent of the persons photographed, regardless of the size of the camera.

Che, however, was not so indulgent with other people's mistakes. On April 19, for example, he notes that the English-Chilean journalist George Andrew Roth—before finding the new encampment "thanks to some boys at Lagunillas, by following our tracks"—had visited the former camp, and there was shown "a diary of Braulio telling of his experiences and travels." Che was furious: "It's always the same story. Lack of discipline and irresponsibility prevail. . . ."

To keep a diary was certainly not unusual among the rebels led by Che, who set the example; to lose it was not unusual either. Braulio himself (Lieutenant Israel Reyes Zayas) was to start another diary immediately, and it too would fall into the hands of the authorities.

Braulio had forgotten his first diary under the oven at the moment of the evacuation "in good order" of the Nancahuazú camp. That was bad enough, but Che had forgotten the medical supply bills, which was much worse. Daniel James reprints Braulio's second diary, along with the notes of Rolando (Captain Eliseo Reyes Rodríguez) and Pombo (Captain Harry Villegas Tamayo) in his *The Complete Bolivian Diaries of Che Guevara and Other Documents.*° Braulio's indiscretions do not appear very damaging: he speaks mainly about food. Nowhere in all the notes of Che's lieutenants can one find anything as fantastically careless as the blunders displayed in the diary of Che himself.

These begin in the earliest pages. On December 2, 1966, Che relates an interview with El Chino. The latter is to bring him several Peruvians, and there is a discussion about setting up a liaison for shipment of arms through the region near Puno, on the other side of Lake Titicaca. Meanwhile, El Chino is to leave for La Paz† and Che adds—in

° New York: Stein and Day, 1968.
† El Chino never left. He was with the group of guerrillas killed or captured on October 8 in the Quebrada del Yuro.

writing—the following details:

> He is taking with him some photos of us. Coco has instructions to prepare the contacts with Sánchez (whom I shall see later) and to contact the chief of the press service at the Presidency who has offered to pass on information since he is the brother-in-law of Inti. The network is still in its diapers.

Even the use of such a transparent alias as El Chino (the Chinaman) marked an unbelievable negligence, for Che might as well have used the real name.

Juan Pablo Chang Navarro was Chinese on his father's side, and he looked it. He was known to the police for having played a public role in support of the Peruvian guerrillas. There was every reason to expect that if a man like Chang Navarro was walking the streets of La Paz, he might be recognized, apprehended, and at least searched. In this case, while an incredulous world would have talked of a CIA provocation, the "photos of us" would have supplied from the start, as early as December 1966, authentic proof of Che's undertaking.

Coco and Inti were the brothers Roberto and Guido Peredo Leigue, two young Bolivian Communists expelled from their pro-Soviet party. Coco was slain in an ambush on September 26, 1967. A survivor of the Quebrada del Yuro and official successor of Che Guevara as head of the National Liberation Army (ELN), Inti was killed on September 9, 1969, at La Paz. His identity, like Coco's, had been known very early. If not, the police, once they had Che's diary, would only have had to search for the brother-in-law of the man who in December 1966 had been chief of the presidential press service.

This well-placed figure, nonchalantly revealed by Che as ready to supply information to the guerrillas, does not seem to have risked much, but Che could not have known that.

His name was Gonzalo López Muñoz, and it reached the press for the first time, other than through presidential statements or releases, when it was found in an address book of Che's main liaison agent in La Paz, the mysterious Tania.

The woman known as Tania was Tamara Bunke Bider, Argentine-born daughter of German refugees. According to former agent Gunther Maennel, who claims that she was under his orders, she worked for East Germany's secret service. Apparently, the "lack of discipline and irresponsibility" Che complained of in Nancahuazú—about others— was contagious, even for a German-trained militant. After having brought Régis Debray and Ciro Bustos to the camp, she had remained there with them, also awaiting the return of Che. During all this time her jeep was parked in a street of Camiri. It finally attracted the attention of the police, who soon found that Tania had left her address book and other compromising papers in the vehicle.

In a minutely detailed study of "Castroist Guerrillas in Latin America," published by the *Forschungsinstitut der Friedrich-Ebert-Stiftung* in West Germany,° Professor Robert F. Lamberg expresses the suspicion that "Tamara Bunke was not guilty of any negligence, but acted deliberately, in conformity with the aims of her bosses in Eastern Europe."

Personally, I believe that Tamara Bunke could have found methods simpler and less dangerous for herself, if she wanted to sabotage Che's guerrilla movement.

Cuban propaganda, in any case, has made an immaculate heroine of her, naming schools, hospitals, and a *batallón de macheteras* (female cane-cutters) in her honor. A book was put out in an edition of 500,000 copies, as well as in the

° *Die castristische Guerilla in Lateinamerika,* Bonn-Bad Godesberg, 1971.

form of detachable supplements of *Granma*. The book, *Tania, la guerrillera inolvidable,* is a sort of hagiographic album, with photos and testimonials—no doubt the 1970 Cuban equivalent to the 1952 Argentine petition for the canonization of Evita Perón.

An incidental point: *Granma* reported on December 6, 1972, that a group of "young pioneers" (a Communist children's organization) from East Germany visited the Tamara Bunke boarding school near San José in Havana province. After they were cheered by the Cuban pioneers in their red berets (*Alemania, Alemania! Ra, Ra Ra*), sixth-grader Aracelis Martínez stepped forward to promise the visitors that "we will be worthy followers of the example of *Tania la guerrillera.*" Does that mean that when *pionera* Aracelis Martínez grows up to be a *guerrillera,* she too will do her best to leave her notebooks behind in a car so that the police will have no trouble finding them?

Another observation, more important: On January 17, 1969, the Cuban official weekly *Bohemia,* paying homage once more to Tamara Bunke, made an interesting admission. Tania, the magazine recalled, had belonged to the East German "Free Youth" (the official Communist youth organization), and then to the SED, the East German Communist Party or, as *Bohemia* puts it, "the organization in power in the German Democratic Republic." It was during her Communist youth work, the weekly adds, that she began to concern herself with Latin-American problems, and before coming to Cuba she went "to Moscow, Prague, and Vienna on revolutionary missions."

No one has pointed out—and *Bohemia* does so only unwittingly—that Tamara Bunke happens to have been the only participant in Che's guerrilla who, unlike the Bolivian or Peruvian members, for example, or even Régis Debray, belonged to an orthodox Communist organization, that is, one loyal to Moscow.

In its haste to polish the halo of the new saint, *Bohemia*
once even—accidentally or deliberately—confused *Tania*
with *Tuma*. Learning of the death of Tania, the magazine
says in its March 8, 1968, issue, Che wrote in his *Diary* that
he felt this loss as that of a child. This, *Bohemia* concludes,
should be "sufficient to establish the revolutionary and
human qualities of the *guerrillera* Tania." Che's *Diary*, in
the entry for June 26, 1967,° speaks of *Tuma*, not of Tania.

The Bolivian authorities obtained the notebooks of Tania
in March 1967. One month later, on April 21, at the time of
the arrest of Debray and Bustos at Muyupampa, police
found on them letters of introduction written on the
stationery of the presidential press service and bearing the
signature of Gonzalo López Muñoz. The same stationery
and signature had already been used for a letter of
recommendation dated September 3, 1966, which the
Bolivian authorities were to find in August 1967 in one of
the guerrillas' caches. The letter was written in the name of
the Uruguayan citizen Adolfo Mena González, "special
envoy of the Organization of American States, assigned to
study and compile data on economic and social relations in
rural Bolivia." And all authorities of the country were asked
to cooperate with Adolfo Mena—that is, with Che Guevara.

Tania, who died on August 31, 1967, with the group led
by Joaquín in the Vado del Yeso ambush, had worked for a
time as secretary-interpreter in the office of the chief of the
press service. So López Muñoz explained that Tania, known
in La Paz as Laura, had forged his signature after having
stolen the stationery. He obviously had good friends in high
places, for his story was accepted. He lost his post, but
nothing else happened to him.

Gonzalo López Muñoz was not arrested until October 23,
1967. Confirming the arrest and explaining it three days

° See Chapter I.

later, Antonio Arguedas Mendieta, the *ministro de gobierno*, simply showed the newsmen a photocopy of the December 2 entry in Che's *Diary*, which mentioned the friendly press service chief.

Freed under conditions which remain obscure, Gonzalo López Muñoz resumed his activities as a journalist specializing in economic issues, as if nothing had happened. He was arrested again on March 21, 1970, released a few hours later, arrested once again and released on March 23. After his fourth arrest, on March 25, he was deported as an "undesirable element." A communiqué issued by one of the successors of Arguedas Mendieta at the *ministerio de gobierno* said that the former press chief, conspiring with a former director-general of the Bolivian petroleum industry, had tried to sell to Gulf Oil for $5,000 a secret document concerning negotiations then under way for the "commercialization" of the country's petroleum.

Che apparently never realized that he was jeopardizing people by naming them in his diary, and not all the victims of his carelessness were such ambiguous and rather well-protected characters as Gonzalo López Muñoz.

On July 20, 1967, for example, he mentions "a man named Melgar" who gave him information about the movements of the army, and who, Che notes, was willing to be of further help. The same day and on the basis of indications given by "the man named Melgar," the *Diary* tells us that "a major named Soperna" seemed to be a "halfway sympathizer or admirer" of the guerrillas. I do not know the fate of Major Soperna, but I fear he had reason to regret having expressed even a halfway sympathy or admiration for Guevara.

The most pathetic case, however, is that of Loyola Guzmán Lara, a philosophy student at San Andrés University in La Paz.

Then 25 years old, Loyola Guzmán was treasurer of the

urban guerrilla organization. She had been expelled from
the pro-Soviet Communist youth group after having been
one of its leaders. Arrested on September 15, 1967, she
attempted suicide on the 17th by jumping from a fourth-
floor window in Arguedas' *ministerio de gobierno,* where she
had been interrogated. Fortunately, she landed on an
awning and suffered only relatively minor injuries.

When Loyola Guzmán left the hospital on September 21
and was led back to her cell, she was able to talk to
newsmen and to explain the reasons for her suicide attempt:
"I could not bear the idea," she said, "that through my
fault, because of the documents found at my place, other
people were jeopardized."

Loyola Guzmán had been arrested following the discovery of Che's caches in August 1967. She had been unfortu-
nate enough to spend two days at the Nancahuazú camp,
and the camera maniacs—as unavoidable among these
guerrillas as the *paperazzi* among the starlets in Rome—soon
were snapping pictures. When Arguedas' men sifted
through the photos found in the caches, they recognized
Loyola in one of them, sitting between Coco and Inti and
posing for the camera with a machine gun in her hand.

The dossier against Loyola Guzmán Lara was completed
by the discovery of Che's diary, in which she was mentioned
several times. Guevara had not even tried to complicate the
work of the police by giving the young girl a different name.

In the January 1, 1967, entry we read: "Loyola will be in
charge of the finances and she is being sent 80,000,° out of
which 20,000 is for a truck. . . ." When he meets the
young girl on the 26th, he adds this note of appreciation,
which certainly could not be used in her defense if the diary
were to fall into the hands of the authorities: "Loyola made
a very good impression on me. She is very young and gentle,

_____

° The Bolivian peso was worth 8 U.S. cents at the time.

but one notes a firm determination. She is on the point of being expelled from the youth group, but they are trying to get her to resign. I have given her the instructions for the cadres and another document. I also reimbursed her for the money spent, amounting to 70,000 pesos. We are beginning to find ourselves short of money."

Loyola Guzmán Lara was one of the ten prisoners freed by the Bolivian government on July 22, 1970, in exchange for two West German hostages kidnapped by the guerrillas in the small community of Teoponte. Later she secretly returned from Cuba, and was again arrested on April 4, 1972, when police raided a house in La Paz which was the hideout of a group of armed militants. In the gun battle, one of the militants was slain and one of the raiders was critically wounded (by Loyola Guzmán, according to the police).

Her visit to Nancahuazú on January 26, 1967, had coincided with the arrival of Moisés Guevara Rodríguez, a leader of the miners union who had been expelled from the pro-Chinese Communist Party. Moisés was to be among the dead of the Vado del Yeso on August 31. In Che's *Diary* he is calmly identified by his real name, though this name happens to be Guevara. A few days before, on January 21, Che's *Diary* had unhesitatingly spelled out the following sentence: "Doctor Pareja will be named chief of the network."

Doctor Pareja Fernández was arrested in mid-October, his name having been found neither in one of the caches nor among Loyola Guzmán's belongings, but in Che's *Diary*.

To the extent that they concerned only himself, one could explain the monumental indiscretions of Che by his complete indifference to death, indeed by the apparent attraction that death had for him. One might even explain these blunders by his sudden waves of optimism, irrational and almost delirious; the *Diary* offers a number of striking

illustrations of this. If he saw nothing wrong with being
photographed as a guerrilla with the bald head and glasses
which were part of his "civilian" disguise, wasn't this
because he had decided he would never again be using that
disguise?

Victory or death. . . . With Che Guevara, the slogan
allows for no evasion: either the guerrilla is defeated and he
has no need of a false passport because he will be dead, or
the guerrilla triumphs and he has no need of any passport
because he will be in charge.

But indifference to his own safety does not explain Che's
negligence in jeopardizing others. Does he name Loyola or
Doctor Pareja in his journal because this notebook never
leaves him and the enemy would have to find it on his body?
Without mentioning the possibility of an accidental loss, this
would imply an attitude of *"après moi, le deluge!"* There is
no basis for such an insulting implication.

Perhaps Che was simply not as competent a guerrilla
leader as was generally assumed? Perhaps there were
certain things he didn't think of, or he didn't grasp, or he
couldn't bring himself to face.

In his *Pasajes de la guerra revolucionaria,*° Che tells how,
in September 1958 during the march toward Santa Clara,
his column lost several bags including one which held "the
book with the names, addresses, weapons, ammunition, and
equipment of each member of the column, one by one."
Although these stories often display a didactic aim, with the
author rarely missing the chance to draw a lesson from
events, he goes on here without a word of comment.

° Various foreign-language versions depart in a number of
places from the Spanish text as contained in *Obra revolucionaria*, the 663-page volume published in Mexico in December 1967 under the supervision of the very official Cuban writer
Roberto Fernández Retamar (Ediciones Era, S.A.). *Obra revolucionaria* is considered the authorized edition of Che's writings,
and most quotations in this book are translated from it.

When he reports in the *Diary* on July 31, 1967, the loss of eleven bags (one of them containing "Debray's book annotated by me and a book by Trotsky"), he at least emphasizes "the political capital that represents for the government."

If the month of August was a fatal turning point for Che's enterprise, it was not because of the Vado del Yeso disaster on the 31st and the extermination of an entire group of the guerrillas. The event was tragic, but no more irreparable than the setback at Alegría de Pío on December 5, 1956, in the Sierra Maestra. What was irreparable was the army's discovery in August of all of the guerrillas' storehouses, with their reserves of ammunition, medicine, and foodstuffs. And it was irreparable because the authorities, at the same time, were able to get their hands on documents which allowed them to destroy the urban network in La Paz.

Contrary to all expectations and to the theoretical convictions of their leader, the guerrillas of Nancahuazú did not draw any strength from the land, from the peasants among whom they were supposed to be spreading out. They depended entirely on the city, and the distraction of the urban underground deprived Che both of any hope of replacing the supplies he had lost and of any possibility of reinforcing the thinning ranks of his guerrillas.

Thus the arrest of Loyola Guzmán, with its consequences, was for Che a setback as crucial as it was avoidable. Was he aware of his responsibility for the disaster? If so, he does not show it. One cannot even be sure he measured the full impact of what had happened, although he immediately guessed the cause. "The radio announces the arrest of Loyola," he writes on September 15, 1967. "That must be the fault of the photos." Nothing else that day, about Loyola or the photos. The following sentence speaks cheerfully of the slaughter of their remaining bull, and the prospect of a good meal seems to prevail over all other feelings.

The personal circumstances in which Che learned of the
loss of the first of seven or eight caches found by the army in
August were profoundly dramatic. But there was a disturbing absence of analysis and initiative on the part of Che, a
clear lack of efficiency, or even a conspicuous incapacity in
dealing with the issues.

Since the end of July he had suffered from an unusually
severe and painful bout of asthma. On the 31st, when the
loss of the eleven bags had just cut off his medicine supply,
his asthma was running *a todo vapor*. On August 2 he writes:
"The asthma has been shaking me up badly and I have used
up the last anti-asthmatic injection; there are only some pills
left for about ten days." On the 3rd he wonders how he will
get through it, since "there is no quick solution in view"; he
has given himself an intravenous injection of novocaine, but
"without result."

On August 4 the asthma is "a little better," but on the 5th
it is again "implacable" and Che thinks "reluctantly" of
sending a group "forward," that is, to one of the secret
caches where medicine is stored. On the 7th he announces
that he will decide this on the next day. On the 8th his
decision is that three men "will go as far as the Nacahuazu°
to get my medicines." On the 12th the asthma remains "at a
tolerable level." And then comes August 14:

> A black day. It was grey as to the activities and there
> were no incidents, but at night the radio news an-
> nounced the capture of the cave where our envoys
> were heading, with details so precise that there can be
> no doubt. Now I am condemned to suffer from asthma
> for an indefinite time. They also took away all sorts of
> documents and some photographs. This is the hardest

° The correct Bolivian spelling is Nancahuazú. The term
designates both the river and the mountainous zone traversed
by it.

blow they have struck at us. Someone has talked. Who?
That's what we don't know.

There was not much to know and no use knowing it. On
September 7, noting that the radio speaks of "precious
information given by José Carrillo (Paco)," Che writes that
"it will be necessary to make an example of him." But Paco
was not captured until August 31, at the Vado del Yeso, the
only survivor of the Joaquín group. The discovery of the
caves in August must have come about through Chingolo
(Hugo Choque Silva) or Eusebio (Eusebio Tapia Aruni),
who deserted in July. In any case, indulging in vain dreams
of revenge on September 7 could not alter the catastrophe
of August.

Was it possible for Che to prevent this catastrophe, or at
least to limit or soften its consequences?

An attempt to answer this question would be idle
speculation. Perhaps Che had good reasons, at the time and
under those circumstances, for not attempting to move the
storage caches known to the deserters as soon as their
desertion had become clear. But even after August 14,
couldn't he still have tried to reach some of the remaining
caches ahead of the enemy, in order to save or destroy the
most compromising documents? I can only say that if Che
ever thought of doing something of that kind, he makes no
reference to it in his diary.

One might also note, at this point, that if Che had been
fully aware of the unnecessary danger represented, for
example, by the photographs, he would never have allowed
them to be taken and stored away.

What went on in Che's mind? The *Diary* often reflects a
certain incoherence, not only in his attitudes but in his
evaluations and reactions. The summary of August thus
contains this enigmatic commentary: "The loss of all the
caves with the documents and medicines was a hard blow,

above all psychological." Only a *psychological* blow, the absence of medicines and, with the arrest of Loyola Guzmán, the end of all possible aid from La Paz?

Che's deep though intermittent optimism seems, here again, to be the only explanation for such attitudes, if they are not to be ascribed to just plain ineptitude.

This optimism remains latent even during his "black days," ready to burst out suddenly at any time, sometimes in the midst of crisis. If he had been religious, one would say he had absolute faith in Divine Providence. He did have faith in his own star. He thus became so sure of victory that as he wrote someone's name in his book, his main concern seemed to be to give each one the place he deserved in the history of this victory, rather than to keep him out of the place that might await him in the prisons of the enemy.

How can we interpret in any other way the note of September 24 on the arrival of the guerrillas at the hamlet of Loma Larga?

This was only two weeks before the end. The men are weary from the long, useless marches. On that day at least they will eat, and Che isn't going to forget the peasant to whom they are indebted for it: "We killed a pig sold to us by the only peasant who stayed in his house: Sóstenos Vargas; the others fled when they saw us." The former *comandante* of the Sierra Maestra knew how Batista's men treated peasants such as Sóstenos Vargas. He has forgotten that it would be prudent not to point out a friendly peasant to the men of Barrientos.

Even if he had thought of that, it probably would have been more important in his eyes to preserve the name of Sóstenos Vargas for posterity; the possible misfortunes of the present could not interfere with his vision of the future.

I believe that to understand something about Che Guevara, and not simply dismiss him as a helpless blunderer, one must see in him the man for whom unrestrained ambition and acceptance of total sacrifice were inseparable. Since his own ambition was the ambition he dreamed of for the masses, he found it perfectly natural that the masses should sacrifice themselves to his ambition, which ought to be theirs. Even the disconcerting photomania appears less confounding in this light. If the revolutionary nucleus—the *foco*—of Nancahuazú was to spread to Peru, Argentina, all of Latin America, it was necessary to popularize by all means, including photographs, the importance of the movement started in Nancahuazú, particularly by emphasizing the presence of Che Guevara at its head. That's why El Chino, after his first talk with Che on December 2, 1966, was to take with him "some photos of us."

Chapter 8 of this book deals with the Bolivarian dream of a second Latin-American liberation that Fidel Castro and Che Guevara had shared. Che pursued this dream relentlessly in the name of Trotsky's "permanent revolution"; Fidel Castro, although continuing to invoke the spirit of Bolívar, slyly or pragmatically soon turned toward the Stalinist conception of "socialism in one country." In Bolivia, Che was alone. Bolivia would be his tomb or his springboard.

Before going further, we must first examine the relationship between Castro and Guevara in Havana, and then between Guevara and Castro in Bolivia.

IV

Castro and Guevara

Celebrating the seventh anniversary of his regime on January 2, 1966, Fidel Castro started the day with a four-hour parade of artillery, tanks, troop carriers, and goose-stepping soldiers whose somber mass heavily outweighed the "popular militia" units of boys and girls. Then came a three-hour speech in which the 500,000 people in the Plaza de la Revolución were told that their rice ration was being reduced from six to three pounds per month.

When a leader wants to teach his people that guns must come before butter, it is natural for him to first display the guns—and helpful to blame someone else for the lack of butter. But Fidel Castro's choice of a scapegoat was startling. On this solemn occasion, with the Tricontinental Conference about to open, he publicly put the blame for the cut in rice rations on the People's Republic of China.

The Chinese, Castro said, had reduced by half the rice shipments due under the existing rice-sugar trade agreement, thus forcing the Cuban government to impose the same reduction on its people. True, Castro mentioned the possibility of a "misunderstanding." He knew, however, that a misunderstanding, even between two "socialist" governments, was bound to grow when trumpeted before 500,000 people and when one of the two "brotherly" countries is made responsible for the privations of the other.

A statement on January 9 by the Ministry of Foreign Trade in Peking, broadcast by the official Chinese News Agency, conveyed the expected reaction: it "deplored" Castro's assertions, branding them as having been made "unilaterally and untruthfully."

According to the statement, China had agreed to supply Cuba with 250,000 tons of rice in exchange for 370,000 tons of sugar, but this was to apply only to 1965. For 1966, the Cubans were asking for 285,000 tons of rice, while the Chinese could offer only 135,000. Castro himself, the statement reminded him, had listed the reasons as "(1) the need to create a reserve in case of any attack by the U.S. imperialists; (2) the aid they have to give to Vietnam; (3) a deficit in the production of other grains which forces them to import from the capitalist area and hence to use some rice in order to obtain foreign exchange for that purpose. . . ."

In any case, the negotiations were not finished, the statement concluded: the Cuban negotiators were still in Peking, and the Chinese Ministry of Foreign Trade considered the attitude of the Cuban Prime Minister "extraordinary in the normal relations between States."

On January 12, 1966, came the first volley from Havana, with light artillery preparing the ground for the bombardment to come. A communiqué of the Cuban Ministry of Foreign Trade proclaimed that "the Revolutionary Government of Cuba is not in the habit of issuing statements which do not rigorously conform to the facts" and that "the strict veracity of our Prime Minister cannot be questioned." It repeated that the reduced trade with China was "an unexpected heavy blow to our economy, creating a problem without an immediately possible solution in regard to the feeding of our population."

The heavy artillery was unleashed at point-blank range on February 6, when *Granma* came out with an enormous headline: "The Chinese government has betrayed the good faith of the Cuban revolutionaries, and by aggravating our blockade aligns itself with Yankee imperialism."

The headline was taken from a statement signed by Castro, which filled two pages of *Granma*. Castro denounced "the obvious extortionist position taken by China" and explained it as "a display of absolute contempt toward our country." The question, he said, was whether big powers could be allowed to practice "blackmail, extortion, pressure, aggression, and strangulation," whether they had the right to resort to "the worst methods of piracy, oppression, brigandage ever seen in the world since the appearance of class societies: slavery, feudal regimes, absolute monarchies, bourgeois States and, in the contemporary world, imperialist States."

Directed against the People's Republic of China, such an orgy of imprecations—remarkable even for Castro—obviously could not be explained by a mere shortage of rice; Cuba's "revolutionary" government had been quite satisfied before to blame Washington alone for the many other privations the Cuban people had undergone.

Nor could it be explained by the fact that China, despite the objections of the *jefe máximo*, had been flooding Cuba (especially its army officers) with the contents of "more than 800 diplomatic pouches full of propaganda." As the Chinese later retorted in Peking's *Jenmin Jih Pao*, why should Communist "printed matter" from China be "dreaded like the plague" in Cuba? It is hard to imagine that Castro was so afraid of the possible effects of that printed matter, or that he would betray to such a degree what the Chinese editorial called "lack of confidence in one's own cadres and officers, and in one's own people. . . ."

Before Castro's outburst of February 6, the Foreign Trade Ministry in Peking had replied to his January 12 attack that his accusations were "contrary to the truth."

Apparently hoping to confer some plausibility on Castro's artificial rage the next day, *Granma* published the Chinese statement on February 5, taking care to emphasize that it came from a "spokesman" of the Ministry, nothing more. Castro's wild anger on the 6th thus could be attributed to the fact that he had felt personally insulted, and there was indeed one sentence in the two pages of *Granma* which sounded sincere: "An obscure Chinese bureaucrat cannot be permitted to call the Prime Minister of a socialist country a liar," Castro indignantly protested.

It was nevertheless clear that the time bomb that went off on February 6 had been set long in advance, and was already ticking in Castro's January 2 speech in the Plaza de la Revolución. What was Castro's motive?

According to the New York *Herald-Tribune*, still being published at the time, this was Cuba's response to a Chinese plot. Reflecting a theory popular among certain Cuban émigrés,° an editorial of February 7 declared: "Mao Tse-tung has been trying to overthrow Fidel Castro and to install a new Communist dictator in Cuba—one who would respond to Peking rather than to Moscow." The editorial had something more to say about Castro: "Does he not, better than anyone, know the whereabouts of his mysteriously missing chief lieutenant, Ernesto 'Che' Guevara, outspoken supporter of Mao Tse-tung in Havana? Was 'Che' the man Mao had assigned to liquidate Castro?"

No. The initiative had come from Castro, and Mao had no part in it. Neither did Che, for that matter. But nothing better illustrates Castro's real problem with Guevara, and the reasons for Che's Bolivian adventure later that year, than Fidel's artificial quarrel with Mao early in 1966 over a matter of rice.

Fidel Castro had a debt to discharge, and shipments of

° See Chapter II.

essential goods had to be paid for in advance. With his
juvenile assistants—*les Enfants au Pouvoir*, as Jean-Paul
Sartre admiringly called them—he had ruined the country's
economy, and the doting approval of French philosophers
or Italian filmmakers could not help it survive. Soviet aid
could help, but the Russians wanted to be paid, and not
only in sugar. Castro paid, royally: in his speech of March 13
at Havana University, the "misunderstanding" about rice
had become "a true betrayal of proletarian internationalism," and "the ballet-masters" of China, he sneered,
were "cut-rate revolutionaries." (*Los corifeos de China
Popular son revolucionarios de pacotilla.*)

Peking, naturally, knew what was going on, but its leaders
tried to leave the door open as long as possible, while
omitting the usual description of Castro as "the great leader
of the Cuban people." On February 21, having thought it
over for two weeks, they answered Castro's February 6
statement in the official organ of the Chinese Communist
Party:

> In the midst of the concerted attacks on China by
> the U.S. imperialists, reactionaries of all countries, and
> Khrushchev revisionists, Cuban Premier Fidel Castro
> has added his voice to the anti-China chorus.

The winners were the Russians. The Chinese had hoped
that the Tricontinental Conference would allow them to
expand their "third world" influence to Latin America. The
flank attacks led by Castro cut the wings of Peking's
offensive, created disarray among those who wanted to be
friends of both Cuba and China, and gave Moscow a victory
over Mao which was also a victory over Che. The ovations
which greeted Che's name on January 7 were window
dressing. The day before, in fact, the same delegates (except
the Chinese) had given a standing ovation to the Uzbek
author Sharaf Rashidov, head of the Soviet delegation.

"As Comrade Castro has said," Comrade Rashidov proclaimed to set off the acclamations, "divisiveness before the enemy has never constituted a revolutionary strategy." These had been Castro's words, in reply to Wu Hsueh-tsien, head of the Chinese delegation, who on January 5 had denounced the USSR as an "accomplice of imperialism."

The long and fierce diatribe of Wu was scarcely mentioned in the Cuban press. "The third speaker of the morning," *Granma* reported, "was the delegate of the People's Republic of China, who greeted the Tricontinental and paid tribute to the revolutionary struggle in Asia, Africa, and Latin America. After denouncing the imperialist policy in Southeast Asia, he advocated intensifying the struggle and the solidarity of the peoples of the entire world." That was all.

But Comrade Wu had not only attacked "those persons who call themselves partisans of the struggle and who cooperate with the United States in all domains, becoming in fact their main ally." He had also proclaimed, according to foreign correspondents' dispatches from Havana, that "the best way to hasten the final defeat of Yankee imperialism lies in supporting other wars of liberation such as that of the Viet Cong."

What Wu said here was later spelled out in the famous message of Che: "Create two, three, many Vietnams." And it was to be the leitmotif of the OLAS conference in the following year. No one considered it suitable to recall that the idea wildly acclaimed in 1967 had been scorned in 1966, and that Che's proposals had been launched first by a certain Wu. This did not mean that Castro had suddenly been converted to the concepts of Wu Hsueh-tsien and Che Guevara. In Havana people were beginning to realize, at least since the disappearance of Che, that Castro's words should not be taken too literally, and that his obligations

toward the Soviet Union did not exclude a ration of verbal
liberties.

This was part of the game. The Russians were perfectly
aware of the asset they had in Castro's reputation for
independence, his renown as an *enfant terrible*. If not for
that, why would Castro's support be valued more by them,
in their Tricontinental rivalries with China, than the
support of Ulbricht or Gomulka? Or of Todor Zhivkov, who
did not know how right he was when he said in the Plaza de
la Revolución on July 26, 1970, that "with each passing
year, Bulgaria and Cuba grow closer."

The official Kremlin spokesmen themselves had permission to play the game of "supporting revolutions everywhere" when necessary, and Sharaf Rashidov, like many
others before him and with still more applause to reward
him, unhesitatingly urged "progressive humanity" to stop
"the international banditry of the United States in Vietnam." The Uzbek writer, in his Tricontinental speech, went
so far as to express "a special solidarity with the armed
struggle of the patriots of Venezuela, Peru, Colombia,
Guatemala, and all of Latin America° against the lackeys of
imperialism." This was not new, he explained: "The Soviet
people have always supported the people's wars of liberation and the armed struggle of oppressed peoples."

Sharaf Rashidov was no less and no more sincere than
Fidel Castro who, in his closing speech of January 15,
hammered away at the theme "the duty of each revolutionary is to carry out the revolution," and unwisely added:
"and to do so in deeds, not words."

Speaking of deeds, three days earlier the Cubans had
exerted their influence in favor of a Soviet "suggestion" that

---

° When the Uruguayan Foreign Ministry later summoned the
Soviet Ambassador in Montevideo to ask for "clarification," it
was told that Rashidov had been speaking "privately."

a reference to "peaceful coexistence" be included in the general policy statement of the Conference. The words were retained over vehement Chinese objections, 31 votes to 9. Castro's associates had succeeded in holding a number of reluctant delegations to the Soviet side of the line. But the nine in the Chinese minority included—in addition to China, North Korea, and the Communist Parties of Japan and Indonesia—the delegations of North Vietnam, the Viet Cong, and the representatives of the "fighting groups" of Peru, Guatemala, and Venezuela.

Had Che been present, it would have been unthinkable that the Cuban delegation could have found itself even momentarily opposed to the Vietnamese and to the few guerrilla bases existing in Latin America. But Che was not there. His absence was necessary, since Castro, despite his revolutionary words and gestures, could not afford any untoward moves apt to displease the Kremlin.

The turning point had come in the spring of 1963, with the lengthy visit of Castro to Moscow and the public "reconciliation" of Castro and Khrushchev.

Nearly every newspaper in the world must have printed that photo of Castro in a fur hat, enthusiastically greeted at Murmansk by a group of Soviet women on April 27, 1963. Everyone wondered at the time about the reasons for this hurried journey. The Cubans themselves had been taken aback. Only *Hoy*, the orthodox Moscow-line newspaper (*Revolución* still retained a 26-of-July type, now old-fashioned audience) managed to come up with an editorial, limited to celebrating the "brotherly love" uniting the two "socialist" countries.

According to Washington, where the "experts" of the State Department had taken credit for having driven a wedge between Havana and Moscow, Nikita Khrushchev was trying to repair the damage and was beseeching Castro to patch up their quarrel. Others believed such a sudden departure was due to the haughty orders of an exacting master rather than to the tearful entreaties of an abandoned mistress. Fidel Castro was to have presided over Cuba's May Day celebration. If he so suddenly gave up the plan to be among his people on that day, it was because Khrushchev had deemed his presence more important in Moscow's Krasnaya Ploshchad than in Havana's Plaza de la Revolución.

The *Herald-Tribune*, recalling that Peking had accused Khrushchev of capitulation to Kennedy in the missile crisis, wrote: "Cuba is a scalp destined to be hung on Khrushchev's belt during the Communists' great war dance of May Day."

The Moscow trip paid off handsomely for both sides. Economically, Castro obtained "long-term credits on favorable terms," and better prices for the Soviet purchases of sugar, as he reported in a speech on June 4 after he returned from Moscow. Castro did not mention it then, but the Cubans soon found out for themselves when buying their gasoline: the Russians, in exchange, had increased the price of petroleum products—in fact Cuba now had to pay twice as much. What Castro stressed most on June 4 was the promised delivery of new military supplies which guaranteed, he said, "the maintenance of our armed forces in the best combat conditions."

But the real meaning of the trip became obvious when Castro in the same speech offered Khrushchev a tribute whose deep political implications, if not high literary virtues, could hardly be missed by anyone, and certainly not by the Chinese:

I have returned with the impression that comrade Khrushchev is a great leader, a formidable adversary of imperialism. . . . He is a man of extraordinary mental energy, of complete mental lucidity, and not only of

great mental lucidity but great mental agility, an active
mind. . . . Without a doubt one of the most luminous
intellects I have ever met. . . .

Not only was the missile affair forgotten, but Castro was
certifying explicitly that contrary to what he had apparently
thought at first, the Soviet Union "had not hesitated to take
the risks it ran concerning our country."

As Theodore Draper wrote at the time in *The Reporter*,
no one else could have been of greater help to Khrushchev
in turning aside the Chinese menace, and that was "well
worth its weight in rubles or in pesos." Indeed, the Soviet
note of July 14, 1963, to Peking pointed to "the manner in
which the leaders of the Cuban revolution themselves have
judged the policy of the Soviet government, which they
have called a policy of fraternal solidarity and genuine
internationalism."

Castroism, even after Castro himself discarded it by
officially embracing Communism, has always been and still
is a kind of pragmatism, stressing practicality or immediate
usefulness as the essential criterion. Among statesmen,
pragmatism might be considered a virtue, but militants call
it by another name: opportunism. Che Guevara was a
militant, and opportunism in his eyes was something hateful.
Could he go along with Castro's concessions when they
aligned Cuba with Khrushchev against Mao, and sacrificed
principles, including the concept of the "anti-imperialist
struggle" he and Fidel were supposed to share?

I imagine Fidel at first persuaded Che that these concessions were only temporary and that his policy had not
changed. A certain balance had remained on the surface. In
August 1963, for example, the review *Cuba Socialista*
published in full China's reply to the Soviet attack. In the
September 1963 issue it published Guevara's essay, *Guerra
de guerrillas: un método*, which included this remark: "No

matter how distant the socialist countries, their beneficial influence will always be of help to the struggling peoples, and their instructive example will give them greater strength."

Nothing prevented the Kremlin from taking this as a compliment to the USSR. But China, geographically the most distant of all the "socialist" countries, had even better reason to feel flattered, and showed it by reprinting Che's article in the *Peking Review*.

It was Che, moreover, who in December 1963 gave the official closing speech of the "Week of Solidarity with South Vietnam." He did so as if Castro, on the preceding May 23, had not signed the Moscow communiqué with Khrushchev, proclaiming that "in present-day conditions the most important problem for humanity is the struggle for peace." Che praised the "new wars of liberation" which were beginning everywhere, and he did not seem unduly afflicted with a sense of proportion or even of accuracy, since he placed on the same level "the great victories won during the last months of this year by the people's forces of Venezuela on our continent and by the liberation army of South Vietnam."

In fact, one of his more trenchant comments could have been meant as a challenge:

> There can be neither compromise nor halfway measures. There can be no peace agreements which only partly guarantee the stability of a country. The victory must be total.

But Che Guevara, like Fidel Castro, was well aware of the need for Russian assistance. It took him some time to lose his illusions that this assistance was motivated only by Soviet generosity. In a "lecture for the education of the people" on March 20, 1960, he spoke of the agreements signed with the USSR as an act of "economic liberation." He admitted that the Russians would pay 80 percent of the bill for Cuban sugar purchases in goods—priced unrealistically high—and only 20 percent in dollars. But he had an instructive if not "educational" explanation for this: "The dollar has no value other than its buying power, and when we receive manufactured products or raw materials, we are simply using sugar in the same way as the dollar."

Again in October 1964, in his article for *International Affairs*, he saw in the agreements with the USSR "one of the main bases for the development of our sugar industry, as well as for the development of the country as a whole." For him, such economic accords provided "an example of the relationship that can exist between an underdeveloped and a developed country when both belong to the socialist camp."

Meanwhile Fidel Castro had brought back from his two trips to the Soviet Union (the second one was in January 1964) serious doubts about Che's capabilities. His dependence on the USSR was the result of Cuba's total economic chaos. Since it was out of the question that he, Fidel, could have placed the country on the wrong road, the only possible conclusion was that the man assigned to deal with these questions had not been equal to the task. He didn't need the Russians to tell him that all was not well in Cuba, but the Russians were happy to provide the details, documents, and experts to show the errors committed by Che Guevara.

Thus even before Che's first misgivings about Castro's new political orientation, Fidel had already reached his first conclusions about Guevara's old economic orientation.

Being a pragmatist, the fact that this orientation had once been his own did not trouble Castro. What disturbed him, he said in his speech on June 4, 1963, after the first Moscow trip, was to see the seriousness with which the Russians dealt with economic questions, while Cuba remained "vaguely idealistic," which apparently amounted to "an excuse to let things drift."

The truth was somewhat different. It was simply that Che had persisted longer than Fidel in holding to a conviction shared by all the men of the Sierra, derived neither from Marx nor Lenin but from José Martí, the thinker and pioneer of Cuban independence. The vague idealism now rejected by Castro emphasized the necessity of the country's escape at any price from the "slavery of sugar."

"In Cuba," Che wrote in 1959, "we are the slaves of the sugar cane, an umbilical cord which attaches us to the great North American market. We must diversify our agricultural production, stimulate industry. . . ."

This was certainly true, and it was pure Martí. Again pure Martí was the prescription set forth by Che in 1960: "The pillars of political sovereignty erected on January 1, 1959, will be totally consolidated only when we have obtained absolute economic independence." What was not at all in the Martí spirit was to replace one umbilical cord with another, longer, more inconvenient, less nourishing than the first, and no less incompatible with the country's independence. But in 1963–64, this was already a *fait accompli;* and Cuba no longer had any choice.

The diversification of agriculture was the responsibility not of Che, but of Fidel himself. Together with his team of arrogant and incompetent juveniles, he mismanaged it at his whim, sheltered from all criticism and from any popular control.

The plain result was to reduce the main export resource, sugar, without supplying any other product in its place, even for internal consumption. I have related some of the exploits of the "children in power" in my book *Autopsie du Castrisme*, published in France in 1962. The ballyhooed "battle of the rice" was one of them. In 1960, when Cuba imported more than half of its rice, Castro announced that by 1963 Cubans would eat their own rice and depend on others no longer. But in 1966, a "misunderstanding" with China was enough to reduce the rice ration by half. And Castro, switching from "misunderstanding" to "blackmail" and "strangulation," did not explain why his government had left its people to the mercy of a big power capable of such methods.

Industry was advancing no better, and this was entirely Che's responsibility. Cuba constructed factories at great expense, only to realize later that the raw materials or qualified workers, or both, were lacking. Complete plants were imported with no idea of what to do with them; if the plants did begin operating, the goods they produced were of poor quality and prices were prohibitive.

Che Guevara complicated matters by refusing to use material incentives for industrial production; these he considered characteristic of capitalist society, and the only incentive he wanted to build on was "socialist conscience." But the Cuban workers did not appreciate cuts in their wages, even in the name of "socialism." When Castro's regime dismissed and arrested elected labor leaders and replaced them with obedient Communist bureaucrats, depriving the workers of any possible defense through their unions, they cared even less about the quality of their work, and production declined. We shall come back to that in our later discussion of "socialism and man in Cuba."

After Castro's two journeys to the USSR, absolute priority was given to sugar, and the Minister of Industry had to hurry to modify what remained of his plans.

Che's speech of February 26, 1964, is not included in the *Obra revolucionaria* selected by Roberto Fernández Retamar, but it was reported in the press at the time. In that speech, Che declared that only 70 percent of the anticipated imports of industrial raw materials had been received, and production had therefore fallen 16 percent below expected levels. He announced that industrial production would remain at a reduced level during the coming years, but would resume on a full scale after 1970. The assumption was that by 1970 Cuban sugar production would have reached 10 million tons, assuring the financial resources needed for industrial development.

Although all activity in the country was concentrated, in 1969–70, on this single objective—*la zafra de los diez millones*—to the detriment of all others, production fell short of the goal by 1.5 million tons, and the Cuban economy was even more disorganized in 1970 than it had been in 1964. Che, meanwhile, had died in Bolivia.

In 1963 and 1964, as Minister of Industry Che had carried out his new orders with discipline, but not without a certain bitterness. This shows clearly in his speech of February 26, 1964, implicitly criticizing the Cuban people: "When we invest in a factory, we are working for the future. In doing so, we slow down the building of the present, in other words that which can be consumed immediately." Obviously, he was annoyed with the Cubans for not choosing to sacrifice the present to the future, thus delaying the construction of "socialism."

If there was a conflict between Guevara and Castro on this point, it remained hidden. Soon enough, on another issue, conflict appeared inevitable. On July 5, 1964, Richard Eder reported in the *New York Times* that in an eighteen-hour interview over a period of three days, Fidel Castro told him that "Cuba would commit herself to withhold material support from Latin-American revolutionaries if the United States and its American allies would agree to cease their material support of subversive activity against Cuba."

What was going on? True enough, the Cuban press had indirectly revealed the discontent of Cuban workers by publishing indignant resolutions, menacing decisions, or editorial sermons against "absenteeism," "indiscipline," and "the poor quality of work which is equivalent to sabotage." There had also been some attempts at real sabotage, and signs of underground activity. But the regime did not seem to be in danger. After reporting Castro's prediction that a constitutional government would be formed "not later than January 1, 1969" (!) Eder observed in a matter-of-fact tone: "At present, Dr. Castro has the authority, if he wished, to declare Cuba anything from a monarchy to a vegetarian State."

Even if Castro desperately needed to halt "subversive activity against Cuba," his statement seemed unbelievable. Wasn't he publicly offering the United States what he denied having secretly pledged to the USSR? Unless he had been misinterpreted, Castro was repudiating all his promises about the struggle of the Latin-American peoples. For he was offering to abandon support of this struggle in exchange for some advantage for Cuba.

Castro had *not* been misinterpreted. He returned to the subject in his July 26, 1964, speech in Santiago de Cuba, and in fact confirmed Eder's story. "If other governments stopped meddling in our internal affairs," he asked, "would the Cuban government get involved in what's going on in their countries? Of course not. . . ." Here was a bewildering turnabout, since it implied that his aid to Venezuelan guerrillas, for example, was merely an act of reprisal against a nonexistent interference by the Caracas government in Cuban affairs. Until this speech, such aid was supposed to be an act of revolutionary solidarity with "the heroic struggle of the Venezuelan people against the lackeys of imperialism."

Che said nothing, at least publicly, after Castro's speech. His own opposite view had been stated *before* Castro spoke. The date was May 18, 1964. Che was in Sagua la Grande, in the province of Las Villas, to dedicate a spark plug factory imported from Czechoslovakia. But he had not come to talk about spark plugs.

In reading the speech, we first discover that the internal situation in Cuba must indeed have been somewhat uneasy during the weeks preceding Eder's interview. The United States, Che said, "continues to send explosives and saboteurs to our shores." He warned against "men who, through various religious sects, try to sow confusion and fear." And he still remained strictly a member of the Cuban establishment, a worried member, when he added: "Fear is the most subtle method to make a counterrevolution; beware of the one who spreads fear because he is a counterrevolutionary. . . ."

But that applied only to Cuba, where to be revolutionary consists of obeying the government and not listening to the subversive talk of the Jehovah's Witnesses, guilty of adoring a *jefe máximo* other than Fidel. Che had something else to say to the workers of the new spark plug factory. He had come to preach the gospel of disobedience and subversion as the true path for the other peoples of Latin America, and this against all counsel of moderation, present and future:

> The struggle against imperialism is a struggle to the death, and it can end only with the destruction of imperialism or the disappearance of one of the two systems in conflict. It may seem pedantic and absurd to speak of a mortal struggle between a small country like Cuba and a gigantic country like the United States. But it is not a struggle between two countries, it is a struggle between two ideologies, between two diametrically opposed ways of thinking. Our mission is to add our little grain of sand so that imperialism will be destroyed.

Although there was no direct personal confrontation

between the two men in 1964, it became apparent well before the end of the year that the authority of the Minister of Industry was no longer what it had been before. The powers of the ministry itself were progressively reduced. No matter how scrupulously Che followed Castro's economic directives, anyone else now could do the job. And anyone else would not embarrass the *jefe máximo* in other areas.

Che's departure on a political mission in December 1964 was to provide the means to replace him as head of the ministry.

It is probable that Che was aware of this, and possible that it suited him as well. The ministry now needed a mere administrator. Che must have been eager by then to try something else. Perhaps tricontinental coordination? A new third world program based on an Algiers-Havana axis? The idea of an African junket must have been appealing to Guevara, and could not have displeased Castro. Fidel knew he could not get rid of Che by making him an ambassador. In Africa, Che could even become useful again; like Che, Fidel had been very impressed by Ben Bella.

The visit to Africa had two preludes, and the first gave rise to some questions. For it was not clear why, on November 4, 1964, *comandante* Guevara flew to Moscow as chief of Cuba's delegation to the traditional celebration of the October Revolution. Did Castro wish to give the Russians a chance to influence the troublemaker and to persuade him to support the developing new Soviet-Cuban policies? Perhaps Castro was anxious to prevent Che from standing in the way of the conference of orthodox Latin-American Communist Parties, which was to take place later that month in Havana? He certainly must have thought it useful to show the Russians that he had to reckon in Cuba with people like Che, and that he needed some helpful gesture in order to neutralize such people. For the moment had come to work out the details of the economic accords for 1965.

If that was indeed what Castro had in mind, the presence of the Minister of Industry in Moscow doesn't seem to have done much good. Shortly after his return to Havana his main rival and adversary on economic matters, Carlos Rafael Rodríguez, an old-line Communist, left for Moscow to take over the negotiations. Che himself boarded a plane for New York and the second prelude to his African trip: the United Nations.

Although Castro could only have been pleased with Secretary-General U Thant in the missile crisis two years earlier, the United Nations never played an important role in his plans. Che was even less inclined to build on the sands of Turtle Bay. The visit to the United Nations nevertheless gave him an opportunity to meet, and impress, the famous Afro-Asian group. He was obviously aware of this when he mounted the rostrum, his olive green uniform carefully pressed and freshly starched, his boots gleaming.

While he was talking, Cuban refugees fired a bazooka shell at the rear wall of the building. They succeeded only in making a splash in the East River. In the General Assembly hall, the shot was not even heard.

Che began his speech with all the required diplomatic niceties, *Señor Presidente, Señores Delegados.* . . . He even followed the tradition of welcoming the new members: in 1964 these were Malawi, Malta, and Zambia. But he added to his good wishes the hope that these three countries would join without delay "the group of nonaligned countries which struggle against imperialism, colonialism, and neo-colonialism. . . ."

Courting systematically the third-world applause, he piously intoned all its slogans, repeated all its hypocrisies. He dutifully went down the list: Rhodesia, South Africa, Portugal's colonies, French Somaliland, Aden, "the Arab people of Palestine." In the same spirit he silently passed by the blacks of southern Sudan, Yemen, the Kurds of Iraq. He dodged the question of Sukarno's aggression against Malaysia with one of those platitudes customary at the United Nations, and better suited to striped pants than to an olive green uniform: "The Cuban delegation expresses the hope that there will be a just solution to the conflict facing our sister republic of Indonesia in its relations with Malaysia."

United Nations correspondents also remember the barely suppressed giggling in the solemn hall when Che denounced, among the 1,323 provocations of the Yankees at the Guantánamo base in 1964, "the commission of acts of sexual exhibitionism by North Americans of both sexes."

It is probable that Andrei Gromyko did not particularly relish Che's definition of coexistence: "As Marxists, we have maintained that peaceful coexistence among nations does not encompass coexistence between the exploiters and the exploited, between the oppressors and the oppressed." But the Soviet Foreign Minister was as zealous in his applause as the Saudi Arabian delegate; after all, Che also had said that it was for the oppressed peoples to demonstrate their concept of coexistence "in alliance with the socialist camp."

The trouble began only in Algiers, with Che's speech of February 26, 1965, before the "Conference of Afro-Asian Solidarity."

This time Che Guevara's sermon was addressed directly to the USSR. It is wrong, he said, for a "socialist country" to base its economic relations with "countries entering the path of liberation" on a concept such as "mutual benefit." He brutally added: "If we establish this type of relationship between the two groups of nations, we must agree that the socialist countries are, in a way, accomplices of imperialist exploitation." Even more explicitly, he supplied his prescription for the future: "The socialist countries have the moral duty to put an end to their tacit complicity with the exploiter countries of the West. . . . Foreign trade should not be what determines policy; on the contrary, foreign trade should be subordinated to a fraternal policy towards the peoples. . . ."

The Algiers speech, without doubt Che's most daring criticism of the "socialist" establishment, inevitably set the Kremlin firmly and finally against him. But Kosygin's dislike of the *comandante* probably hardened a few weeks earlier in Peking.

Contrary to a general belief, there was nothing secret about Che's visit to Peking on February 3, 1965. It certainly was no secret for Fidel Castro, since Che went to Peking as chief of a very official Cuban delegation which included two *apparatchiks* considered above reproach in Havana: Emilio Aragonés and Osmany Cienfuegos.

Linked to Moscow by economic needs, Castro intended to hold onto his Chinese trump cards as long as possible. They could be played in different ways. On September 30, 1964, for example, when the annual negotiations for the renewal of economic agreements were approaching, the game consisted of devoting an entire page of the newspaper *Revolución* to Mao. On February 3, 1965, it called for Che's visit to Peking.

While the USSR at that time had not signed anything, China had granted Cuba on December 31, 1964, an advantageous rice-sugar exchange agreement, the one which Castro said in January 1966 was to be in effect for five years, but which in any case arrived in the nick of time for 1965. Moscow kept Fidel waiting to teach him to behave. Fidel replied by showing Moscow that he was not entirely at its mercy. These were the rules of the game. What upset them was the fact that Che found himself in Peking at the same time as Alexei Kosygin.

Che hardly could have known, when he took off for the

Chinese capital, that the Soviet Premier would be landing there two days after his arrival. Mao, however, knew very well that Kosygin, en route to Hanoi, planned to make a stop in Peking. The Cuban Minister of Industry was warmly received by Mao Tse-tung himself. The Soviet head of government was received politely by Chou En-lai. Such things do not pass unnoticed in the "socialist camp."

It may be assumed that the Russians made Havana aware of their displeasure. To make sure that Castro would share it, they only had to remind him that the Che-Mao idyll could prove as dangerous to Fidel as it was disturbing to the Kremlin. By a fortunate "coincidence," the new Soviet-Cuban economic agreements were signed on February 17, that is, shortly after Che's visit to Peking; they provided for a 12 percent increase in trade and sizable credits to cover Cuba's deficit.

Che returned from his journey on the evening of March 14, 1965. He disappeared soon afterward, and did not appear again until October 10, 1967—in the laundry shed of Vallegrande.

The Dominican affair in April 1965 no doubt contributed to his complete break with Castro and I am not the only one, nor the first, to express this opinion. A U.S. expeditionary force had landed on the territory of an independent state, against the will of the constitutional provisional regime established in the capital. It was clearly an imperialist intervention in favor of the Dominican military, who were in trouble after failing in an attempt to grab power. The Cubans had always proclaimed their desire to shed their blood against imperialism in Vietnam, but Vietnam was far away. Here they had a chance to show they meant what they were saying, since Santo Domingo was nearby. For a Che Guevara, the appeal must have been irresistible. Fidel Castro resisted it very well.

Nothing could have been more revealing in this regard than Castro's own angry self-defense on January 15, 1966, at the Tricontinental Conference.

Adolfo Gilly is an Argentine journalist of the "new left," who lived in Cuba for a year (1962–63) and was completely devoted to what he continued to call, under Castro, "the Cuban revolution" (just as the Trotskyites under Stalin continued to speak of the "Russian revolution"). His articles in *Marcha* (Montevideo) and other "leftist" Latin-American magazines also were published in New York in the *Monthly Review*. In one of these articles, speaking of Che's disappearance in 1965 and of the Cuban internal conflict which it reflected, Gilly had emphasized the impact of the Dominican affair.

Trembling with rage, Castro was now publicly taking the journalist to task from the rostrum of the Tricontinental. Adolfo Gilly, he shouted, was "villainous enough to write the following paragraph, which is well worth analyzing, on the crisis of the Dominican Republic." Castro quoted the paragraph:

> The culminating point of this crisis must have been the Dominican revolution, where the State of the Cuban workers was paralyzed by its own policy, without openly supporting the revolution, although in Cuba there was tremendous internal pressure for a policy of active support. . . .

The first of two arguments invoked by Castro in reply to this accusation suggested that the interest of the Dominican Republic as well as that of Cuba justified nonintervention:[*]

> This person has the vileness to accuse the Cuban revolution of not having given active aid to the

[*] Every word here is taken from the official translation as published in the English edition of *Granma*.

revolution in the Dominican Republic. And while the imperialists were accusing Cuba, while they were trying to justify their intervention with the pretext that leftists and Communists trained in Cuba were heading the uprising there; while imperialism was accusing Cuba and presenting the Dominican revolution not as an internal question but as an external problem, this person accused the revolution of not having given active aid. . . .

With unexpected modesty, Castro based the second argument on the disproportion of Cuban and American military power:

And what does active aid mean? Did they expect that Cuba, whose weapons and resources are well known, could stop and should stop the landing of U.S. troops in the Dominican Republic? Cuba has weapons to defend itself, and has these defense weapons in an infinitely inferior number with relation to the imperialists. And these gentlemen are so despicable, so shameless that they blame Cuba for not having prevented . . .° Because what else does active support mean? Because all that Cuba could do under those circumstances, all that it could have done, and should have done, it did. To ask Cuba to prevent the landing is like asking Cambodia in Southeast Asia to prevent bombings of North Vietnam, and to prevent occupation of South Vietnam by Yankee marines. [Applause] Unfortunately, the forces of Cuba are limited. . . .

Both arguments, naturally, were quite valid. One might even say they were self-evident—if they had not been expounded by Fidel Castro.

For on March 3, 1965, less than two months before the

° Castro leaves the sentence unfinished.

invasion of the Dominican Republic, he had stated: "We
regret that we are not closer to North Vietnam in order to
help them with everything we have. . . ." On March 12,
1966, less than two months after his protestations of
powerlessness at the Tricontinental, there was a week of
solidarity with Vietnam. Its theme, repeated on countless
banners, was this phrase of the same Fidel Castro: "For
Vietnam, we are ready to shed our own blood!"

Then all that was nothing but words? Yes, nothing but
words. Because when the opportunity arises for action,
"unfortunately the forces of Cuba are limited. . . ."

Rarely has a demagogue more openly confessed his
demagoguery than did Fidel Castro in that speech at the
Tricontinental Conference. But Castro here was not just
attacking a journalist named Adolfo Gilly, who certainly
counted for little in his eyes. He was replying to Che
Guevara. Desperately, furiously, he repeated the arguments
which he must have used in opposing Che, but which Che
could not accept because Che practiced what he preached.

*Your father has been a man who acts as he believes and,
certainly, he has been faithful to his convictions.* This
sentence in Che's farewell letter to his children is one of the
keys to the Guevara case.

V

Guevara and Castro

Hoy comienza una nueva etapa. . . . "Today a new stage begins. . . ." This is the first line of the diary Ernesto "Che" Guevara kept in Bolivia, from November 7, 1966, to October 7, 1967. It consists of two books. The first is an ordinary notebook with blank pages. The other is an appointment book for the year 1967, published by Karl Klippel, Kaiserstrasse 75, Frankfurt, and the dates are printed in German. On the last page covered with a compact handwriting often difficult to decipher is the printed date: *Sonnabend, 7 Oktober.* The pages that follow are blank.

In the ordinary notebook he used for 1966, Che inscribed the dates in his own hand, beginning with *7 de noviembre.* "In two days and two vehicles," and "conveniently disguised," Che arrived in Nancahuazú by way of Cochabamba on November 7, 1966. . . . With what? With whom? On what road?

By what it tells us of Castro's aid to the guerrillas, or lack of it, Che's *Diary* gives a clear idea of the final relations between the two men. It punctures the official legend of the fraternal and revolutionary team, one mind and one will, a bronze medal with two superimposed heroic heads. It also shows that after the disagreements there came a compromise. Finally, it allows us to perceive the three major points of this compromise:

(1) Che Guevara must have promised not to return to Cuba, not to meddle in Cuban politics, not to say or do anything that might hamper Fidel Castro's policies in Cuba;

(2) Fidel Castro must have promised to aid Che Guevara by facilitating preparations for setting up the guerrilla force, furnishing funds and equipment, allowing Che to choose a core of volunteers from among his old Cuban companions, and also offering to send along any Bolivians trained in Cuba who might wish to join him;

(3) Much more vaguely, the two men must have agreed to consult on political problems which could have direct effects upon one or the other.

Che had reason to be satisfied with the false passports supplied by the Cuban secret service: they never gave him any trouble. These were in fact "false genuine passports," as we used to say in France under the Nazi occupation—not copies or imitations, but originals with false identities. There were two different passports not only for Che himself but for Pacho, who went with him on the last stage of the journey to Nancahuazú on November 7, 1966. Pacho was Captain Alberto Fernández Montes de Oca, former Director of Mines under Guevara. He was slain on October 8, 1967, in the Quebrada del Yuro.

Though he occasionally expresses in the *Diary* some concern about running low on money, Che had nothing to complain about in regard to Cuban financial aid. The guerrillas of Nancahuazú failed to forge the slightest bond with the peasants they were supposed to liberate, but they never lacked money to buy them. The *Diary* shows that to get anything from the peasants, the guerrillas either had to scare them or pay them, and pay them well. Lack of money had no part in the problems of supply faced by the guerrillas, and this remained so even after "the loss of a package of dollars which fell from Pombo's bag" on April 22, 1967.

From statements made by arrested Bolivian deserters, it appears that the unemployed miners recruited by Moisés Guevara were expecting, rightly or wrongly, some kind of regular and substantial pay.

Che never had any illusions about these men. He called them "dregs" (*resacas*) and complained to Moisés about the deplorable quality of the recruits. But the use of material incentives apparently was not as objectionable to him in the Bolivian guerrilla force as it was in a Cuban factory. On December 13, 1966, he notes in his *Diary*: "We spoke to Apolinar, who will go to his house in Viacha for a few days, we gave him money for his family and recommended to him absolute discretion." Apolinar Aquino Quispe did not betray them. He was to be killed on August 31, with Joaquín's group, in the Vado del Yeso.

Money was also used by Che when he tried to silence the old woman goatherd who came upon the guerrillas in the Quebrada del Yuro on October 7, 1967. He knew, of course, that it wouldn't make much difference. "We gave her 50 pesos," he writes on the last page of his *Diary*, "asking her not to say a word, with little hope that she would keep her promises." She did talk, and it meant the end for Che.

As for arms and equipment, it is evident that the Cuban revolutionary government, after a short-lived initial effort, mobilized no more than a very small fraction of the means it had available to ensure at least the survival of the Nancahuazú guerrillas, if not the triumph of the Bolivian revolution.

The two heavy and burdensome radio transmitters soon became useless, first because they were damaged by the humidity and second because no one in the group really knew how to handle let alone repair them. Lost in the tropical forest, the guerrillas had no system of communication or signals. For months Che tried in vain to reestablish contact with Joaquín's group, which had been separated from the main force. Several times the two groups were quite close to each other. A pair of walkie-talkies might have helped. Didn't the Cuban armed forces—or *comandante* Guevara himself for that matter—foresee that walkie-talkies often are handy in guerrilla operations?

Broadcasts from Havana received by transistor radio could have been used more effectively, moreover, to provide not only a regular and essential source of intelligence but also an auxiliary system of relays and communication.

This was not the case. In the beginning, Havana's messages sometimes offered information about contacts or new arrivals. They soon lost any practical value, and even reached a point of futility, considering the message deciphered on September 5, one month before the end. Che had just lost all his supplies in storage; he had no more medicine for his asthma; the Bolivian radio had announced the extermination of Joaquín's group; and on the same day, to get something out of the peasants, "it was necessary to resort to threats." Havana's message for Che was that "the OLAS has been a triumph but the Bolivian delegation was a pile of shit (*una mierda*)."

On April 15, when Che was beginning to receive disturbing reports about the army's discoveries in the abandoned camp at Nancahuazú, "part of a long message from Cuba" was decoded, indicating that "Lechín knows about me, and he is going to prepare a declaration of support, returning secretly to the country in twenty days." What does this mean?

According to Che, not much. On the 12th, after glancing at "part of a message" which must have been the same, he had noted that it "did not appear very important." On the 15th he has no comment at all on the decoded part. Juan Lechín Oquendo, head of the miner's union and former vice-president of Bolivia under Víctor Paz Estenssoro, could lead militants from the mines to join the guerrillas, and they would be far more efficient than the *resacas* of Moisés. But Lechín was a politician, and Che probably was not enthusiastic about collaborating with him. Is that the meaning of his silence? In any case, the question did not arise since there was no further mention of Lechín in the *Diary*.

Another question remains: Who took the initiative to inform Lechín about Che's presence in Bolivia? This question brings us to another which is at the heart of this chapter: Was Che's presence in Bolivia supposed to be a secret or not? From the April 15 entry we learn nothing. Che says only: "A note is written to Fidel (No. 4) to inform him about the latest events. It goes coded and in invisible ink."

The "latest events" meant the victorious ambush at Iripití on April 10, which was costly for the army but also took the life of El Rubio. Apparently Che did not consider taking up with Fidel the possible role of Lechín, or any other matter: he simply wanted to tell Fidel about a brilliant success of the guerrillas in the tradition of the Sierra Maestra, and about the heroic death of one of the men who had been with Che at the Ministry of Industry, who had followed him out of it, and whose qualities Fidel had failed to appreciate.

As Che had mentioned the day before, the messenger who was to carry this note to Havana was to be El Francés, in other words Régis Debray. The message thus never reached its destination.

One more observation. On April 15 Che refers to Fidel by name. This is not the worst example of his carelessness in the use of names, since in this case nobody's safety was jeopardized. But it takes on a preposterous and even nonsensical aspect in light of the only rule followed by Che with childish tenacity: to call Havana "Manila." Here we have Che cautiously saying on April 14 that "message No.

4" is prepared "for Manila," but nonchalantly referring on
the 15th to the same message No. 4 as "written to Fidel." A
Philippine Fidel?

With regard to the political-personal, not to mention
diplomatic relations between Nancahuazú and Havana, the
Diary shows that in general, the formalities were observed.

On April 29 a pompous message asked Che to authorize
the use of his signature on a statement by Bertrand Russell
against the Vietnam War. Che doesn't say whether he gave
his approval; it would have been difficult for him to do so,
since his transmitters did not work. Apparently Havana
dared not use his name without authorization. I have no
knowledge of any appeal by Russell at the time bearing
Che's signature.

But good manners sometimes were disregarded. On
September 12 Che learns through Radio Havana that the
OLAS has received a message of support from his ELN. He
knows better than anyone that there has been no such
message from his National Liberation Army, but he is not
upset: "Miracle of telepathy" is his good-humored comment.

Perhaps the *comandante* of the ELN would have been
less complacent if he had read the account of the OLAS
Conference by Cedric Belfrage, British-born co-founder of
the American "progressive" publication *National Guardian*.
This account appeared in the October 1967 issue of another
"leftist" but quite different American publication, *The
Minority of One*. Thus it was written before the fate of Che
and the contents of his *Diary* were known.

On July 28, 1967, at the time of the opening of the
Conference, Che was still, in the words of its organizers,
"fighting imperialism in some part of the world." Belfrage
noted that "wherever 'El Che' was, his myth was even more
potent than his presence would have been, and Guevara

revolutionary slogans were plastered over the tower of guerrilla weapons erected in the conference-hotel lobby. . . ." True, Belfrage added: "Topping all in dramatic interest was the appearance of the U.S. militant black leader Stokely Carmichael as honored guest."

According to Belfrage, one could hear at this first OLAS conference in July–August 1967 not only the representatives of "the most revolutionary groups that can be called serious in the hemisphere" but those of "guerrilla movements already in action: fighting leaders from Venezuela, Bolivia, Guatemala, Colombia who laid down their guns to come to Havana or who spoke by tape."

The question arises: As far as Bolivia is concerned, who was the "fighting leader" who laid down his gun or spoke by tape?

Since Guevara speaks of miracles of telepathy and not of marvels of tape transmission, we know that he did not record any tape. Any tape attributed to Che, say a "message" composed of bits of earlier recordings spliced together, certainly would have topped in dramatic interest even the appearance of Stokely Carmichael, and the world would have heard about it. In fact, the "fighting leader" from Bolivia who became Che's self-appointed "telepathic" spokesman was Aldo Flores, one of the orthodox Communist Party bureaucrats who made up the official Bolivian delegation.

Curiously, the message from Havana decoded on September 5, the one which described the Bolivian delegation as *una mierda*, mentioned that Aldo Flores "pretended to be the representative of the ELN"; Che notes that "they had to give the lie to him." But on September 12, Radio Havana was still broadcasting, as genuine, the fake ELN statement read by a representative who supposedly had been exposed as an impostor. Strange. . . . Strange and instructive;

obviously Castro had tried to please Che by telling him about the unmasking of Aldo Flores, while Radio Havana (and Cedric Belfrage) apparently knew nothing about it.

In general, Fidel does not seem to have taken up much room either in Che's thoughts or in his *Diary*. And what little space he occupied at the beginning seems to have shrunk with the passage of time.

On January 2, 1967, Che's visitors (Tania, Sánchez, and also Coco, who had not yet joined for good) listened to a broadcast by Fidel before returning to La Paz. "He spoke of us in terms which make us even more committed, if that is conceivable . . . ," Che writes, as if addressing a meeting. Perhaps that was exactly what he felt he was doing, or was supposed to be doing. After all, the speech they had solemnly listened to marked the commemoration of the Cuban victory.

Later on in the *Diary*, Fidel's speeches no longer appear to be listened to with such solemnity. But twice Che briefly cites passages where Castro has changed his position of 1964–65, and he does not seem much impressed by the fact that Fidel now belatedly talks like Che: "We have heard part of the speech in which Fidel castigates the Venezuelan Communists with utter harshness, and speaks with severity of the USSR's attitude towards the American puppets . . . ," he writes on March 14.

And on August 10: "Long speech of Fidel in which he goes after the traditional parties, especially the Venezuelan; there must have been a big brawl off stage. My foot is being taken care of again; it feels better. . . ."

We have come a long way from the time when Che swore only by Fidel, and when his adoration took the form of bad poetry and worse prose, ludicrous in its flattery but sincere in its feeling. A book entitled *Mi amigo, el Che*, published almost simultaneously in 1968 in Buenos Aires, New York, and Paris, brought us precious and definite information about when and how the break occurred between Che Guevara and Fidel Castro.

Ricardo Rojo, the author of *My Friend Ché*, is an Argentine lawyer who had known Ernesto and the Guevara family for many years. Politically, he had started as an anti-Peronist in his youth, like all the members of the liberal bourgeoisie in Argentina, including the Guevara family. Later he became Peronist, whatever that means.°

It must be emphasized here that there is not the slightest trace in *My Friend Ché* of any anti-Castro bias. Quite the contrary: when Rojo gives some "historical background" about the early years of the Castro regime, he rather slavishly follows the official version, with all its blatant omissions and distortions. Rojo even has Castro "completing his sentence" under Batista, when in fact he was pardoned with nearly fourteen years of his fifteen-year sentence still to go.

Castro nevertheless tried at first to ignore Rojo's book; and to make sure others ignored it, too, he banned its sale in Cuba. But *Mi amigo, el Che* had caused much comment abroad, and when some copies began to circulate inside the country, Castro decided to destroy Rojo, unleashing a violent barrage against him. He went so far as to mobilize Federico Evaristo Méndez and Juan Héctor Jouve, two survivors—and the only ones still in prison—of the absurd guerrilla movement led by the journalist Jorge Masetti, a

---

° There was, and is, a good deal of "Peronist" sympathy in Castro's Cuba. On May 25, 1962, the Cuban press published a photo showing Che Guevara side by side with John William Cooke, who had been Peron's right-hand man during the dictatorship. They were presiding together at a banquet of the newly formed "Institute of Argentine-Cuban Friendship." In January 1966 it was John William Cooke (an Argentine by birth despite his Anglo-Saxon name) who represented the "anti-imperialist" Argentines at the Havana Tricontinental Conference.

close friend of Che, in northern Argentina where it vegetated from late 1963 to early 1964.

On October 3, 1968, *Granma* published an aggressive, poster-like article with the following headline in the English weekly edition: "From the Prison at Salta, Argentina, Open Letter from Combatants of the People's Guerrilla Army." The letter, dated July 8, 1968, was preceded by an editor's note worth quoting in full:

> Sr. Ricardo Rojo, an Argentine lawyer closely linked to the CIA, released a book a few months ago about Major Ernesto Che Guevara entitled *My Friend Ché* in which he maliciously tried to twist the revolutionary ideas and personality of the heroic guerrilla combatant. Ricardo Rojo had the undeserved honor of knowing Ernesto Guevara during those restless years in which Che toured Latin America prior to coming to Cuba with Fidel. Of course, Mr. Rojo was not able to understand, much less follow, a single one of Che's revolutionary ideas. Guided by thoughts of personal gain and ambition, and due primarily to his ties with the CIA, he wrote a book which was published in Europe, the United States, and some Latin-American countries, among them Argentina. And it is from there that combatants of the People's Guerrilla Army (EGP), founded by the heroic Major Segundo, Jorge Ricardo Masetti, have sent, from their prison cell, an open letter to Mr. Ricardo Rojo, exposing and condemning his reactionary maneuver. *Granma* reprints the complete text of that important document below.

This "important document," spread over three columns, contains nothing to refute the book, which Cubans were forbidden to read but which they nevertheless were asked to judge on the basis of the refutation. The only point worth quoting is found in the conclusion, where the authors of the "open letter" signed by Méndez and Jouve "waste no time in exposing your lie and rejecting any revision by faithful agents of imperialism such as that *New York Times* 'expert on Latin-American affairs' to whom you are so grateful for having 'revised' your book."

In the preface to the Argentine edition of his book (published by Jorge Alvarez, Buenos Aires, 1968), Rojo not only acknowledges the "help and advice" of Juan de Onis, a well-known *New York Times* reporter; he also thanks two others who thus are included among the "faithful agents of imperialism." It seems that the letter's authors, while imprudently drawing attention to them, preferred not to mention their names. The first was Rogelio García Lupo, one of the most pro-Castro writers in Argentina. The other was Dr. Salvador Allende, then President of the Chilean Senate and a few years later President of Chile.°

Why Castro's ferocious campaign against a book which had not shocked such a personal friend of the *jefe máximo* as Allende, and whose author apparently was not considered by Allende to be "closely linked to the CIA"?

The reason is that Ricardo Rojo, when he states what he knows from personal experience rather than what he has read in Castro's propaganda leaflets, brings to light facts of major importance. It is thanks to Rojo that we know today of the existence of a letter which dispels any doubts about Che's state of mind in the spring of 1965. Written to his mother, this letter from Che had been sent through another of his Argentine friends, also a lawyer, Gustavo Roca.† I do

---

° Strangely enough, while the Argentine edition explicitly acknowledges *la ayuda y el consejo de tres* [3] *personas,* the American paperback edition (Grove Press, New York, 1969) mentions only "the advice and assistance of two persons": García Lupo and Allende. The French edition (Seuil, Paris, 1968) has no preface at all.

† Gustavo Roca and Ricardo Rojo had both been members of

not know what became of it. As far as I know it was never
published; nor have I ever heard its existence denied. In
fact, as will be seen later, its existence was unwittingly
confirmed by *Granma* in its campaign against Rojo. Gustavo
Roca had given the letter to Che's mother on April 13, 1965,
and Celia de la Serna de Guevara showed it to Ricardo
Rojo. In his book, Rojo sums up two passages of the letter:
The first:

> Guevara tells his mother that he is going to give up
> his revolutionary leadership in Cuba, that he intends to
> work for thirty days cutting sugar cane, and that he will
> then spend five years in a factory, to study from the
> inside the workings of one of the many industries he
> has directed from the top.

The second passage is even more revealing:

> He also tells her that she is not to travel to Havana
> for any reason.

Ricardo Rojo then discloses for the first time the text of
the letter written by Che's mother on April 14, in reply to
her son.

She has read Ernesto's letter, she says, "as I read the news
published in *La Prensa* or *La Nación* of Buenos Aires,
tearing out or trying to tear out the true meaning of each
sentence and its full implications." She is aware "there must
be reasons I don't know about." She thinks she knows "half
the answers"—for instance that "if you go to manage a
factory, you are not Minister of Industry any more." She
suggests that "if for some reason the road is blocked for you
in Cuba," he should go elsewhere, to Algeria for example,

---

the group of lawyers which defended the survivors of Masetti's
guerrillas in the court of Salta.

where there was "a Mister Ben Bella who would be grateful
to you for organizing his economy or assisting him in it." In
any case, she cannot accept the idea of Che's spending five
years in a factory. She tries to say things which will strike
home:

> It's not the mother who is speaking. It's an old lady
> who wants to see the whole world converted to
> socialism. I believe that if you do what you have said,
> you will not be a good servant of world socialism.

This letter never reached Che. It was supposed to have
been delivered, Rojo tells us, by an Argentine Peronist
invited to Havana for May Day, but his invitation was
canceled at the last minute. Rojo recovered the letter and
tried to find another messenger. Meanwhile Che's mother,
suffering from cancer, became gravely ill.

Rojo's account of the last hours of Celia is a moving one,
and it attests to the physical isolation in which Che was
living in Cuba at the time he discovered that "other parts of
the world are calling for my modest efforts." On May 16 the
doctors think Celia's death is imminent. Rojo telephones
Aleida, Che's wife, who "seemed rather embarrassed."
According to her, "Guevara was not in Havana, but he was
in Cuba." Rojo explains to her that Celia has only a few
hours to live and that a way must be found to notify Che.
Here is what follows:

> On the 18th, Aleida called the clinic directly from
> Havana. Celia was almost in a coma, but she drew
> herself up in her bed as if she had received an electrical
> shock. It was a painful conversation in which she had
> to shout and which brought no hope. At noon I sent a
> telegram: "*Comandante* Ernesto Guevara. Ministry of
> Industry. Havana. Your mother gravely ill wants to see

you. Regards from your friend Ricardo Rojo." Still there was no answer, and on May 19 Celia de la Serna de Guevara passed away in Buenos Aires.

This is about all we know of the details, except for one other bit of information, also from Rojo. In giving his letter to Gustavo Roca, Che told him that he had "talked for nearly forty hours with Fidel Castro." Che did not mention any quarrel to Roca, but it may be imagined that if the conversation had been friendly, Che would not have insisted that his mother should not come to Havana "for any reason."

A second attack on Rojo was launched by *Granma* on October 5, 1968, and was reprinted in the same weekly English edition containing the open letter attributed to the prisoners of Salta. This used excerpts of an article in the Chilean "new left" magazine *Punto Final* by a childhood friend of Che, José (Pepe) Aguilar. The article, according to *Granma*'s note preceding it, "gave the lie to Argentine lawyer Ricardo Rojo, who, in his book *My Friend Ché*, was the instrument of imperialism in its latest maneuver to try to discredit Che's memory among the peoples of the world."

In his *Punto Final* article quoted and analyzed by *Granma*, Pepe Aguilar magnanimously declined "to use my long-time friendship with Che . . . to recall what Ernesto really thought of Rojo and how far he was from considering him his 'friend.' " Denouncing "the effrontery" of Rojo in recalling such a friendship, he preferred "to let Rojo himself show us with his own record that people of his ilk were never worthy of Che's confidence and friendship—if we are going to use the term 'friendship' in its true and profound meaning." After which he sets out to demonstrate that Rojo must have been an agent of the CIA, even a very important one, since he was informed in advance of its enterprises: "What an amazing coincidence that Rojo made a 'timely' departure from Cuba in 1961, only a few days before the imperialist landing at Playa Girón, just as he had fled Guatemala in 1954."

The most important fact about Aguilar's article, however, was its acknowledgment—and the indirect confirmation by *Granma* and thus by Cuban officialdom—of the existence of Che's letter to his mother.

Of course, *Granma* did not publish the text of the letter, even though Ernesto Guevara Lynch, Che's father, must have found it among his late wife's effects and could have brought it to Havana, where he had become a constant visitor. *Granma* does not explain its nonpublication. It just mentions an "evasive letter" from Che to his mother, and leaves to Aguilar the task of telling the Cubans not the contents but the supposed motive of the letter:

> In March 1965, Gustavo Roca arrived in Havana bearing a letter from Celia Guevara, Che's mother, in which she requested that a ticket for her to visit Cuba be sent. Ernesto had just arrived in Cuba (on March 15) from an extensive trip through Asia and Africa, and his secret plans for his leaving Cuba were being set into motion. He was to remain in Cuba only a short time, and there was no sense in sending his mother the tickets. It was necessary, however, for Gustavo Roca to return with some sort of answer, and the only solution was to put her off with some sort of excuse until she could be told the truth.

The vast majority of Cubans had been denied the opportunity to read Rojo's book, and thus were unaware not only of his summary of the letter shown to him by Celia but of Celia's reply, which gave a rather precise idea of Che's arguments and motivations.

I wonder, however, what Chilean and other Latin-Ameri-

can readers of *Punto Final*, who could buy *Mi amigo, el Che*
in any bookstore, thought of Pepe Aguilar's line of argument. According to him, to protect his "secret plans"
(which, by the way, were far from being set into motion
since he had just arrived in Cuba), Che Guevara simply was
looking for any innocent excuse to dissuade his mother from
coming, without upsetting her or arousing her curiosity. And
what excuse does he find? He will abandon his post as
Minister of Industry to go cut sugar cane for a month, and
then spend five years in a factory. How clever! . . .

"Aguilar," *Granma* commented, "points out that it was
this evasive letter which moved Che's mother—most probably under Rojo's advice—to write a letter to her son, which
Rojo never delivered. Moreover, displaying an utter lack of
morals, he kept the letter and now makes it public to
support his lies."

Was *Granma* displaying an "utter lack of morals" or just
brazen "effrontery," as Pepe Aguilar would say, when it
reproached Rojo for not having sent Che the letter from his
mother? Where was Rojo to find him in May 1965, in order
to deliver the letter, when not even Che's wife was able to
reach him, and when Rojo's telegram on the worsening
condition of Celia went unanswered? According to Aguilar,
when Che asked his mother not to come to Havana for any
reason, it was because he was too busy, since he was leaving
soon to carry out his "secret plans" and therefore "there
was no sense in sending his mother the tickets." Was there
also no sense in speaking to his mother one last time by
telephone, in the clinic where she lay dying?

Ricardo Rojo, who well knew the close ties between
Ernesto and Celia, thinks that "if Guevara did not answer
the last call of his mother, it could only be because he
simply was unaware of what was happening."

Che, Rojo says, must have been in a place without a
telephone. Apparently it was also a place without newspa-

pers, since the Havana papers on May 21 carried the news of the death of Che's mother. Rojo nevertheless believes that Che was "in seclusion, not in prison." According to him, it was "an act of political discipline which presumed a long session of perfectly voluntary self-criticism." This is not totally impossible, but it is not likely. In any case, we enter here the realm of theory. My own theory is that Che did indeed have a long period of self-criticism, or rather introspection, but in prison, or in some isolated, well-guarded cottage equivalent to a prison.

The decision to go cane-cutting or to work in a factory did not constitute a solution. It was not acceptable, in the final analysis, either to Che Guevara or, above all, to Fidel Castro.

Cuba is a small country, where it is not easy to get rid of someone, even with his consent, by naming him administrator of a hydroelectric plant in East Kazakstan. Cubans are Cubans and not Russians. No doubt Castro could have brought them, in a well-orchestrated rally in the Plaza de la Revolución, to demand *el paredón*—the firing squad—for Guevara as a "traitor." But he could not have expected them to lose interest in Che as the manager of a factory in Pinar del Río or Santa Cruz del Sur.

Furthermore, Guevara was no Malenkov. True, in his October 1964 article for *International Affairs* he spoke of errors made in industry and of the serious agricultural problems which had only begun to be solved during recent months. But he did not get overexcited about it; he did not blame himself or display any personal dejection. He wrote in the name of a collective "we" which tended to include the whole government. He explained the deplorable food situation by "the way in which we carried out diversification"; the responsibility here, applying to "many of us" and with attenuating circumstances, rested with the "fetishistic idea (that) connected sugar with our dependence on imperialism." Should this be seen as a *mea culpa?* At most a *culpa nostra,* in which the responsibility of one and all was diluted in such a way as not to trouble anyone's sleep: "It is for history to judge how much was our fault and how much was caused by circumstances. . . ."

As far as the industrial situation was concerned, Che quite obviously did not intend to await the judgment of history. The balance, he stated, showed successes as well as failures. He was not at all unhappy with the results of certain textile and chemical enterprises, and there was "a new and vigorous search for fresh mineral resources."

Self-criticism? Well, he did not deny that in many of the factories set up under his direction, "the technical efficiency was insufficient when measured by international standards." But he promptly added: "So far, the industrial development achieved can be described as satisfactory, if we take into account the problems caused by the American blockade and the radical changes which have occurred in only three years as regards our foreign sources of supply."

Such self-criticism sounds more like self-justification: despite the errors made and admitted, Che did not feel in any way disqualified as chief of the Cuban economy, and we have to look elsewhere to find the reasons for his despair.

Shortly after the publication of the article in *International Affairs,* there had been his journey to the USSR. Several years before, in his "educational" lecture of March 20, 1960, Che had said something which must have haunted him later. Deploring the fact that at the time the ties with the United States had not yet been completely cut off, he declared that "we cannot yet proclaim at the tombs of our martyrs that Cuba is economically independent," because "it cannot be so as long as a freighter delayed in the United States can force a Cuban factory to shut down." That was exactly what was happening now, more than ever before,

when a ship was delayed in the USSR, and Che knew that
sometimes the ship was intentionally held up.

Fidel Castro certainly must have repeated this truth to
Che again and again, telling him it was his fault that Cuba
was in such a fix economically, his fault that Cuba could not
get out of it politically. Did Che bow his head? I doubt it. I
can easily picture him arguing about it during at least part
of the "nearly forty hours'" talk with Fidel, maintaining
that if only the Cuban people were willing to make an
effort, everything would work out. But sooner or later,
beyond the wretched economic realities, another reality
must have entered Che's mind.

Two walls, Che must have felt, were looming up in front
of him—dark, sinister, and inexorable—the first between
him and life, the second between him and Castro.

I do not believe that Che Guevara, once converted, ever
doubted the necessity of socialism. The gnawing doubt that
never left him concerned the capacity of the masses to
realize that necessity. Here we have the problem of the
"socialist conscience," the questions of "socialism and
man," not only in Cuba but in the mind of Che. His
fundamental failure came about in confronting these questions, and this is the theme of the next chapter.

Che could not bring himself to admit such a failure. For
him it was a question of example, education, perseverance.
He had to convince Fidel that the meager results in this
domain were a much more serious matter than the miscalcu-
lations of the Ministry of Industry. But if Fidel answered
that the joke had gone on long enough, and if he deprived
Che of the chance to keep trying to awaken that "socialist
conscience" in which he saw the mark of the new man,
what remained for him?

No, Che Guevara did not think of spending five years in a
factory in order to learn how to run one better than he had

managed the Ministry; he was not the type to believe that what he lacked was technical competence. It is easier to imagine Che questioning himself desperately about the deeper meanings of socialism as seen by the ordinary worker. He was sure of his socialism as a priest is sure of his God. If the worker was not carried along, it could only be because he had not been approached in the right way. Like a worker-priest, Che thought of going to the factory not to learn a trade, but to understand the mentality of the working man. And in the final analysis, like the worker-priest, to save the people's soul.

Such an idea could not be put into practice, and Castro may even have seen in it a potential source of agitation which risked being turned against him.

Was that why Castro did become angry, and why the place where Che was awaiting a decision became a cell where not even the news of his mother's death could reach him? One can speculate endlessly about what Fidel expected of Che. Probably he expected nothing more, and was wondering only what to do with him.

The idea, first of the Congo then of Bolivia, must have had great appeal for both men: a journey far away, followed by a useful death. Could the thought of a useless death, of ordinary suicide, ever have occurred to a man like Che?

In *Pasajes*, Guevara tells a story which is particularly painful, not only because of the event related but also because of the way the author relates it.

Pasajes de la guerra revolucionaria is a collection of personal reminiscences by Che Guevara which appeared in *Verde Olivo* and other Cuban publications after the 1959 victory. It was first published in book form, with eighteen stories selected and reworked by the author, in 1963.* The

* La Habana, Ediciones Unión.

American edition I have° contains twenty-four stories, including some reprinted in *Granma* after Che's death. John Gerassi, in *Venceremos,*† publishes nineteen stories which he dates "1956–1963" and groups in a chapter titled *The Revolutionary War.* The nineteenth is taken from the official Cuban government translation published by the Havana Book Institute in 1967. The French edition, also published in 1967,‡ utilizes the same and other sources to wind up with twenty-seven stories. The most complete, with thirty-four, is in Roberto Fernández Retamar's *Obra revolucionaria,*§ used here.

The episode which I am referring to, headed "Pino del Agua," does not figure in the above-mentioned English editions.

During the marches in the Cuban Sierra which were to end in the first battles of Pino del Agua, a young guerrilla named Roberto Rodríguez had been disarmed by his lieutenant as a disciplinary measure. The young man grabbed another man's revolver and shot himself in the head. Che called this "a disagreeable accident." A day or two earlier, he explained, Roberto had told him his story. He was "an oversensitive boy" who had trouble adapting to the life of the guerrillas, because of his "rebellious instinct" (the criticism is Che's).

The disagreeable accident had been followed by a "little incident" described by the *comandante* as follows:

° *Episodes of the Revolutionary War* (New York: International Publishers, 1968).

† *Venceremos, The Speeches and Writings of Che Guevara* (New York: The Macmillan Company, 1968).

‡ *Souvenirs de la guerre révolutionnaire* (Paris: François Maspero).

§ Mexico: Ediciones Era, S.A., 1967.

We had a little incident because I opposed granting him military honors, while the fighters considered that he had fallen as one of them. We tried to show that to commit suicide, under the circumstances in which we found ourselves, was a reprehensible act no matter what the virtues of the comrade were. After an attempt at insubordination,* it was decided to hold a wake, without rendering military honors.

In his Cuban solitude during the spring of 1965, did Che ever think of Roberto Rodríguez and of his regrettable "rebellious instinct"? There was not much in common between Guevara and Koestler's Rubashov who, confronted with his past, accepted his fate so that he would not have to disavow himself. Among the various states of mind, or of soul, reflected in the *Diary*, one never encounters a sentiment resembling remorse.

For Fidel Castro, meanwhile, the idea that Che might kill himself must have been disquieting. How would he explain it, how would he prevent people from drawing conclusions putting him in a bad light? Such an act could not be permitted, at that time or later. We do not know whether the threat of suicide served Che in 1965 as a weapon to extract concessions from Castro. But we do know that in 1967, in his October 15 speech announcing "the bitter news," the *jefe máximo* betrayed his concern over heading off any suggestion that Che could have sought death in Bolivia. That was why he insisted so much on Che's scorn of death during the Sierra Maestra days: "Always," Fidel said, "in all the time we knew him, he displayed an extraordinary

* Che does not give details about this "attempt at insubordination," nor about how the compromise was reached. In the
French version of Robert and Magali Merle (Maspero, Paris),
the words *Tras un conato de insubordinación* became: "The
men finally calmed down. . . ."

lack of fear, an absolute disregard of danger, a constant readiness, in every moment of difficulty and danger, to do the most difficult and dangerous things. . . . Frequently we had to adopt measures concerning his safety somehow or other. On more than one occasion we had to oppose certain actions which he wanted to carry out. . . ."

Castro seemed to be making an effort to protect himself against the Che of Bolivia by presenting the Che of Cuba as a sort of daredevil who exposed himself to danger through indifference, if not for the fun of it, and who had to be saved from his own recklessness. Castro thus was obliged to gloss over not only Guevara's theoretical writings, but also his account of his adventures.

Che wrote in his *Guerra de guerrillas*:

> Just as the general of a division does not have to die at the head of his troops in a modern war, the guerrilla, who is his own general, should not die in each battle. He is ready to give his life, but the positive quality of this war of guerrillas is precisely that each is ready to die, not to defend an ideal, but to transform it into reality.

In his recollections of the Sierra, the best pages are those where he pokes fun at himself, and his own caustic humor speaks more in his favor than the heroic tales of a fawning propaganda. Only a truly courageous man could speak so openly about his moments of fear, as Che Guevara did.

During the attack on the small garrison of Bueycito, Che found himself face to face with a soldier armed with a Garand. Che fired, but his Thompson submachine gun jammed. The man accompanying him, Israel Pardo, was armed with a small and defective rifle and also was unable to fire a shot. "I don't know exactly how Israel got out of it alive," Che relates. "All I remember is what I did, and that is, that under the rain of bullets from the Garand, I ran with a speed I have never since been able to attain."

In another account titled "*Interludio*," Che describes a night ride, with a guide he did not know, heading back to his command post. Suddenly, under the full moon, he saw a row of dead mules. The two men dismounted. The mules had been part of a supply convoy intercepted by Batista's troops. The guide's face, as he inspected the bullet holes, reminded Che of the Cowboy films in which the hero finds a horse killed by an arrow and murmurs: the Sioux! "Perhaps," he adds, "it was also the face I was making, but I was not much interested in looking at myself."

The guide abandoned him then and there, pretending not to know the route, and Che went on alone, Beretta in hand, across the coffee plantations. "Arriving at an abandoned house, a terrible noise made me jump, and I was about to shoot. But it was only a pig, frightened, as I was, by my presence. . . ."

This "Interlude" has a second movement. The troops which intercepted the convoy launched a direct attack, and the guerrillas, still unaccustomed to battle, broke ranks. With a thousand cartridges in a leather bag over his shoulder, Che made a running zigzag retreat under another hail of bullets. Cut off from his companions and not knowing the results of the attack, he dropped to the ground behind a large boulder in the middle of the forest, to catch his breath. But was he really out of danger?

"The asthma, charitably, had let me run a few yards, but it was getting its revenge, and my heart was jumping in my chest. I heard the sound of branches cracking, people approaching, and already it was no longer possible to run as I really had the urge to do."

It was only one of Che's men, a new recruit. He says something to Che, "to console me," something like "Don't be upset, *comandante*, I am going to die with you. . . ." And Che, not afraid to show that he was by no means indifferent to fear and danger, reveals himself to be a man like others: "As for myself, I had no desire to die, and I was tempted rather to tell him something about his mother. . . ."

No, Fidel Castro could not explain Nancahuazú by referring to the Sierra. He could not dispel the impression that Che was seeking death in Bolivia by pretending that Che had always seemed to be courting death. But in Cuba, Che was anxious to survive because he had the future—a big future—ahead of him. Where was his future in Bolivia?

During that dramatic spring of 1965 in Havana, the first wall Che hit his head against was the absence of "socialist conscience" among the Cuban masses. There was still the need for armed struggle to give the masses elsewhere a chance. Che's fanaticism could coexist with Fidel's pragmatism as long as there remained a common goal and an equal will to achieve it. But what if Fidel did not really mean what he said when he spoke of the duty of the revolutionary to make revolution everywhere? A second wall had begun to rise before Che, a wall of doubt about Fidel, cemented by Cuba's inertia during the Dominican invasion. This wall could not be moved. But Che could move around it. He could and would do what Fidel now appeared unable or unwilling to do. For whatever Che was not, he *was* a man of his word.

This leitmotif returns everywhere. It was the key sentence of the letter to his children. We find it again in the letter to his parents:

> I believe in armed struggle as the only solution for the peoples who struggle to free themselves, and I act in accordance with my convictions. Many will call me an adventurer, and I am one, but of a different kind, one of those who risk their skin to prove their truths. . . .

One of the goals of the Bolivian campaign, clearly

conceived by Che before his departure and solemnly spelled
out as a tenet in his April 1967 message to the Tricontinental, was to create "a second Vietnam," forcing the United
States to send troops, to disperse forces, to exhaust them.
Since Che proved incapable of gaining the peasants'
support, absolutely necessary to achieve any positive result
(such as starting a Bolivian revolution), the "second Vietnam" idea finally was the *only* goal left to him. It meant
sacrificing himself and his guerrillas to gain worldwide
attention and United States intervention. This in turn meant
intensifying dramatically both military operations and international propaganda. But this goal also proved beyond
reach, and most of the blame lay with Castro. At no time
was Che Guevara given the technical means which might
have made it possible for the Bolivian guerrillas to shake up
the feeble Bolivian army. And at no time did the Bolivian
guerrillas profit by the sensational fact—sensational if it had
been echoed throughout the world—that their *comandante*
was Che Guevara.

To judge by the numbering, there were thirty-nine
messages from Havana. The last, No. 39, was dated August
26, 1967. On that day, "everything went wrong," the *Diary*
tells us; Che blamed Antonio and was so furious that he hit
him. Message No. 39 was decoded only on September 5.
This was the one informing the guerrillas that the Bolivian
delegation to the OLAS conferences was *una mierda*. Che
apparently expected something else, for he ends with the
melancholy remark: "That's all. Obviously, they did not
receive our last message."

We do not know what Che was asking in the lost
message. We do not even know whether he did ask for
something. But none of Havana's messages, as published in
a supplement to *Bohemia* on July 5, 1968, was of much
practical or immediate help to the guerrillas.

Message No. 38, undated but probably sent in July 1967,

announced the arrival of a badly needed radio technician, a young Bolivian *becado* (scholarship student), trained in Cuba and receiving a stipend from the government. But he was not to arrive before September, and since all contact was lost in the meantime, he never did arrive. A new liaison agent for La Paz was announced for November. The dispatch of a group of 23 Bolivian *becados* who wished to join the ELN was planned, but no date was set. "We are also working on the *becados* who are in the USSR and Czechoslovakia to integrate them into the battle under the guidance of the ELN," says message No. 38. Clearly there was no great hurry in Havana.

And what about the propaganda? Except for its separate campaign for Régis Debray, Havana exerted far less effort in behalf of Che's guerrillas than it did for the other guerrillas who did not have Che as leader—in Venezuela, for example, where Castro seems to have pursued a kind of personal vendetta against Romulo Betancourt and his successors.

Che certainly expected more from Fidel. If the Tricontinental secretariat was able to distribute a selection of Che's photos along with his message in April 1967, it was because Che supplied those photos. Why? Was it not because he believed the time had come, and the occasion was appropriate, to announce his presence in Bolivia?

On April 13, he notes in the *Diary*:

> The North Americans announce that the sending of advisors to Bolivia is in accordance with an old plan and has nothing to do with guerrillas. Perhaps we are in the process of witnessing the first episode of a new Vietnam.

In his summary at the end of the month, he is happy about the attention finally given to the Bolivian guerrillas by

Radio Havana, and adds with evident satisfaction: "After
the publication of my article in Havana, there can no longer
be any doubt as to my presence here." This hope was
quickly dashed. The Cuban radio continued its "information
offensive on Bolivia," sometimes even "with exaggerated
reports," as he observes on July 2. But it did not mention
Che or it spoke of him without connecting him with Bolivia;
this kind of "propaganda" was of no use to Che.

News of his presence in Bolivia, Che knew, would be
headlined throughout the world, including of course Bolivia
and the United States. Yet Radio Havana kept the "secret."
A short sentence on July 26 shows Che's resentment. This
was the anniversary of the attack on the Moncada barracks,
starting point of the Cuban revolution. At night, Che talks
to his companions about "the significance of July 26: a
rebellion against oligarchies and against revolutionary dog-
mas." After this somewhat unexpected definition he adds,
without transition or further comment: "Fidel came out
with his little mention of Bolivia."

I have said earlier that unless Che Guevara was a maniac
who didn't know what he was doing, his photographic
recklessness can be explained only by the importance he
attached to the photos as a propaganda device. The *Bolivian
Diary* abundantly confirms that any concern for protecting
his anonymity was merely a secondary preoccupation.

This was true even at the beginning. From the first page,
on November 7, 1966, he recounts with good humor and no
sign of anxiety how the young Bolivian driving the second
jeep nearly went over a cliff when he recognized him. On
the 20th, after meeting a liaison agent, Che reports that the
agent had been informed of his presence "contrary to
instructions," but he does not seem very upset about it. He
evidently preferred not to attract attention as long as his
operation was not fully organized; it was therefore impor-

tant that his presence not be known too soon. It was even more important that it not become known too late.

The question of timing must be considered as having been settled by March 21, 1967. The date is important. Che has just returned from an exhausting march and finds "terrible chaos" in the camp. The preparatory stage thus is far from over, and the military operations have not yet begun; the first engagement does not take place until the 23rd. Yet when Che confers with Régis Debray on March 21, the record of their talk implies nothing less than the end of Che's anonymity.

Debray was not particularly eager to stay with the guerrillas and Guevara was not particularly eager to hold him. It is decided that he will organize a network of support in France. Che is to write—*yo debo escribir*—to Bertrand Russell and Jean-Paul Sartre "to get them to organize an international fund for assistance to the Bolivian liberation movement." Did he intend to sit down and personally write Russell and Sartre to get their support for the Bolivian guerrillas, without telling them—and without letting them tell the international movement they were supposed to start—that he was the leader of those Bolivian guerrillas?

The idea is absurd. In March 1967 Che's whereabouts were still unknown. It was possible, as was done a month later in Havana, to publish an undated general message from him concerning Vietnam. But could letters seeking aid for a Bolivian operation come from "somewhere in the world"? Why then would he be asking only for aid to Bolivia, when the newspapers were full of stories about the guerrillas of Guatemala or Venezuela but had not yet printed a word about the guerrillas of Bolivia, since up to March 23 they were militarily nonexistent?

Thus it appears plain that on March 21, finding that his guerrilla movement wasn't going well, Che Guevara decided to wait no longer to play his trump card: his name. The letters he planned to write could make sense only if they were to spread the word that Che had reappeared, that he was alive, that he had taken charge of a group of Bolivian revolutionaries struggling against the Yankee oppressor. The sensational effect of such an announcement would place Bolivia at the top of the news, send Washington into an uproar, push the United States to take the first steps toward that "second Vietnam" of Che's dreams.

The following weeks and months could only have convinced him that this was indeed the only outcome he could still hope for. His companions were being killed off one by one, and not a single Bolivian peasant—*not one*—had come to take their place. They were dying for nothing, but their death could be made a signal to the world if people everywhere learned that these guerrillas in Bolivia were unlike any others, these were *Che's* guerrillas.

On July 1, 1967, there is a sentence in the *Diary* as startling as it is revealing: "Barrientos has held a press conference in which he admitted my presence." Yes, in the midst of the conspiracy of silence surrounding Che, Barrientos *admitted* his presence. But not Castro. The Castro-Guevara agreement may have reserved to Fidel the right to decide at what moment to make public Che's presence in Bolivia. In choosing to keep silent until the end, Castro took on a heavy responsibility.

Régis Debray does not impress me as a great thinker, and he was perhaps not a great hero, but he was not a traitor either. It was false and ridiculous to blame him for having "revealed" Che's presence to the Bolivian authorities. False because the authorities had known about it for a long time, not only through the deserters but as a result of the discoveries in the abandoned camp of Nancahuazú;° ridicu-

° In an interview with the three Cuban survivors of the Quebrada del Yuro—Pombo, Urbano and Benigno—which

lous because after his talk with Che on March 21, Debray was rightly convinced that Che's presence in Bolivia was no longer a secret.

The statement delivered by Régis Debray to his lawyer on October 11, 1967, for the officers of the Camiri court martial should have given some food for thought to Castro and his friends. In it, Debray explained that if Che did not want him in his guerrilla organization, it was because "my mission to inform the world about his presence here and about his activity was as important as that of fighting." Che's *Diary* amply confirms that this was indeed Che's opinion.

Che knew his fate depended not on discretion but on propaganda. He had little personal attachment to Debray, as we learn from the way he writes about him before Debray leaves camp and immediately after his arrest. But the May summary declares: "The uproar caused by the Debray affair has given a greater warlike impact to our movement than ten victorious battles."

The publicity offered Che by Debray's arrest was not a substitute, however, for the official proclamation refused him by Castro. Did Che ask him for such an announcement? Perhaps his pride did not allow him to do so. Or perhaps this was the purpose of the "last message" mentioned on September 5, 1967, which went unanswered. In any case, Che knew—and Fidel, too, must have known—that the guerrillas' best potential weapon was denied them: a proclamation that Che Guevara was their leader.

In his message to the Tricontinental Conference, Che Guevara had harsh words for those who had left the Vietnamese "tragically alone":

---

appeared in *Bohemia* on October 17, 1969, Pombo explained that Che chose the pseudonym Fernando after the army had found Braulio's diary, because "Ramón had been identified as Che."

The solidarity of all progressive forces of the world towards the people of Vietnam today is similar to the bitter irony of the plebeians coaxing on the gladiators in the Roman arena. It is not a matter of wishing success to the victim of aggression, but of sharing his fate; one must accompany him to his death or to victory. . . .°

In Bolivia the bitter irony was not in Castro's coaxing but in his silence; before enshrining Che as a dead hero, Castro kept him waiting, alive, in the tomb of the unknown soldier.

° Official English text distributed by OSPAAAL secretariat.

VI

Socialism and
Man in Cuba

or

The First Failure of Che Guevara

O ne of the last statements issued by the "Revolutionary Committee" of Kronstadt in 1921 was entitled "Socialism in Quotation Marks." It was a fiery denunciation of the "shining kingdom of socialism to which the dictatorship of the Communist Party has brought us." *

The sailors of Kronstadt had been in the vanguard of the October Revolution in 1917, because they thought it was the revolution of the workers and peasants. They did not wish to be either victims or accomplices of the rigid dictatorship later imposed upon the workers and peasants by fanatics who were certain they held the keys to the future, and who were convinced that the end justified the means. Fifty years after the *Commune de Paris*, the sailors of the Baltic fleet started their own "Commune" in Kronstadt.

On March 16, 1921, when the final battle was raging and Trotsky's Red Army was ready to repeat Thiers' bloody victory of 1871, the Kronstadt Commune published its proclamation to explain what it was fighting against.

It was fighting against a "socialism in quotation marks," a "State socialism with soviets of functionaries who vote obediently according to the dictates of the Party committee

---

* I quote from the translation by Paul Avrich in *Kronstadt 1921* (Princeton, N.J.: Princeton University Press, 1970).

123

and its infallible commissars," in which the worker now was
"a slave of State enterprises," in which the peasant was a
serf "on the estates of the new landlord, the State," in
which "all independent thought, all just criticism of the acts
of the rulers became crimes, punished by imprisonment and
sometimes even by execution. . . ."

The Cuban revolution in January 1959 did not want
"socialism in quotation marks" any more than "democracy
in quotation marks." This revolution opposed both the rule
of oligarchy and the excesses of dictatorship. Its aim was to
reform society as well as to reestablish a constitutional
regime. That was what Fidel Castro had proclaimed before
his judges in 1953, after the failure of the July 26 attack on
the Moncada barracks at Santiago de Cuba. Revised and
amplified, distributed by the hundreds of thousands, the text
of this court statement—*La historia me absolverá*—represented Castro's program in January 1959.

All the Cuban revolutionaries were "socialists" of the
Castro type, not of the type represented by Blas Roca, Juan
Marinello, or Lázaro Peña, Stalinist bureaucrats who were
scarcely "destalinized" and whose *Partido Socialista Popular*
(PSP), tolerated by Batista, had taken care not to let itself
be identified with the "putschists" of July 26.

The Cuban revolutionaries owed nothing to Karl Marx, of
whose writings they were almost totally ignorant, and they
did not know Lenin any better. They followed only José
Martí.

Sons of the middle class, indeed often of the upper
middle class, they were idealists; but their idealism was not
based on books. The young fighters of the mountains had
seen for themselves the misery of peasant life in the *bohíos*,
those primitive thatched huts which lay beyond the casinos
and palaces. The young fighters of the towns had discovered
for themselves the corruption of government and economy,

profiteers and exploiters being as much a part of Batista's regime as were his executioners.

There was no place in such a movement for what "socialism" meant in Moscow, what it had just proved to be in Budapest. Cuban socialism was intensely libertarian.

"We want to establish in Cuba a true democracy, with no trace of Fascism, Peronism, or Communism . . . ," Castro declared in New York on April 23, 1959. He spoke no differently one month later in Havana: "Capitalism can kill a man with hunger. Communism can kill him by destroying his liberty." This was the era when, to avoid confusion, the new men in Havana preferred to speak of *humanismo* rather than *socialismo,* and when the watchwords proposed to the Cuban crowds were carefully differentiated from those which had served to deceive crowds elsewhere: "Bread, with liberty and without terror. . . ."

It is almost forgotten today that the first post-revolutionary disagreements in Cuba were not about Communism but about casinos and brothels.

The rebels always had considered that victory would bring an end to the humiliating state of affairs which made Havana a red-light district for the *gringos.*° But Fidel Castro now was saying that tourism should not be discouraged, and the others finally went along. Che Guevara was among the others.

On May 1, 1961, when Castro officially announced in the Plaza de la Revolución (then called Plaza Cívica) that Cuba was henceforth a "socialist State," there were still brothels, but the tourists weren't coming any more. And much else had changed.

Installed in the fort of La Cabaña, Che had been the

° In Latin America *gringo* is the popular term of insult applied to North Americans, rather than *yanqui,* which is a relatively recent political import.

military commander of the capital. It was his view—and he did not conceal it—that the *ejército rebelde*, the army of the resistance, should constitute the main instrument of the revolution rather than any political organization. That did not please the Communists of the PSP, who had no influence in the *ejército rebelde*. It also did not please Castro very much, because he knew that the men of that army, although personally devoted to him, remained rebels at heart as well as in name.

A few years later, speaking of the suicide of Roberto Rodríguez in the Sierra Maestra, Che Guevara retrospectively depicted the "instinct of rebellion" as something reprehensible. But Fidel Castro was on guard against his soldiers, and their instinct, as early as the summer of 1959. In that year Che still was first of all a soldier, and a soldier of the *ejército rebelde*.

There had been no incident, not even any noticeable ill feeling, only a difference of opinion which could contain the seed of future conflict. Fidel took care of such potential conflict in advance, during Che's first long journey abroad. On his return from this trip, in September 1959, *Comandante* Guevara discovered that his place at La Cabaña had been taken, and that no other military post awaited him. He was never again to exercise any active military command in Cuba.

While suspicious of Che the soldier, Castro nevertheless had great respect for him as an organizer. The economic career of *Comandante* Guevara began at the start of this same autumn, when he became director of the industrial branch of the all-powerful National Institute of Agrarian Reform (INRA).

Named president of the National Bank in November 1959 and Minister of Industry in February 1961, Che loyally supported his chief when Castro whipped the labor unions into line, liquidated the 26th of July movement, and undertook to "reorganize" the *ejército rebelde*—beginning by jailing Huber Matos, former military commander of Santiago de Cuba, the provisional capital of the revolution. And it was Che who, in an "educational" television lecture on April 30, 1961, prepared the Cuban people for the announcement Castro was to make the next day.

"We are on the eve of a day when the Cuban people will proclaim that their revolution is the first socialist revolution in Latin America," Che revealed. The Cuban people had heard such rumors, but this was the first time they learned what *they* were going to proclaim the next day. Che added, significantly if not educationally: "This is not the time to define socialism. . . ."

He went on to define it anyway, and quite unwisely, since in making "socialist conscience" a fundamental condition of socialism, he set forth the great dilemma which he was never able to resolve: "It is important to emphasize that if the people do not clearly realize their rights and their duties in the new phase, it is impossible to really arrive at the socialist society we want. A socialist society is absolutely democratic. It is based on the needs and aspirations of the people. . . ."

Here we have the difference between Castro and Guevara. Castro had no qualms about expressing the aspirations as well as the needs of the people; Guevara had no doubts as to their needs, but he wanted the people to show their aspirations themselves.

The Cuban workers were ready to parade by the hundreds of thousands for Fidel on May Day, but Che knew well enough on April 30 that they were not marching for "socialism." The massive exodus which had begun at the end of 1959, long after the departure of the last elements linked to the Batista dictatorship, involved not only the managers and technicians who, according to Havana, had been bought by Washington gold, but also those viewed by

Che as perhaps "quite simply" unable to bear "the new climate in Cuba." The exodus from then on included workers, peasants, and many fishermen (they had boats), along with an increasing number of former Castro partisans. On the eve of the CIA plot in the Bay of Pigs° resistance to Castro had begun to reach the level which had brought about Batista's fall three years earlier.

Che, however, considered "socialism" as within reach: "This is the miracle which a people can accomplish when it is possessed by the sacred idea of production and by the desire to realize its aspirations." But he was alone in being possessed by this sacred idea; the people showed no desire to realize the aspirations of Che. Returning to earth, the Minister of Industry shook his head:

> The working classes are not always aware of their potential, of their duties, of their rights. . . . If the worker stops working on Sunday when work remains to be done, simply because he has earned enough to cover his most urgent needs, that shows that there is no spirit of betterment in his life, that there is a lack of understanding as to the needs of the revolution. . . . What I wanted to make clear is that the working class is not making a sufficient effort.

Proclaiming that "socialism is not only a word," stressing that it involves "elements of conscience" as well as "economic factors," Che concluded finally that "we still have much to do in this regard."

° I believe I have demonstrated in *Autopsie du Castrisme* that the CIA operation was designed to head off a victory of the new resistance—anti-Communist and anti-totalitarian, but revolutionary and "socialist" in its way and thus, in the eyes of the CIA, no less opposed to the interests of the United States. In fact, the CIA saved Castro.

It was useless to tell the Cuban workers that to have "the honor of belonging to a socialist country," they must consent to sacrifices: the Cuban workers had never asked for that honor. They went to the Plaza de la Revolución because everyone was going there, because Fidel was there, and everyone loved Fidel. It was impossible to convince them that because they were now in power, as Fidel said, they had to accept reductions in salaries, work extra hours without extra pay, and give up all the advantages they had won through past labor union battles.

Go on strike? Against Castro? Unthinkable. After all, one could not treat Fidel as a capitalist boss. It would also be dangerous; no one had forgotten the years of prison which befell the electrical workers when they dared to demonstrate in December 1959 in front of the Presidential palace. There had been sporadic walkouts among printing industry, hotel, and restaurant employees, as well as incidents involving transport workers. But most of the workers contented themselves with grumbling and taking it easy on the job. It was the task of Che, as master of the economy, assisted by Labor Minister Augusto Martínez Sánchez, to see to it that the "authentic results of the revolution" celebrated by Castro on May Day 1961 would at least begin to emerge by the end of 1962.

On April 15, 1962, Guevara spoke before the national council of the *Confederación de Trabajadores Cubanos* (CTC). Its former leader, David Salvador, had blindly submitted to Castro in the elimination of his own friends and the transfer of control to the Communists. Now Salvador, Castro's first labor leader, was in prison, and under the direction of the old Stalinist bureaucrat Lázaro Peña the CTC became a strictly governmental organ. This did not prevent it, of course, from adding to its name the adjective *revolucionaria:* CTC-R.

In his address to the CTC-R, Che for the first time spoke

of the "dictatorship of the proletariat," defining it as "the democratic dictatorship of the working class at all levels in the countries carrying out the construction of socialism."

This "democratic dictatorship," he explained, stemmed from "the basic decision of our people to construct socialism." Workers and their organizations had to adapt to the "new social order," and to do so they must "struggle against the old mentality." They must do away, he insisted, with "the mentality of an exploited and deprived working class, which fights only for economic improvements at the level of national unions." Had the Cuban workers then simultaneously taken "the basic decision" and kept "the old mentality"? Che doesn't say: he cannot defend his logic and his "socialism" at the same time.

Che's "socialism" asks the worker to interest himself in the problems of his factory, to analyze these problems and make suggestions. The worker has "the duty and the right to make sure that all orders of the government, all the main lines of development established by the government, are accomplished." No other "rights" are mentioned. In his own ministry, Che had to "categorically impose the principle of authority, of single responsibility, in order to avoid the improper interference in the management of a factory on the part of certain labor organizations and, at times, of active revolutionary groups."

The Minister, however, recognized the need for a brief transitional phase before finally disposing of trade unionism.

He thus mentions the problem posed by "the comrades who, in other times, obtained higher pay through often harsh struggles against the capitalist sector." What is one to do, for example, with the machinist who earns 15 pesos a day—a survival of capitalism—when his work, according to the new "socialist" standards, is worth no more than 8 pesos? Well, he will keep his salary, as an individual, as long as he occupies the same job. But the man who replaces him—or he himself if he moves to another job—will receive no more than regular "socialist" wages.

For Che, such evidence of flexibility showed the happy blend of "socialism" and "man." He had no doubt that with the "progress of conscience," all such problems soon would be resolved.

The workers earning wages considered too high did not have to wait long for their "problem" to be resolved. Where the progress of conscience was not enough to incite them to voluntarily give up their advantages, the remedy was simply to transfer them to another job, and the result was the same. The mere existence of this remedy, moreover, made it unnecessary to use it. By the end of 1962 there were hardly any machinists or other specialized workers in Cuba earning the higher pay they had received under the capitalist regime.

The true problem of Che Guevara, the one that really preoccupied him until the end, was defending the purity of Cuban "socialism" against concessions to "human nature" which other "socialisms"—and the pragmatism of Fidel Castro—judged desirable in the interest of production.

Che believed that any *estímulos,* work incentives, should be moral and not monetary, and that nothing could inspire workers worthy of the name more than the hope of "seeing themselves, individually or collectively, as the best among the best." Under pressure from Castro, he reluctantly considered "certain material encouragements, suited to the era in which we are living," but did not spell out what those might be. Obviously he thought it humiliating to go into details. While distributing "certificates of Communist labor" in January 1964, he thus announced that there were also "some little gifts, not so little as that," but added: "I am not going to show them here, because they are rather pretty, and they could be taken as material incentives. That is not my intention."

In October 1967 the Uruguayan Castroites published a collection of "unpublished letters" of Che.° One of them, dated May 31, 1963, is addressed to the workers of a motorcycle factory in Santiago de Cuba. When Che had visited this factory, the workers proposed that each of them should have the right to one of the motorcycles they were producing. After turning down this idea in his capacity as Minister, Che informed them that as a "socialist," he considered it "an error" to believe that the workers had a right to the product of their labor: "The workers responsible for the production of any article have no rights over it. Bakers have no right to more bread, cement-makers to more bags of cement, and you, you have no right to a motorcycle. . . ."

The Uruguayan intellectual who wrote a preface to the book saw in Che's letters "the very pure stream of humanity which runs through the guerrilla and the statesman, which will have to flow, inexhaustible, in the new socialist man foretold by Guevara." But while waiting for the "socialist conscience" to take effect, Che saw nothing wrong with using a little coercion to do the job.

Wages would depend on meeting the government's quotas, he reminded CTC-R leaders on April 15, 1962. The worker who did not fulfill his quota was to earn less. The same rule would apply to anyone who did his work badly, and apply even more to the absentee. Che's doctrine, later picked up by Castro,† was that the "undisciplined" worker was robbing his comrades:

> The worker who steals from another worker at the place of work is not a true member of the working class. . . . There are infractions of a social type which

° Montevideo: Editorial Sandino.
† See page 254.

we must judge and punish. The worker who, in
moments of danger, deserts his trench, that is to say his
machine, is failing in his fundamental duty.

The "socialism" of Che required workers to labor like
convicts. Yet he assumed they would do so of their own will,
even with enthusiasm. This was to assume the impossible,
although Guevara's Cuba, like Stalin's Russia, soon was
displaying cases of genuine, that is pathological, "Stakhano-
vism." Did Che really believe this was socialism? The
answer is *yes,* since he considered Comrade Arnet, who had
worked 1,607 hours in six months, a socialist and not a
simpleton or madman.

The Minister of Industry had sharpened his pencil and
figured it out. Had his faith been religious rather than
"socialist," he would have fallen on his knees to thank the
Lord for having shown him a saint. On the basis of an
eight-hour day, Che marvels, 1,607 hours amounted to
nearly 201 days, and there were only 182 days in the
six-month period. Comrade Arnet, in six months, not only
had not taken a single day off but had added 151 extra hours
to his normal days. Hallelujah!

Like Trotsky in 1920, and forgetting the lessons history
later taught Trotsky and ourselves, Guevara wanted the
workers to think of themselves as soldiers. For those who
were reluctant, he set up militarized "labor brigades." For
the *vagos,* the idlers, caught in movie houses or on street
corners, he revived the compulsory labor service.

Isaac Deutscher, in *The Prophet Armed,*° devoted to
Leon Trotsky and not Che Guevara, cites Trotsky's formulas
which had been "unceremoniously" and sometimes "literally" taken over by Stalin and "remorselessly carried into
execution" by him. Today those formulas are the rule in

° New York and London: Oxford University Press, 1954.

Cuba, Castro having taken them over from Che Guevara, just as remorselessly but at the same time officially and even ceremoniously.

"Display untiring energy in your work," Trotsky proclaimed in 1920, "as if you were on the march or in battle. . . . The political departments must cultivate the spirit of the worker in the soldier and preserve the soldier in the worker. . . . A deserter from labor is as contemptible and despicable as a deserter from the battlefield. Severe punishment to both! . . . We must become conscious, self-sacrificing builders of the socialist economy. Only on this road shall we find a way out, salvation, warmth and contentment. . . ."

Trotsky went so far as to put down as "the most wretched and miserable liberal prejudice" the idea that compulsory work was not productive. "Chattel slavery, too, was productive!" he stated, and "serf labor did not grow out of the feudal lords' ill will" but was, in its time, "a progressive phenomenon." May God save the unbelieving workers from the prophets armed with "socialism"!

"Carried away by his desire to justify the measures he sponsored," Deutscher comments, "he, the rebel *par excellence,* the expounder of permanent revolution, came very near to talking like an apologist for past systems of coercion and exploitation." We have to make an effort to remember that Deutscher was writing in 1954, that he was talking about the USSR of 1920 and not Cuba in 1962, and that the rebel he portrayed was not Guevara but Trotsky.

In the spring of 1962, when Che addressed the CTC-R national council, his ministry's publication, *Nuestra Industria,* disclosed for the first time the existence of "rehabilitation camps for workers." The magazine—which, far from intending any criticism, only wanted to show the Ministry's unceasing efforts—said the camps already were in operation in the Guanahacabibes peninsula of extreme western Cuba.

The last refuge of the Guanahatabeyes Indians pushed back by the Spanish conquistadors, this peninsula is considered the most inhospitable part of Cuba. Captain Antonio Núñez Jiménez, a geographer by profession before becoming (temporarily) director of the INRA, described the desolate area in his *Geografía de Cuba,** stressing that it was formed of "sandy and silicious terrain which gives the landscape the look of a desert." The only thing that workers, government officials, or factory managers being "rehabilitated" could do there would be to clear away stones, cut brush, and build roads.

The Ministry publication said "the natural conditions there are difficult." It did not say how long the men remained for "rehabilitation," but gave assurances that "the high direction of the Ministry determines and imposes the penalty after having made appropriate inquiries in each case." Imbued with the "socialist conscience" of the Minister heading this "high direction," *Nuestra Industria* tells us in this same issue of March 1962 that work at Guanahacabibes was "voluntary."

Perhaps these administrative measures were indeed carried out voluntarily, if not willingly, since the alternative was the "revolutionary" court which could issue a sentence of death or an indefinite prison term.

But Che himself continued to wonder why his "socialism" was not shared by the masses. He was perplexed, for example, by the poor quality of the products made by nationalized enterprises. "It wasn't that way under capitalism," he lamented. "Why should it happen under socialism?" His faith was not shaken, however: "This cannot be an intrinsic evil of socialism. It must be remedied by more conscience, more vigilance, better control. . . ."

* La Habana: Editora Pedagógica, *año de la agricultura* (1963, third edition).

It was not remedied, and the situation was getting worse. At the end of 1962 the Ministry of Foreign Trade recorded a drop in cigar exports to Europe. What had happened?

The blame in this case could not be put on Washington. The *yanqui* blockade had cut off the North American market for Havana cigars, stimulating sales in Europe; lighting up a Havana cigar was a most agreeable way for a smoker to show his independence from Washington. The truth is that many fans of Havanas found the cigars no longer had quite the same taste; their quality seemed to have deteriorated. That's why Comrade Alberto Mora, Minister of Foreign Trade, complained to Comrade Guevara, Minister of Industry, in the hope of shifting responsibility from his ministry to the other. This did not prevent Alberto Mora from losing his post before the end of 1964.

It has never been known why Miguel Castro Reyes, Communist secretary of the *tabacaleros* (tobacco workers' union), committed suicide on January 27, 1963. The only information given by his wife was that shortly before, he had left a meeting at which Che Guevara had spoken.

The *tabacaleros* have an old union tradition, but all their leaders elected in the 1959 convention under Castro had gone to prison or into exile by 1960. The Communist functionaries who replaced them were careful above all to report favorable statistics, and statistics tell of quantity, not quality. The best specialists, moreover, had emigrated to Tampa and other U.S. East Coast areas, as well as to the Canary Islands, Central America, and Mexico.

The first direct popular revolt was that of the housewives. Not only were food rations inadequate, but the women had to line up for hours to get them. In June 1962, first in the city of Cárdenas, then at the gates of Havana itself in El Cano, housewives went into the streets beating on empty pots and chanting *Hambre!* (Hunger!).

Cuban "socialism" mobilized. Raúl Castro sent a parade

of tanks through Cárdenas, and President Dorticós warned the "counterrevolutionary parasites" that if their "provocation" was repeated the armed forces would intervene. After the El Cano incidents, Fidel himself had something to say: "For those who go out with pots to play Kennedy's game, let's break the pots on their heads."

Che Guevara had no comment about this method of reconciling socialism and man, or woman, in Cuba. Together with Labor Minister Augusto Martínez Sánchez, he was busy drawing up ways to impose rigid "labor discipline" in the factories to make up for the lack of a "socialist conscience."

A decree of August 29, 1962, ordered specific penalties for tardy workers: a fine of a half day's pay for being more than fifteen minutes late, or for three instances of arriving from one to fourteen minutes late. The same penalty applied to workers leaving the job ahead of time. In case of a repetition in the same month, the worker could be transferred to another job, at the Ministry's discretion. The decree added that the transfer of a worker to another place of work could be ordered "in any case where necessities of production may so require." In this case the government could even suspend the worker's one-month paid vacation obtained by the Cuban industrial workers in the Batista period.

It was during that same month of August 1962 that Cuba saw the birth, or rebirth, of the *carnet de trabajo,* later called the *tarjeta de control.* This was in fact a special worker's identity card and report book, a "worker's passport." The first of these passports were distributed without official announcement, and the event was publicized only in September, when the national council of the CTC-R mentioned them—naturally, for the purpose of approving the idea.

Essentially, the aim of the *carnet de trabajo* was to subject the worker to his job. The book indicated the conditions under which the worker had left his previous job; if his departure was not authorized, he could not obtain another job. The book also listed his good points (extra hours worked without pay, voluntary work on Sunday, participation in meetings and political rallies) as well as the bad (lateness, absences, nonachievement of quotas, nonparticipation in political activities). This system of worker identification had been introduced by some capitalist bosses and fought by all socialist organizations in the nineteenth century. It has been used for many years in South Africa to control the movements of black workers and maintain the apartheid system. But only Stalin up to then had found "socialist" virtues in such policing of the workers.

The difficulties in applying this measure in Cuba must have been considerable; although it was approved by Industry Minister Guevara, introduced by Labor Minister Martínez Sánchez, and endorsed by the Board of the Unions (Lázaro Peña) in 1962, it did not become law—Law No. 1225—until seven years later, on August 29, 1969. As *Verde Olivo* said in an enthusiastic comment, this system permitted "a just evaluation of the attitude and conduct maintained by each worker, without having to rely on the caprices of memory or the chance availability of known persons who could testify to it."

One of the headlines trumpeting the *Verde Olivo* article proclaimed that this was "a unique system of organizing work." The official organ of Raúl Castro and the Cuban armed forces refrained from recalling that this unique system was not without precedent in the history of the working classes.

As for Guevara and Castro, we are back to Trotsky and Stalin. As Isaac Deutscher put it, "there was hardly a single plank in Trotsky's programme of 1920–1921 which Stalin did not use during the industrial revolution of the thirties."

Che had resorted to all available means, even the most cruel, to awaken the "socialist conscience" of the masses. Fidel took over Che's vocabulary, but the means had become the end.

Though the methods, generally, were more brutal than ever, Fidel Castro's masterpiece remains his clever manipulation of the retirement system and of allowances for sickness or injury, as revealed in his speech of July 26, 1968, at Santa Clara.

After paying assorted tributes to the "civilization without money" dreamed of by the slain guerrilla, he announced a great new "socialist" innovation. From now on, in all enterprises which showed themselves to be "worthy of Che"—that is, where the workers followed a "schedule of conscience" by putting in a certain number of extra unpaid hours—those who fell ill or who reached retirement age would be pensioned at full salary, rather than at a fraction of it.

This was Sartre's *No Exit* at the factory: for each worker, hell will be the other one. Any worker who relaxes his effort jeopardizes the quota of extra hours the factory must meet if it is to obtain the new benefits; the other workers will be sure to remind him of that fact.

In the same speech, Castro offered in passing an unexpected example of "socialism" in action: the elimination of ticket-takers on buses, so that "each passenger, fully conscious of his obligations, pays, puts his money (in a box)." This, Fidel proclaimed, was "a system which can only be established in a revolution."

New Yorkers, among others, have been dropping their money into coin boxes of subways and buses for quite some time; have they been taking the road of the "new man" without knowing it?

Che's "socialism" in 1963 was first of all a military affair, and his ideas were being put into practice by Raúl Castro,

the commander-in-chief of the armed forces. On November
12, Raúl Castro announced the start of compulsory three-
year military service for all men aged 17 to 45, and a
"voluntary" term of two years for women aged 17 to 35.
While he made much of the "forty-seven provocations"
committed by the *yanquis* at the Guantánamo base between August 3 and November 3, he did not conceal that it
was mainly a matter of saving the sugar and coffee harvests.
The contingents of conscripts would serve as "workers'
brigades."

"The three-year service will give our soldiers a bursting
will to fight," said Raúl Castro in his telecast, "and it is
indispensable, moreover, in order to solve our production
problems."

A Minister of Labor, even a Minister of Industry named
Guevara, could not have done better than Raúl Castro,
Minister of the Army, in telling the Cuban workers what
was expected of them in 1968. Speaking in Camagüey on
May Day 1968, he said that in the province of Las Villas,
"where our Che has left his indelible mark," 35 enterprises
had given 90,217 hours of voluntary work. And he praised
the success of the "magnificent campaign to uproot the old
vice of a narrow economism among the workers." He
carefully avoided mentioning on this May Day 1968 in
Camagüey that since May Day 1886 in Chicago, May Day
battles throughout the world, including Cuba, had been
fought, and won, in the name of the eight-hour day.

Since the old vice of narrow economism was being
successfully uprooted, had Che's "socialism" finally given
birth to the "new man" in 1968, *año del guerrillero heroico?*

Well, if the "new man" is the worker who consents to
work himself to death, there seem to have been quite a few
representatives of the species extant that year. According to
Granma, the 8,000 workers of the huge El Moro cement
works were going to work 12 hours a day for two weeks,

"refusing pay for the extra hours." According to *Bohemia*, the cement works *Veintiséis-de-Julio* had accumulated 120,000 "voluntary hours" and there were "men who had been forty or fifty days without leaving the plant." At a State farm called *Juventud Heroica* (Heroic Youth), young boys had worked "15, 16, and 17 hours." At the William Soler children's hospital, nurses, already subjected to "normal" working days of 10 to 12 hours, were taking an extra 24-hour shift once a month.

Even so, however, there were misgivings, and not about the sick children at the William Soler hospital, exposed to what *Bohemia* called the "feverish enthusiasm" of their nurses. *Granma* during that same period had other worries. In a half-page editorial in large type, the official party and government newspaper was demanding measures to impose "worker's discipline," a problem of "far-reaching importance." *Granma* called for "a daily struggle against absenteeism, the careless manner of working, the poor quality of the products, and other factors raising questions about the productivity of the workers." After which it gave this illuminating definition of what Cuba's Communist Party meant by "voluntary work" and "worker's discipline":

> We must detail in a categorical manner what the production quotas are, the quality, the quantity and the nature of the work that each worker must require of himself. The administrative leaders in the brigades or in the production units must demand that these norms be strictly applied. . . .

Of course, the best way to get the workers to require all that of themselves is to require it for them. This concept of Fidel Castro conforms to the traditional line of Communist totalitarianism. And it is not in the least at odds with the concepts of socialism and man set forth by Che Guevara in his *El socialismo y el hombre en Cuba*, a work often considered to be Che's outstanding contribution to the new socialist thought.

For the young and spirited John Gerassi, son of a Spanish Civil War refugee, and editor of *Venceremos*, this work is even "one of the great documents in the history of socialism." This kind of "socialism," however, must begin by finding a place in its dialectic for that magical phenomenon which Jean-Paul Sartre defined for Castro under the name of "direct democracy."

Che has an explanation for it, the magic as well as the "democracy." The Cuban people follow Castro unswervingly because "the degree of confidence accorded to him corresponds precisely to his exact interpretation of the desires and aspirations of the people, as well as his sincere struggle for the accomplishment of the promises made."

Describing this "quasi-intuitive method" in which Fidel has become "a master" and which allows him to sound out the feelings of the people about any problem, Che manages to graft an acoustical experiment onto the magical phenomenon:

> In large concentrations of people, one observes something like the dialogue of two tuning forks, the vibrations of each one starting new vibrations in the other. Fidel and the crowd begin to vibrate in a dialogue of increasing intensity until the climax which comes in an abrupt conclusion, crowned by our cry of battle and victory.

Such an extraordinary "definition" at first appears to be a rather crude parody, one with some sexual overtones since the word "climax" used in the original is somewhat unusual in Spanish. The sad truth, however, is that this bit of buffoonery was indeed written by Che, shortly before his disappearance in 1965, in a document which in a way is his last will and testament. Composed in the form of a letter to Carlos Quijano, director of the weekly *Marcha* in Montevideo, *Socialism and Man in Cuba* also contains some of the most sinister formulas about the "Party" and the "individual" ever set forth since Trotsky declared that the individual could not be right against the Party, and since Stalin undertook to prove it with executions, concentration camps and, in the case of Trotsky himself, with Ramón Mercader del Río's ice-axe.

The individual, Che nevertheless states, is "the actor in this strange and moving drama which is the construction of socialism," and he fulfills this role "in his dual character of a unique being and a member of the community."

Does this mean there is to be some hope of survival for that half, or at least that fraction of the individual considered to be "unique"? Not at all. For Che, once he puts down his tuning forks, does not beat about the bush. Man, he says, is an "unfinished product" who bears within him "the flaws of the past." He must be subjected to "an unceasing effort to eradicate them." Even when thus cleansed, however, the individual is not yet acceptable to Che Guevara, for the individual interests him only to the extent that he is no longer one.

Contrary to his initial statement, one does not find any further trace in this manifesto of the "unique being" which he claims to be a part of the actor in the drama. The only "individual" he recognizes is "the member of the community," or what the individual without quotation marks has become, must become, after having undergone the direct and indirect education of "socialist" society, and after submitting himself to "a conscious process of self-education."

True "individuals," as seen by Che, cannot be "those whose lack of education turns them toward the solitary path." The new men he envisions will take other paths: "They no longer march completely alone, over meandering roads, toward distant goals. They follow their vanguard, constituted by the Party, by the advanced workers, by the advanced men who march linked to the masses and in close communion with them."

Self-education for Che is nothing more than a product of indirect education, which in turn is the result of direct education. In the molding of the "individual" according to Che Guevara, we thus have three stages.

First, direct education: "This is carried out through the educational machinery of the State . . . by means of organisms such as the Ministry of Education and the propaganda apparatus (*aparato de divulgación*) of the Party." Next, indirect education: "The new attitude called for tends to become a habit; the masses assimilate it and bring pressure on those who are not yet educated." Finally, self-education: "The individual continually undergoes the influence of the new social power and perceives that he is not fully adequate to it. . . . He seeks to adapt himself to a situation which he feels to be just, but which° lack of development has prevented him from doing until then. He educates himself. . . ."

° The translation of this part of the sentence presents quite a problem. The Spanish text, as literally, and officially, translated by Margarita Zimmermann in the Cuban government version reprinted by John Gerassi, says: ". . . whose lack of development has kept him from doing so thus far." It is doubtful that Guevara was referring to the lack of development of the "situation," but that is what the Spanish text says: . . . *cuya propia falta de desarollo*. . . . The French edition, published by François Maspero, translated by a (later dissident) group of the Union of French Communist Students, justifiably dared to reverse and correct Che's faulty grammar: ". . . something he has not been able to do up to then because of the inadequacy of his own development."

But what if the individual does *not* feel the situation is just? Is he supposed to adapt himself in spite of it? Che cannot imagine that any such question might arise. So he dispenses with any appropriate answer. If *El socialismo y el hombre en Cuba* is "one of the great documents in the history of socialism," then the history of socialism will have to resign itself to including the most cynical justifications of gutless servility. For education—direct, indirect, or "self"—as outlined by Che means nothing but brainwashing, and the ideal "individual" he describes, the "new man" he holds up before our eyes, is the submissive follower, the obedient executor, the perfect, simple-minded, well-drilled human robot.

One is horror-stricken—and if not, one should be—at the fact that Che, once a rebel before he became a "revolutionary," did not draw back from such odious definitions. He was perfectly aware of the political consequences of his concept of the individual, and he crudely spelled them out, without bothering about those of his supporters who continue to call themselves "libertarians" or indeed "anarchists." Candor was his only innovation in dealing with the question.

If the masses are to follow the vanguard, Che concluded, they "must be subjected to influences and pressures of a certain intensity." Before him, others had by their actions carried this idea to its furthest limits. But Che sets it down in black and white in a "socialist document" which indeed should not be ignored: "It is the dictatorship of the proletariat, exercised not only over the defeated class but also individually over the victorious class."

Yes, that was Che Guevara's definition of "socialism," as no "socialist" before him had been mad, stupid, or cynical enough to utter publicly: *Es la dictadura del proletariado ejerciéndose no sólo sobre la clase derrotada, sino también individualmente sobre la clase vencedora.*

In its definition of the relation between the individual and
society, between "man" and "socialism," *El socialismo y el
hombre en Cuba* openly advocates an unrelenting totalitarian "socialism," a "socialism" without liberty and without
humanity, where there could be no talk of either thaw or
spring, and no more room for a Dubcek or a Solzhenitsyn
than there is in Brezhnev's "socialism."

Much has been made of Che's scornful attitude toward
"socialist realism," as if this attitude established his independence of thought. Che says socialist realism was born
"on the foundations of the art of the last century," and asks:
"Why pretend to seek in the frozen forms of socialist
realism the only valid recipe?"

At the time Che was writing, socialist realism had already
ceased to be sacred, and to express doubts about it proved
nothing, certainly not any defiance. While cracking down
on unofficial long hair and unauthorized homosexuals,
esoteric poets and the *Tres Tristes Tigres* of Cabrera Infante,
Fidel Castro had made it a point to show tolerance of
abstract art. The question is whether Che's "socialism"
offered Cubans any artistic freedom beyond that of not
practicing "socialist realism."

One wonders for a moment when Che deplores the
absence of "an ideological-cultural mechanism which would
permit research and pull out the weeds growing so quickly
in the ground fertilized by State subsidies." The intention
here seems praiseworthy, but the ideological-cultural mechanism Che seeks would hardly seem to be the best method
for realizing his aim. There is some hope again in his
warning that "we should not create hirelings subject to
official thinking, nor subsidized students who, living under
the patronage of the budget, exercise a freedom in quotation marks." But all the rest is negative.

Che carefully stresses that the opposite of "socialist

realism" is not "freedom"—freedom, for Che, is also in quotation marks—because freedom "does not yet exist and will not exist until the complete development of the new society." We are thereby given notice: What Che calls "freedom" can be attained only by the kind of "individual" he has in mind when he speaks of the necessary three-stage process of "education" discussed earlier; this "freedom" will become available when there is no one left who knows how to use it.

And when Che—quite refreshingly, it seems at first sight—admits that "we revolutionaries very often lack the knowledge and the intellectual daring which are necessary to face the task of developing a new man by methods different from the conventional ones," the illusion is quickly shattered by the conclusion: "The men of the party must apply themselves to this task, and seek to realize the main objective: to educate the people."

There have been more lasting but even less justified illusions about the often quoted sarcasm of Che: "If one respects the rules of the game, one receives all the honors, the same as a monkey could have by inventing pirouettes. The condition is not to try to escape from the invisible cage." Che of course is talking about the intellectuals of the capitalist world, probably including those who refuse the Nobel Prize. He could not have meant the intellectuals in the service of "socialist" governments such as his own, for he does not object to monkeys inventing pirouettes as long as they do so for the benefit and under the control of the Party.

Socialism and Man in Cuba also includes the portrait of the man whom Che considers "a true revolutionary." It does not resemble Castro, but comes appallingly close to a self-portrait. Both a religious fanatic in the style of the Crusaders and a professional revolutionary in the tradition of the first Bolsheviks, Che's true revolutionary is a sort of superman, explicitly different from the "ordinary man" or *hombre común:*

> He must combine an impassioned spirit with a cool mind and make painful decisions without flinching. Our revolutionaries of the vanguard . . . cannot come down with their little dose of daily affection to the places where the ordinary man practices it.° The leaders of the revolution have children who, with their first faltering words, do not learn to call their father; wives who must be part of the general sacrifice necessary to carry the revolution to its destination. The circle of friends is strictly limited to the circle of revolutionary companions. There is no life outside the revolution. . . . A man† who devotes his entire life to the revolution cannot let himself be distracted by the thought of what a child needs, of his worn shoes, of the basic necessities which his family lacks. If he lets himself be haunted by such preoccupations, he creates favorable ground for the development of corruption.

Che is not unaware of the fact that his "revolutionary" prototype is a sort of visionary, not very likable and possibly

---

° . . . *los lugares donde el hombre común lo ejercita.* The Maspero edition, embarrassed by this "common" or "ordinary" man thus distinguished from the man of the elite, translates it as *les autres hommes* (other men). The official English translation by Margarita Zimmermann, reprinted by John Gerassi in *Venceremos,* is more honest: "ordinary men. . . ."

† Here begins a tortuous sentence in which Che ends by saying the opposite of what he obviously intended to say. The literal translation of Margarita Zimmermann distorts thus not the text but the thought of the author. Not knowing how to get out of this dilemma, I decided in translating this sentence to use the very free but logical and at least intelligible French text of the Maspero edition.

dangerous. He recognizes that "under these conditions, it is necessary to have a large dose of humanity, a large dose of sense of justice and truth in order not to fall into dogmatic extremes, into cold scholasticisms, into isolation from the masses." What he seems unaware of is the fact that the "revolutionary" he has just described has already fallen, and could not help but fall into all these extremes.

Even if such a fanatic were to succeed in remaining human during the struggle, he would cease to be so the day he gained power, because for such a fanatic it could only be absolute power. Lord Acton, in this regard, was infinitely more farsighted than Lenin.

As partisan of an all-powerful State, of a party obeyed to the letter, Che presumably would have liked to escape from this dilemma. It disturbs him to imagine that someone, "seeing things from a superficial point of view," could speak of "the subjection of the individual to the State." His problem is of course not easy to resolve. He tries by idealizing the State and the Party, assigning to the revolutionaries in power, at least in Cuba, almost supernatural virtues such as the ability to vibrate in unison with the people. But this utopian vision of the tuning-fork revolutionary is not much different from the ancient philosophy of enlightened despotism. In both cases, the well-being of the people, if not the birth of the new man, depends upon the will—the good will—of an aristocracy.

Che consoles himself by affirming that "the masses carry out with incomparable enthusiasm and discipline the tasks set by the government." This leads us back to the "democratic centralism" of the Stalinist bureaucracy, with only the name of Fidel to give it a Cuban flavor:

> The initiative comes in general from Fidel or from the high command of the revolution, and it is explained to the people who make it their own. At other times,

local experiments are launched by the party and the government to be generalized following the same procedure.

One short paragraph seems to reverse the direction:

> The State, nevertheless, sometimes makes a mistake. When one of these errors occurs, one notes a lessening of collective enthusiasm as the result of a quantitative lessening of each of the elements which make it up, and work is paralyzed to the point of being reduced to insignificant proportions; it is time to rectify.*

Rectification, alas, exists only on paper. Che himself, when confronted with the symptoms he describes, never applied the remedy he recommended. Whenever enthusiasm waned in Cuba and work slowed down, the Minister of Industry denounced the lack of "socialist conscience" of the workers, or their "indiscipline" or the actions of the CIA. Once a mistake could no longer be concealed, it was attributed to an anonymous bureaucracy which had incorrectly followed the orders of the State, or which had incorrectly explained the decisions of the State to the masses. If someone was singled out by name, it was precisely to serve as scapegoat for a State which never made mistakes.

The illustration offered by Guevara in support of his reassuring affirmation shows, moreover, that he doesn't mean what he says: After telling how one recognizes when the time has come to "rectify," he writes that "this is what happened in March 1962 due to the sectarian policy imposed on the party by Aníbal Escalante."

The Escalante affair was one of those dark intrigues

---

* This is Che's style, not mine. See Margarita Zimmermann's official translation. The French text, in the Maspero edition, is more readable but less faithful.

which are chronic events in the top echelon of all Communist parties, periodically resulting in the ritual elimination of one group or another, which is then blamed for all existing evils. Aníbal Escalante was certainly no more responsible than Che Guevara or Fidel Castro for what was going wrong in the Cuban factories or on the sugar plantations. His removal changed nothing. The State continued to make enormous mistakes, but no one could say so, or contribute to any "lessening of collective enthusiasm," without exposing himself to the risk of being dealt with as a counterrevolutionary.

In September 1963, more than a year after the "rectification" performed on Aníbal Escalante, the secretary-general of the CTC-R, Lázaro Peña, was confronted at a union meeting by angry construction workers who protested against the increase in work quotas and the revision of wage scales.

Augusto Martínez Sánchez, Minister of Labor, quickly convened another "union" meeting, which was carefully screened this time and solidly backed by strong-armed militants. It approved the new quotas and the new wage scales, and deplored "the disrespectful attitude" displayed toward the secretary-general at the previous meeting. Then Lázaro Peña spoke and denounced the conduct of "certain leaders who deceive their comrades." These leaders, he said, were "traitors to today's trade union movement."

During the same month of September 1963, Raúl Castro, Minister of the Armed Forces, let it be known that the rectification of errors—not those of the State, of course, but of the workers—might be carried out henceforth by firing squads. "There are cases of economic sabotage," he said, "which appear to be innocent mistakes. But one day it will be necessary to shoot the authors of certain mistakes which are in fact counterrevolutionary acts."

Lázaro Peña lost his job in 1964. Dismissed in his turn,

Martínez Sánchez on December 8, 1964, shot himself in the head. It seems he survived, but no more was heard about him. The communiqué announcing the suicide attempt expressed regrets, but at the same time declared that according to "fundamental revolutionary principles," such an attitude was "unjustifiable and improper." The communiqué bore the signature of Fidel Castro. "A revolutionary," it added, "knows that he does not have the right to deprive his cause of a life which belongs to it, and that he may sacrifice it only against an enemy."

Che Guevara did not shoot himself in the head. He departed for Bolivia.

VII

Guerrilla and
Man in Bolivia

or

The Second Failure of Che Guevara

A curious thing—they avoid meeting the people of the country. Some liberators, not daring to pass the house of a peasant! This is because they know that in each peasant's house there is a fighter, there is a revolutionary. Some liberators!"

Fidel Castro was speaking at the funeral, on April 18, 1970, of Cuban militia members slain in clashes with anti-Castro Cubans who had landed at Baracoa in Oriente province. The anti-Castro Cubans also had been killed in the battles, or caught and shot the next day. Now Castro mocked them for having tried to hide in uninhabited locations: "The less people around, the better for them. Some liberators, really!"

Just like the anti-Castro guerrillas in Cuba, Che Guevara and his guerrillas in Bolivia had been obliged to avoid inhabited areas; just like the anti-Castro guerrillas, they too hardly dared go near the house of a peasant. The peasants of the Nancahuazú region, of course, were not combatants or counterrevolutionaries. But like the peasants of Baracoa, they were wary of "liberators" who came from afar.

Fidel Castro called the Cubans who fought against his regime in Baracoa "mercenaries" and "agents of the CIA."

But these "mercenaries" must have known they had little chance of returning to Miami to make use of their "CIA

153

dollars." Were they willing to give their lives out of pure
devotion to *yanqui* imperialism? Since Castro could not
imply such an explanation, he suggested another one: these
"counterrevolutionaries" were hoping that after hiding at
first from the peasants as well as from Castro's soldiers, they
might succeed later in winning over the peasants. So Castro,
on April 18, 1970, called them "stupid" too.

Were Che Guevara and the "liberators" of Nancahuazú,
who had come all the way from Cuba in the hope of
winning over Bolivian peasants, equally stupid? It has been
said, to avoid that sorry conclusion, that Che never really
intended to stay, and win, in Bolivia. He was only seeking, it
is argued, to hold onto a limited territory, chosen because it
was close to the borders of several countries, in order to
establish a base for training and support of guerrilla
operations aimed at these countries.

The ambitions of Che Guevara certainly went beyond
Bolivia. On July 10, 1967, he complains in his *Diary* about
the statements of Debray and Bustos, who had "made a
confession as to the intercontinental ° purpose of the
guerrilla, something they shouldn't have done." Che thus
had told Debray and Bustos about his aims. Other pages of
the *Diary* show that he discussed guerrilla plans for
Argentina with El Pelado (Bustos), just as he spoke with El
Chino (Chang Navarro) about the chances of renewing
guerrilla operations in Peru.

But the "continental purpose" required a launching
platform which could not be a mere camp lost in the
wooded mountains above the gorges of Nancahuazú. To
carry on revolution in the Andes, to capture Asunción,
Lima, Buenos Aires, it was first necessary to take hold of La
Paz.

° This is obviously a slip for "continental," as the French
translation—but not the English one—corrects it.

This indeed is what Che intended. Listening to his radio, he follows excitedly each minor vicissitude of Bolivian politics. He is transported periodically by absolutely irrational onsets of optimism. At these moments, sometimes amid bitter complaints about his men and about the peasants, he appears persuaded that the regime in La Paz is on the point of collapse. And he seems to have no doubt that, as soon as this happens, the entire country will fall like a ripe plum into the hands of his guerrillas—this isolated, hungry, and powerless band, wasting away in the southeastern forests.

Castro, in his "Necessary Introduction" to the *Diary*, singles out a remark by Che which shows, he says, "how real were the chances of success, and how extraordinary the catalyzing power of the guerrilla."

The date was July 14, 1967. The guerrillas on that day have "led away," or more exactly have kidnapped, two peasants needed as guides, leaving "the wives in tears." That night Che listens to the radio. He learns that two parties are quitting the government coalition, and that "the peasants are threatening an alliance with the *Falange*" against Barrientos. That's when Che utters the exclamation quoted by Fidel (who says only that this was "on a certain occasion," preferring not to recall the context): "The government is disintegrating rapidly. What a pity not to have a hundred more men right now!"

What could Che have done with another hundred men on July 14, 1967? To begin with, he would have had one hundred more mouths to feed. True, another hundred men would have made it easier to take over villages and confiscate food, for payment, but then what?

The La Paz regime may not have been very solid but it was not falling apart because, on July 14, 1967, politicians of the "PRA" and the "PSB" had been replaced in the government by politicians sporting other initials equally devoid of meaning. As to the *Falange Socialista Boliviana*, this was an organization similar to the Spanish Falange— that is, of fascist inspiration—and linked to the oligarchy even if its "social" pretensions sometimes gave it, like its Spanish model, the superficial appearance of an opposition party.

Unlike Che, who at Nancahuazú had no access to the Cuban press, Castro was able to read in *Bohemia* some harsh observations on the "fascist" and "counterrevolutionary" character of the Bolivian Falange.° A rapprochement between this party and the peasants could only mean, for Che, added difficulties and dangers. Was that what Castro meant by the "catalyzing power of the guerrillas"?

The "catalyzing power" on this "certain occasion" would have had at most an involuntary and paradoxical effect, if the peasants' hostility to the guerrillas had encouraged them to support the rightist critics of governmental "passivity," seriously weakening President Barrientos. This was not the case. Che's transistor radio leads him to imagine excitedly that La Paz is gripped by "a tremendous crisis whose outcome cannot be foreseen." His excitement doesn't seem to be dampened by the fact noted in his next sentence: "For the moment, the peasant unions of Cochabamba have formed a political party 'of Christian inspiration' which supports Barrientos. . . ."

From November 1966 to September 1967, Che summed up the situation at the end of each month in his diary. More than half of the eleven summaries repeat in various tones—incredulity, bitterness, irritation, resignation—that the guerrillas are unable to recruit or even interest the peasants, or to deal with them in any way other than as enemies.

° The *Falange* played a major role in August 1972, when reactionary Colonel Hugo Banzer Suárez overturned the regime of General Juan José Tórrez.

"What has gone most slowly," we read in the summary of January 1967, "is the incorporation of Bolivian fighters." For March, noting that the government is beginning to organize a counteroffensive, Che mentions among its elements a "peasant mobilization" *against* the guerrillas. The political downfall of the guerrillas is certified—together, alas, with the moral collapse of their leader—in this monstrous passage from the April summary:

> The peasant base still is not developing, although it seems that by means of systematic terror, we will obtain the neutrality of most of them; support will come later. We have not made a single recruit. . . ."

Mediante el terror planificado . . . Those among Che's admirers who claim not to believe the end justifies the means silently and hypocritically overlook this frightening display of totalitarian cynicism. Some liberators, really, as Castro was to say in 1970, though not in speaking of the *guerrillero heroico*.

In the same April 1967 summary Che returns to the government's peasant mobilization, to minimize its importance: "The peasant mobilization is nonexistent, except for providing information, which proves somewhat annoying, but this is neither very fast nor very efficient, and we will be able to overcome it." The inconvenience must have been rather considerable, and overcoming it not so easy as that, since the "systematic terror" against the peasants, so calmly contemplated by Che, modestly limited its aim to obtaining the mere neutrality of these peasants toward the guerrillas.

The summary of the following month includes a somewhat paradoxical variation, adorned with a slight note of hope:

> Complete absence of peasant recruitment, although the peasants begin losing their fear of us and we are

getting their admiration. It's a slow task which requires patience.

The note of hope has disappeared in the June summary. Again reporting that "the lack of recruitment continues to make itself felt," Che explains it in these terms:

> It is a vicious circle. In order to recruit some peasants, we have to carry on our activities permanently in an inhabited region, and for that we need more men.

In July there are still no peasant recruits, but the note of hope returns in the summary at the end of the month:

> The lack of peasant recruitment continues to be felt, although there have been encouraging indications in the welcome given to us by old acquaintances among the peasants.

The formula is slightly modified in the August summary:

> We go on without any recruitment of peasants, something logical, by the way, if one takes into account the little contact we have had with them recently.

The final monthly summary in the *Bolivian Diary*, for September 1967, gives up all hope, all further ambitions, all attempts of explanation. The formula this time is terse, final, and without illusions:

> The peasant masses are of no help to us whatsoever, and they are turning into informers.

How can a guerrilla movement operating under such circumstances be held up as exemplary by those who claim to be followers of Che's doctrine on guerrilla warfare?

In the first chapter of *Guerra de guerrillas*, in which he
defines the "general principles" and "the essence" of the
struggle, Che explains that a guerrilla movement is "a
struggle of the masses, a struggle of the people," and that
"its great force rests in the masses of the population." He
draws a categorical conclusion: "The guerrilla must count
on the full support of the population of the area. This is a
condition *sine qua non.*"

Published in the summer of 1960 by the INRA (Institute
of Agrarian Reform), Che's book was long considered, by his
enemies at least as much as by his partisans, as a model
handbook for modern guerrilla warfare.

In the United States it was condensed by Major Harries-
Clichy Peterson in several consecutive issues of the *Marine
Corps Gazette.* Later, in a preface to the English edition of
the book printed for the U.S. armed forces,° Major Peterson
stressed that the importance of Che's contribution was in
the dominant role he attributed to the peasants. The
rebellion of Mao Tse-tung, Peterson recalled, failed when it
took the form of workers' revolts; it succeeded when Mao
took to the rural areas and adopted the cause of agrarian
reform. The Marine officer added:

> Guevara has no intention of repeating Mao's abor-
> tive worker's uprisings. . . . He favors rural areas
> where guerrillas and inhabitants can cooperate closely,
> beyond the reach of enemy forces. . . .

This in fact was the *theory* of Che:

> One of the most important characteristics of guer-
> rilla warfare is the considerable difference existing

° Che Guevara on Guerrilla Warfare (New York: Frederick A.
Praeger, 1971).

between intelligence obtained by rebel forces and that available to the enemy. While the latter must pass through absolutely hostile zones where they are up against the unyielding silence of the peasants, the former, that is the defenders, count on a friend, almost a parent, in every house. . . .

In *practice* the contrary was true. For Che's men in Nancahuazú in 1967, as for the anti-Castro commandos landing at Baracoa in 1970, the dream of "a friend in every house" was brutally shattered. It had not been really so even in 1957 in the Sierra Maestra. But among the Cuban peasants, Castro's men had never encountered such an impenetrable wall as the Bolivian peasants raised against Guevara ten years later.

At first, Che relates in his *Pasajes de la guerra revolucionaria,* "many peasants were still running away, frightened, at our arrival for fear of reprisals the government would take when it learned of the least little contact between the inhabitants and our group." Peasant encouragement, however, was never completely lacking for the Cuban *barbudos:* "We always found someone to serve as a guide, to advise us, or to give us the food we needed to go on. . . ."

The Indian peasants of southeastern Bolivia were only beginning to emerge from the slumber of several centuries. The 1952 revolution had given them title to the land they cultivated. They were poor, but free. Having escaped from the servitude which they had known and which continued to oppress their brothers of the Peruvian Andes, they were not on the verge of revolt. Didn't they have their own piece of land?

"The guerrilla is essentially and above all an agrarian revolutionary," Che had said after the Cuban victory in February 1959, when the peasant's desire to work his own soil was not yet considered to be counterrevolutionary.

Che then was stressing the necessity for the guerrilla to grasp the fundamental importance of this desire in the peasants of any region where he planned to operate. Even in April 1961, when Cuban agrarian reform was already following the path traced by the doubtful Soviet experiment, Guevara did not consider it heresy to repeat: "The hunger for land is present at all times among the peasants."

Castro and his companions from the Cuban middle class were well aware of this truth, and this is why they had succeeded in gaining a foothold among the peasants of Oriente province.

In January 1959, speaking of the social role of the *ejército rebelde*, Che had not failed to recall the importance of the first agrarian reform carried out in the Sierra Maestra in October 1958. He even affirmed that this reform had been the "spearhead of the rebel army." The text of the reform, he noted, had been "drafted primarily by Dr. Humberto Sorí Marín and by Fidel Castro," but he also had been given "the honor to contribute to it."

"Through the revolution, land has been given to the peasants," he stated. "Huge estates belonging to servants of the dictatorship were occupied, and portioned out, and we began to turn over to the peasants of the region all lands belonging to the State. The moment came when we were completely identified as a peasant movement, linked to the land, and with agrarian reform for our flag."

We must be thankful to Roberto Fernández Retamar for not having dropped the January 1959 speech from the *Obra revolucionaria* of Che Guevara, and especially for having retained in December 1967 the reference to *comandante* Sorí Marín, shot by a firing squad at the end of 1961 as a "counterrevolutionary." In 1963, at the time his *Pasajes de la guerra revolucionaria* were assembled, and "edited," in book form, Guevara sought to forget this 1959 account— much as the traditional Moscow "historian" would have done—to satisfy the "dialectical necessities" of the moment.

For Che Guevara in 1963, the only Cuban agrarian reform which mattered was that of the *granjas del pueblo*,* imposed on the Cuban people in the name of "socialism."

There was no longer any praise of the original reform which served as "spearhead" for the *barbudos* and to which he had "the honor to contribute." But there still was a mention of Sorí Marín, who refused to approve the later measures and resigned as Minister of Agriculture. "He did not wish to commit himself. . . ." Guevara jeers. He even preferred, finally, to be shot.

As is shown by Theodore Draper, one of the most rational and best-documented critics of Castroism, and as is implied sometimes by Carlos Rafael Rodríguez, the most resilient and astute of old Cuban Communists, the peasants played a more important role in Che's imagination than they did in the Cuban revolution. But even if Che's conviction was based on autosuggestion, it was a conviction, and it dictated an attitude: "The guerrillas have become increasingly aware of the necessity to win over the peasant masses."

When Guevara arrived in Nancahuazú on November 7, 1966, he was sure that his guerrillas could count not only on the help but on the participation of the Bolivian peasants.

On November 13, a Sunday, some young workers employed by the owner of a neighboring farm, on their way back from hunting, pass by the little farmhouse which was the guerrillas' "front." Che eyes them greedily: "They are mountain men, young and single; perfect to be recruited, and intensely hating their boss."

Perhaps they hated their boss, but they had no love for these strange characters who looked like foreign soldiers and with whom they felt nothing in common.

---

* Farms of the people, or rather of the State, like the Russian *sovkhoses*.

Still less attracted were the Indians who worked their own acre and were no longer tortured by the "hunger for land." In their eyes, these armed men from other lands, unable to understand their language, must have seemed more like *conquistadores* than *libertadores*. Amid these Indian peasants with their ignorance, their suspicion, their superstition, Che with his theories, his ambitions, his revolution, was like a fish out of water.

In an additional study of guerrilla warfare published in September 1963 by the magazine *Cuba socialista* and titled "Guerrilla warfare, a method," Che again stressed that to pretend to carry on a guerrilla war without the support of the population was "the prelude to an inevitable disaster."

Che Guevara thus had given notice to himself, but he also seemed to imply that the support of the population was automatically guaranteed to anyone who came to set up a guerrilla base, a *foco*, in their midst. "The guerrilla is supported by the masses of the peasants and the workers in the region and in all the territory concerned . . . ," Che categorically states, and he says "is," not "should be." The next sentence, however, no less categorically states that "without these conditions, guerrilla warfare cannot be permitted." If the second sentence is to suggest that the conditions specified in the first one are to be minutely verified before launching any operation—that is, if the future guerrillas are to make sure of the state of mind of the population in the region where they intend to operate—Che certainly did not follow that rule in Bolivia.

For Bolivia offers us the bewildering spectacle of a guerrilla leader who, having set up his *foco* on November 7 in a certain region, is led to write on the following June 19: "As to the inhabitants, we have to track them down in order to speak to them, since they are like little animals. . . ."

After nearly seven months and two weeks, Che has discovered that the peasants among whom the *foco* was to spread its revolutionary fire behave like *animalitos*. What does he do? Does he move to some other place, or change his methods, or rethink his theories? No. He consoles himself with the political scraps he picks up on his transistor radio. He hangs onto these bits of news as if they were full of promise: "What is interesting," he notes on June 13, "is the political convulsion of the country, the fantastic number of pacts and counter-pacts which make up the atmosphere."

On June 13, 1967, in Bolivia there were signs of increasing tension in the mines, but the "political convulsion" in La Paz consisted mainly of the usual intrigues of politicians and parties maneuvering to grab a larger portion of the government pie.

Che Guevara appears totally uninterested in what is happening in the mines, echoes of which are beginning to reach him by radio, his only source of information. Fascinated by the Byzantine quarrels of La Paz, he grotesquely overestimates their importance. At the same time, he dangerously underestimates the personal popularity of President Barrientos among the peasants. It did not show great foresight, or insight, to have dismissed the man who was going to defeat him by scornfully declaring on May 20 that "there is no one more incapable," or on August 12 that "he was stupid as always."

If guerrilla warfare cannot be permitted without the support of the peasants, the support of "the masses of the workers," according to Che Guevara, is no less essential.

Most smaller countries in Latin America do not have great masses of industrial workers, but Bolivia has a genuine proletariat in the tin mines of the *altiplano*, the bleak plateau lying at an altitude of 12,000 feet between two ranges of the Andes. There are about 25,000 active miners, as well as an undetermined number of unemployed miners, and widows and children of miners, who still try to scrape a living from the mines. Most often this is done through what might be called "private appropriation": COMIBOL, the administration of the nationalized mines, repurchases ore which people recover from the slag, and this is generally augmented by ore directly stolen from the mine.

Their lives are miserable, squeezed by starvation wages and shortened by the *mal de mina*, the miner's disease (silicosis). To forget their hunger they chew *coca*. To drown their despair they drink *chicha*. And from time to time they revolt.

The 1952 revolution was made possible by the miners of the *altiplano*, and the prime example of a popular force routing a regular army was offered by these Bolivian miners, who did it well before the Cuban *barbudos*, and in a more convincing manner. But the revolution did not help them; their situation, unlike that of the peasants, did not improve. The nationalization of the mines having resulted only in replacing the Patiño family with an incompetent and corrupt bureaucracy, their situation after a few years was even worse. It became more tragic than ever following the military take-over in November 1964.

General Barrientos was on good terms with the peasants, leaned on them for support, and did not hesitate to form them into armed militia units. At the same time, he had good reason to be wary of the miners. They did not accept cuts in their pay because the price of tin on the world market had dropped: had their pay been increased when the world tin price went up? And Barrientos knew that miners have something with which to make themselves heard: dynamite.

First in May, then in September 1965, there were bloody battles between the miners and the army of Generals Barrientos and Ovando. Soldiers machine-gunned the miners and fired bazookas at the blocks of dried earth which formed their homes. There were hundreds of victims, including women and children. The miners buried their dead, and then again started putting aside sticks of dynamite to prepare for revenge. Their unions were strong, and they had remained so even when their leaders, as happened more than once, were arrested, murdered, or bought off. Open to all revolutionary trends, notably to the Trotskyite influence which has prevailed over that of the ex-Stalinist bureaucracy, the Bolivian tin mine workers represent an authentic proletarian vanguard.

Marxist or not, and Che Guevara considered himself "Marxist-Leninist," it is impossible to see how anyone could seriously plan to launch a revolution in Bolivia without first winning the support of the miners of Huanuni, Catavi, or Siglo Veinte. Yet this is what Che tried to do.

For Che not only decided to liberate the Indian peasants, when his relations with them were those of *hombre* to *animalito* and when his hope to at least neutralize them was based on the expected results of systematic terror, he also thought that along the way he would liberate the Indian miners, whom he scarcely knew, who knew him hardly any better, and with whose struggles he had never bothered to establish contact and coordination. The incredible futility of the whole Nancahuazú undertaking became particularly evident after the bloody "night of Saint John," June 24, 1967, when soldiers again massacred men, women, and children in the mining centers of Catavi and Siglo Veinte.

The miners, their problems, and their struggles have no place at all in the *Bolivian Diary* up to June 8. On that day Che notes first that he had to admonish Urbano again "because of his insolent remarks." Urbano was Captain Leonardo Tamayo Núñez, who in 1961 had been secretary of the Cuban delegation at Punta del Este, led by Guevara. Late in the evening of the 8th, Che heard the radio telling about a state of siege and the threat of an uprising by the miners. But he thinks, and writes, that all this is *agua de borrajas:* literally borage water (which causes sweating), but figuratively, bullshit.

Then comes June 24, 1967, the date which will remain in the history of Bolivia as *la noche de San Juan.* For Che, it is the date when he and his men have traveled "a total of twelve kilometers," descended "an incredible cliff," and camped near "a small rivulet on the slopes of Durán hill." Only in the last two lines of the day's entry does Che get around to mentioning that "the radio carries the news of fighting in the mines."

Even the day after, the events in Siglo Veinte are given less than two out of twenty-three lines on the page, most of which concern the guerrillas' purchase of a heifer "which was immediately sacrificed." But the Bolivian guerrilla chief is now better informed. He has been able to tune into the Argentine as well as the Bolivian newscasts; the Bolivian radio had withheld the number of victims at Siglo Veinte, but the Argentine broadcast gave the figure as 87.

Finally on June 30 the miners achieve four lines out of thirty-five, while six are devoted to the main event:

> On the political level, the most important fact is the official statement by Ovando announcing that I am here. He also has said the army was facing highly trained guerrillas, including Viet Cong commanders who had beaten the best North American regiments.

Che, however, is pleased by the Siglo Veinte development. The radio broadcasts, he proudly records, say that he is considered "the instigator of the plan of insurrection in the mines, coordinated with that of Nancahuazú." Obviously Che knows better than anyone else that this is not true, but avidly clinging to the calculated statements of the Bolivian generals, the hermit of Nancahuazú is ready to be persuaded that he is at the center of everything. "Things are

taking shape," * he exults; "before long, I will no longer be
Fernando the tooth-puller." †

In his summary of June, written the same night and
including an eight-point balance sheet, the events of Siglo
Veinte are mentioned last, despite Che's wave of optimism.
"The massacre in the mines," he writes, "considerably lights
up the panorama for us. . . ."

It does not seem possible that a human revolutionary, in
contrast to a doctrinaire fanatic, could react so unemotion-
ally to a massacre of workers, even if it offered undeniable
advantages. Moreover, it is difficult to imagine exactly how
the Siglo Veinte massacre could help the guerrillas or "light
up the panorama" for them. Since the government's propaganda has blamed the resistance of the miners on Che—
falsely, but Che didn't mind at all—wasn't the same
propaganda going to present the defeat of the miners as a
defeat for Che Guevara?

Che returns to the miners in his *Diary* for the last time on
July 9. Noting radio reports of a fourteen-point agreement
between the miners and COMIBOL, he concludes without
any reaction at all that this agreement amounts to "a
complete rout for the workers."

Such impassiveness is truly remarkable. It corresponds to
the portrait of the leader painted by Che in *El socialismo y
el hombre en Cuba*: "to flinch" is unworthy of a revolutionary. But perhaps there was nothing to flinch about here.
Without waiting for confirmation of the rout of the miners
on July 9, Che had written in his June summary that their
massacre improved the prospects for the guerrillas. How?

---

* *La cosa se pone linda:* Literally, "things are becoming nice,
pretty."

† *Fernando Sacamuelas.* Having discovered on June 19 that the
peasants were *animalitos*, Guevara (now calling himself Fernando) has tried to win their favor, as he reports on the 21st, by
offering for two days his services as dentist.

In the same June summary the *Diary* mentions a proclamation which, "if it could be sent out," would be of "great help in clearing things up." Today we have the text of this "proclamation," which was communiqué No. 5, published first by *Bohemia* in Havana on July 5, 1968.

"One must not persevere," the proclamation said, "in false tactics, no doubt heroic but sterile, which only lead to a bloodbath for the proletariat and empty its ranks, depriving us of its most combative elements." Then, citing as an example the tactics of his own guerrillas, which he says had "convulsed the country," Che lectures the miners, beseeching them not to heed "the false apostles of the struggle of the masses." The proclamation ends with a grandiose appeal:

> Comrade miner! The guerrillas of the ELN await you with open arms and ask you to join with the mine workers who are fighting at our side. Here, we are rebuilding the alliance of workers and peasants which was broken up by anti-popular demagoguery. Here, we will transform the defeat into a triumph and the lament of proletarian widows into a hymn of victory. We await you.

I don't know whether the miners of the *altiplano* ever learned of this appeal from the guerrillas in the southeast. We know from Che's *Diary* that there was no contact between them. As a matter of fact, if one of the fighters of Siglo Veinte wanted to join the guerrillas, he would not have known how to go about it. "We await you." The invitation had no practical meaning whatsoever.

Why then was Che so pleased with the turn of events in the mines? As guerrilla leader he had gained nothing, since none of the defeated miners had joined, or could join, his band. But there was the theoretician. For a theoretician so wound up in his theories as to be untouched by human sentiments or by a sense of reality, the defeat had a positive side if the crushed miners took it as a lesson. From then on they would be able to abandon the erroneous path of the "struggle of the masses," to regain the only correct "revolutionary" if not exactly "Marxist-Leninist" road: that of *foquismo.*°

A word should be added concerning the "mine workers who are fighting at our side."

The only two Bolivians for whom Che showed any respect, the brothers Guido (Inti) and Roberto (Coco) Peredo Leigue, were not miners: both had been more or less professional Communist Party functionaries, although Coco also worked as a taxi driver. Che had only contempt for the unemployed miners recruited by Moisés Guevara. Most of them probably saw the guerrilla life first of all as a means of escaping from their immediate misery, that is, the hope, soon to be disappointed, of getting enough to eat.

In the *Diary*'s summary of March 1967, Che emphasizes the "generally poor level" of those he pejoratively calls "the band of (Moisés) Guevara." He sketches the following picture: "Two deserters, a talkative prisoner, three floaters, two stragglers. . . ." In short, *resacas*, as they say in Che's Argentina: leftovers.

Moisés Guevara Rodríguez, however, was not a *resaca*. This miner of Huanuni, born and raised in the misery of the

---

° Born in total opposition to Marxism, Leninism, Trotskyism, and even Maoism, out of a complete misinterpretation by Castro and especially Guevara of what had happened in Cuba, *foquismo* is the theory of the *foco*. Pretentiously dressed in doctrinarian finery by Régis Debray, it means that revolution is to be started by setting up small guerrilla bases in rural sectors from where they are to spread progressively to the whole country, while at the same time developing into a rebel army, capable of defeating the regular troops of the State.

altiplano, had been treasurer of his local miner's union. At first a member of the pro-Soviet Communist Party, he switched to the pro-Chinese party in April 1964 and became a member of its central committee. Two years later he was expelled from this party for trying to start a guerrilla movement, which was the first in Bolivia to call itself the *Ejército de Liberación Nacional* and to use the initials ELN. Moisés Guevara, known in the mining region by the name Armando, had always been an admirer of his namesake Che Guevara. He had even named one of his four children Ernesto in Che's honor.

Reporting the arrival of Moisés Guevara in Nancahuazú on January 26, 1967, Che tells how he dictated certain conditions to him, beginning with the need to disband his group. Moisés, he adds, accepted all these "with a great simplicity." This was the last friendly word he was to have for the Bolivian miner until his death in the Vado del Yeso on August 31.

Like Moisés, Willy, whose actual name was Simón Cuba Sarabia, was a militant of the miner's union who had passed through the two Communist parties and had been expelled from the pro-Chinese one for taking part in Armando's group. Che complains about Willy at various times, but in especially strong terms in the final summary, that of September 1967. "I still have my doubts about Willy, who might make use of some incident to try to get out alone if we don't speak to him," Che writes.

That was Che's opinion on the night of September 30, and it is unlikely that in the seven tormented days remaining to him Che had an opportunity for this conversation with Willy. The *Diary,* before it comes to its end on October 7, does not return to the subject.

But on October 8, when Che Guevara was reduced to impotence—a bullet in his leg, his rifle out of action, his revolver empty—the Bolivian miner Willy, far from grabbing his chance to get away, refused to abandon his leader and tried to carry him on his back. Captured at the same time as Che, Willy was slain by a burst of machine gun fire in one of the two rooms of the little school in La Higuera (later razed). This was the prelude to the second machine gun burst in the other room, which marked the execution without trial, that is, the official assassination, of Che Guevara.

Always concerned about his duties as leader, Guevara had pedantically analyzed the behavior of each of his men, recording his approval or criticism. "Bad marks" were given more often than good ones. For this reason, the Cuban press, in trying to transform the dead guerrillas into heroes, had some problems with the *Bolivian Diary*.

Che's meticulously detailed complaints against nearly all of his companions suggest some embarrassing comparisons. There is a big difference, of course, between a real guerrilla band and a fictionalized Navy destroyer, but the numerous references in the *Diary* to the disappearance of sugar or condensed milk bring to mind the image of Captain Queeg in *The Caine Mutiny* with his investigation of the missing strawberries.

Inti Peredo at the age of fourteen had been one of the co-founders of the Bolivian Communist Party, when there was only one. In the *Diary* he appears to be the most stable and reliable of all Che's companions. Che nevertheless has a bone to pick even with Inti.

This is on September 19, 1967, and little time remains for the guerrillas. With his caustic humor so often alternating with a certain pedantry, Che ends his notes for the day with a strangely symbolic sentence: "Sign of the times: I have no more ink left." But earlier he has reported this incident: "I had a conversation with Inti concerning some of his weaknesses about food, and he answered, very embarrassed, that it was true and that he would make a public self-criticism when we were alone,* but he rejected certain accusations."

We can understand why *Verde Olivo*, organ of the Cuban armed forces, in a cover story on Inti two years later citing the numerous references to him in the "vibrant pages" of the *Bolivian Diary*, preferred to jump from the 13th to the 22nd of September without stopping at the 19th.

The "alimentary" incidents begin to occupy an important place in the diary as early as March 1. Guevara, with the main part of his band, is engaged in his troublesome training and reconnaissance march. He has just concluded, in the February summary, that "the last days of hunger have led to a weakening of enthusiasm" and he already knows that "not all the Bolivians will hold up." The next day he finds that one of the Bolivians has eaten his reserve can of milk without authorization, another his milk and his sardines. "A bad sign," Che concludes.

On March 11 the situation is even more disagreeable because the rear guard is short of sugar and suspicions fall on Braulio, second in command of the group.

One of the main "factors of perversion," to use Che's expression, was the condensed milk. On April 14, when one of the secret storehouses is opened, twenty-three out of forty-eight cans are found to be missing, and this "in an inexplicable manner" since "no one would seem to have had the time needed to take them out." On the 15th, Che

---

* This may seem rather contradictory, but is faithful to the text. As to the first phrase of the sentence, Daniel James believes the words *en la comida* following the reference to Inti's weaknesses meant that the conversation took place "during dinner," and that it involved Inti's weaknesses in general, not just related to food. I prefer the translation given here, which is also that of the *Ramparts* edition as well as of the Maspero version in French.

returns to "the problem of the disappearance of the cans of milk," addressing "a stern warning" to all. The milk episodes, however, never ended and on May 11, after the ambush of April 8 in which the guerrillas killed three soldiers and captured ten, Che notes that he must "speak seriously" with Benigno because on the day of the battle he had consumed a can of milk.

Benigno was Captain Daniel Alarcón Ramírez, one of the three Cuban survivors of Che's guerrillas who succeeded in getting back to Havana after a long march through the jungle to the Chilean frontier. A second of these three survivors was Captain, and ex-diplomat, Tamayo Núñez (Urbano); he too was reproached on May 11 for having allowed himself a piece of the *charqui* (dried meat) left in the camp, while Benigno was gulping down his milk.

On May 14, Che assembles everyone to deliver a sermon—or, to use one of his favorite expressions, to "launch a volley"—concerning what is apparently the essential problem with his men, their desire to eat. He publicly criticizes Benigno for having downed the can of milk "while denying it," and Urbano for having eaten the *charqui* "on the sly" (*a escondidas*). The Bolivian Aniceto Reynaga, who was to be killed in the Quebrada del Yuro, is criticized for "his zeal to cooperate as long as it concerns food, and his reluctance to do so when other matters are involved."

One of the most startling pages of the *Bolivian Diary* is that of March 31, 1967, a few days after the first major encounter between guerrillas and troops on March 23.

> During the evening I spoke with Loro and Aniceto. The conversation was very unpleasant. Loro went so far as to say we were decaying, and when I pressed him he beat a retreat to fall back on Marcos and Benigno. Aniceto went along with him halfway, but he later

admitted to Coco that they had been accomplices in stealing some cans and he said to Inti, more or less, that he did not agree with the terms used by Loro about Benigno and also about Pombo, as well as about the "general decomposition of the guerrilla force."

Loro, also called Bigotes (Moustache) was Jorge Vásquez Viaña, son of the historian Humberto Vásquez Machicado, and a member of one of the best-known families of Bolivia. He had studied geology in Munich. At first a member of the pro-Soviet Bolivian Communist Party, he teamed up with the Peredo brothers, and like them left in 1965 for guerrilla training in Cuba. The following year he was assigned to the team which was to prepare for setting up a nucleus of Cuban guerrillas in Bolivia.

It was Bigotes who, en route to Nancahuazú, nearly drove his jeep over a cliff when he recognized Che in disguise among the first of the arrivals. Che recounts the incident on November 7, 1966, on the first page of his *Diary*, giving the impression that he was amused. On December 23 he is amused no longer. Loro, who had been sent to bring a pig to the camp, had allowed the animal to escape. He finally recaptured it, and it was a good pig, "rather fat"; but he had forgotten to bring something to drink, and this was too much for Che: "Loro is incapable of doing efficiently even this kind of thing; he appears very disorganized."

Loro was wounded and captured at the end of April while trying to rejoin his comrades, from whom he had become separated. Despite the efforts of his family and of some highly placed friends, he vanished from the Camiri hospital where he had undergone surgery, and there can be no doubt that he was kidnapped and killed. Among the various stories provided by the authorities, the most cynical was that he had managed to escape without leaving any trace.

Perhaps there was a strain of the former Minister of Industry and his attitude toward the Cuban workers in the way the guerrilla leader dealt with his men. A revealing remark slips into Che's notes for June 29, 1967. Commenting on the mistakes made in the skirmishes of the 26th, which took Tuma's life, he sums them up as having one fundamental cause: *por incumplir normas,* the fact of not complying with the norms. The respect for the "norms" seems as indispensable to Che for the success of the guerrillas in Bolivia as for the construction of "socialism" in Cuba.

Underlying the decomposition of which Jorge Vásquez spoke were the effects of physical and moral isolation. Two observations in the month of September 1967 show that Che sometimes realized this, but give no hint that he had yet seen the inanity of installing a *foco* in a region where the population was as hostile as the natural surroundings.

On September 7, at the beginning of the eleventh and final month of the guerrillas of Nancahuazú, Che has a conversation with Julio (Mario Gutiérrez Ardaya), a Bolivian who had learned guerrilla warfare along with medicine in Cuba, and who was to be slain on the 26th with Coco Peredo and Miguel (Cuban Captain Manuel Hernández Osorio). Julio's state of mind had worried Che. After talking to him, he notes in the *Diary*: "He feels very well, but he is disturbed by the lack of contact and recruitment."

Four days later, on the 11th, it is Pablito's turn. Since the desertion of 18-year-old Chingolo, Pablo or Pablito (Francisco Huanca Flores), who was not much older, had become the youngest member of the band.

Like Chingolo, Pablito was one of Moisés' recruits, but he did not desert: he was to die with the second group of guerrillas exterminated by the army on October 12, after the Quebrada del Yuro operation. Meanwhile, Pablito is bored and restless, and Che speaks "lengthily" with him:

"Like all the others," he writes on September 11, "he is depressed by the lack of contact, and he believes our basic task is to reestablish it with the town. But he shows himself to be firm and decided, 'my country or death,' and to the end."

Here Che appears as a friend, an older brother, but this is not always so. In fact, relations within the group are generally rather disconcerting. Che often must have appeared to his men as cool, disdainful, a bit arrogant. It is clear that they respected and admired him and recognized his superiority, but one would not swear they had much genuine affection for him.

Judging by the way Che speaks of his companions in the *Diary*, there were many moments of tension between him and his men. Each of them sooner or later is the object of an acid comment, an offensive remark, a venomous judgment, or an entirely gratuitous commentary such as the one on Loro touched off by a late pork dinner unaccompanied by drinks.

No one escaped this. A remark about Tuma on March 29, for example, shows that if Che regards him "almost like a son," he also considers him almost like a village idiot: "I spoke with Urbano and Tuma; with the latter, I wasn't even able to get him to understand the origin of my criticism."

There is also the case of Arturo (René Martínez Tamayo, younger brother of the very important Ricardo or Papi, who is José María Martínez Tamayo). Arturo is supposed to be in charge of the radios and even though, according to *Verde Olivo*, he had received ten months of training in the Soviet Union, he does not seem to have been up to his task. But he arouses Che's anger on January 11 mainly because Che's books, which Arturo was also supposed to be guarding, have become wet. "If we add that," Che notes, "to the fact that both radios are broken, we have a sad picture of Arturo's capabilities."

Most of these men were killed (Arturo on October 8 in
the Quebrada del Yuro). Some of them deserted and then
betrayed the others. As for Darío, he was to become a
guerrilla chief, but only after he had shaken off the yoke of
Nancahuazú.

Darío (David Adriazola Beizaga) had come from the
mining center of Huanuni. He had worked in the mines, but
was a peasant, the only one in fact to join the first "national
Liberation Army" of Armando (Moisés Guevara). On September 13 Che reports this conversation:

> I spoke with Darío, raising the question of his
> departure, if that is what he wants. He replied first that
> to go now would be very dangerous, but I warned him
> that this was not a refuge, and that if he decided to
> remain it must be once and for all. He said he would
> remain and would correct his faults. We will see.

On December 30, 1969, at the stroke of noon, a group of
armed men held up the cashier of the biggest brewery in
Bolivia, the Boliviana in La Paz. There was immediate talk
about "urban guerrillas," and the audacious crime was
linked to another one two weeks earlier against a branch of
the Banco Nacional.

Apparently informed by political circles opposed to the
"urban guerrillas," the men of Colonel Juan Ayoroa,
Ministro de Gobierno of General Ovando, raided the house
which was the group's headquarters on December 31,
killing one of the men and capturing two others. The dead
man's papers bore the name Arturo Alvarado Durán. On
January 8, 1970, a communiqué signed with the initials ELN
announced that Arturo Alvarado Durán was David Adriazola Beizaga, "legendary guerrilla who fought at Che's side
under the name of Darío."

Darío certainly was not a legendary figure while he

fought in Che's sterile guerrilla movement. One of the two Bolivian survivors—the other was Inti Peredo—he had taken over the ELN and reorganized it on entirely new lines after Inti, Che's official successor, fell on September 9, 1969. Inti Peredo was killed by a grenade, in a midtown La Paz house raided at dawn by an army of policemen who had been mysteriously informed in the same way.

In an interview given to the Chilean journalist Augusto Olivares shortly before Inti was killed, and published after his death, in the magazine *Punto Final* in Santiago, Inti declared his belief in Che's principles and said "the thesis of the guerrilla *foco* remains the only one suited to the current situation in Latin America." But even while speaking of "going back to the mountains," Inti had set up with Darío's help, first in Cochabamba and then in La Paz, an "urban guerrilla" organization whose program called for attacks on banks, destruction of bridges and railroads, power plant sabotage, etc. Inti had no more success than his predecessor, but at least he was looking for new ways, rather than stubbornly carrying out a peasant and worker battle detached from the workers and against the peasants.

The last words of Inti in the interview were in defense of Che: "It is very important," Inti recommended to the Chilean journalist, "to make clear that we have not formed a new organization. We are soldiers who have followed the example and the practice of one of the greatest strategists of armed struggle in the world. . . ."

The only way, it seems, to prevent the very idea of guerrilla warfare from going under in the catastrophe of Nancahuazú would be to seriously analyze the catastrophe. To do so, it is first necessary not to deny it and it is even more necessary not to present what happened (as does Fidel Castro in his "Necessary Introduction" to the *Diary*) as a perfect model of guerrilla warfare which failed only because "unfavorable factors combined in an incredible manner against it." Is it just a matter of starting all over again in the same pattern, hoping that next time the elements, if not the gods, will be more favorable?

The dilemma, for those who claim to be both partisans of the guerrilla and partisans of Che, is that they cannot preserve at the same time the myth of Che Guevara as a great guerrilla leader and the idea of guerrilla warfare as an effective instrument of revolution.

VIII

The Second Liberation of Latin America

or

The Third Failure of Che Guevara

I t is impossible to discuss Latin America and its problems without mentioning the "Colossus north of the Río Grande." It is possible, however, to discuss the "Colossus north of the Río Grande" without mentioning the problems of Latin America, or indeed precisely to avoid mentioning them. The elimination of Spanish rule in the first half of the nineteenth century obviously did not complete the emancipation of Latin America. There is hope that this might be achieved in the second half of the twentieth century by the elimination of U.S. tutelage. Many Latin Americans today are dreaming of a new Simón Bolívar. This is why panegyrists have been quick to compare Castro and then Guevara to Bolívar. And indulgent critics, seeking to explain the two men, have attributed to them a "Bolívar complex."

Simón Bolívar, *El Libertador*, had no complex. He was driven by a conviction, not by an obsession. But the idea of a second Latin-American liberation had an intoxicating effect on certain temperaments, engendering blind hatred, frenzied demagoguery and, finally, impotence. For those who claimed to heed the voice of their people, the invocation of Bolívar's example justified any sacrifice, beginning with that of liberty, on the pretext that the only thing that counted was to boot the *yanqui* out of Latin America.

"Bolívar entered more lands with the banners of liberty than any conqueror under the banners of tyranny," said the great Cuban José Martí. An English historian also was struck by the fact that "his marches were longer than those of Genghis Khan and Tamerlaine," and concluded that "Bolívar surpassed Alexander, Hannibal, and Caesar." Simón Bolívar, who took himself neither for Joan of Arc nor the Messiah, did not even want to be Napoleon.

He could have become one. Among the volunteers who flocked to him from every land, there were many Frenchmen who dreamed of a new Bonaparte. Bolívar could have conquered even the Spain of Ferdinand VII. On February 13, 1826, the French ambassador in Madrid, Marquis de Moustier, wrote to the French foreign minister, Baron de Damas, that "if an American insurgent squadron appeared within sight of the Spanish coasts, it would be impossible to contain the revolutionary tide." But Bolívar wanted to liberate America, not to conquer Spain.

All his contemporaries were persuaded that the victorious *comandante* would end as *jefe máximo,* and at the time that meant becoming a king or emperor. "If Bolívar dies without being crowned," Benjamin Constant wrote, "he will be, for centuries to come, an exceptional figure." Bolívar did die uncrowned, and he indeed remains an exceptional figure.

Karl Marx despised Bolívar, even if that meant glorifying Napoleon. With that pre-Stalinist arrogance which reached its apex in his campaigns against Bakunin, he wrote (in a letter to Engels) the now famous sentence: "To compare Napoleon I to a rascal so cowardly, so vulgar, so miserable is something that goes beyond all limits." For Karl Marx, Simón Bolívar could only be compared to Soulouque, the Haitian who proclaimed himself emperor in 1850 under the name Faustin I, and who, according to the encyclopedia I had to consult, became "famous for his foolishness and cruelty." So much for *Carlos Marx.*

The "neo-Bolivarians" of Havana, who still pretend to reconcile Marx—and Lenin and Brezhnev—with José Martí, have wronged Bolívar as much with their praise as had Marx with his insults. Despite the "historical materialism" which they profess in theory, they have tried to create a mystical bond between Castro and Bolívar under the common halo of the "man of destiny."

When Castro pretended for a few hours in July 1959 to be ready to step down, it was only to get rid of the scruples of President Urrutia. When he staged the same act for a few seconds in July 1970, it was only to make the crowds forget the failure of the *zafra de los diez millones* (the promised great sugar harvest); he knew the masses would cry: No! No! No! Simón Bolívar was no less powerful, nor less popular, than Fidel Castro when on January 2, 1814, he turned over his powers to the Venezuelan Assembly and rejected the Assembly's request that he run the country for an unlimited period. His response explains why the first pages of this chapter are not a digression but a necessary starting point: "You have given me the title of liberator of the Republic; I will never be its oppressor. . . . One must flee the country where a single man exercises all power. It is a country of slaves. . . ."

On January 20, 1830, when the Assembly in Bogotá offered him the presidency of the new Colombia Republic, he not only refused the offer, he lectured, berated, scolded:

> The Congress should know that its honor prevents it from nominating me, as mine prevents me from accepting the nomination. . . . How could you, without jeopardizing your reputation, give me your votes? Would that not be the same as if I signed my appointment myself? It would be a vile thing to do, for you as for me! . . . If one man were necessary to uphold the State, such a State would not deserve to exist. . . .

This was shortly before Bolívar's death. Meanwhile, on February 10, 1825, in Lima, the Congress of Perú, which had named him "dictator" a year earlier, had also urged him to remain in power. The man who dreamed of a confederation but wanted no empire lost his temper: "There is nothing more for me to do, gentlemen, in this republic. My presence here is an absurd and monstrous phenomenon; it is shameful for Perú. I am a foreigner. I came to help you as a fighter, and not to govern you as a politician."

Perhaps Che Guevara, at a certain time in his life, might have used similar words. It might even be argued that Che, in sending Castro the letter in which he said nothing remained for him to do in Cuba, was following Bolívar's example. But Che Guevara, who had come to aid the Cubans as a fighter, saw nothing improper in becoming their Minister of Industry, and in governing them not only as a politician but as dictator of the economy, master of the conditions of life and labor.

A fighter for independence, Bolívar was ready to go anywhere to defend the insurgent American peoples from the menace of Spanish armies. To liberate Bogotá and New Grenada by surprising the enemy where it least expected him, he crossed the Andes in 1819 under conditions which have been compared to the crossing of the Alps by Napoleon or Hannibal. But Simón Bolívar preached the love of liberty, not hatred of Spain, while Che Guevara was carried away by his hatred of the *yanqui* to the point of losing sight of the world he lived in as well as of the world for which he intended to fight.

Che's program of total war against the United States, made public in April 1967 in his "Message to the Tricontinental," has been praised to the skies as a masterpiece of "socialist thought."

This document reveals no concern with social revolution

or the transfer of power to the working masses. The "autochthonous bourgeoisies" * are mentioned in a single sentence of two and a half lines which dismisses them as having "lost all their capacity to oppose imperialism, if they ever had it." What counts, and what is repeated with hysterical excitement—recalling the tirades of Gustave Hervé and other French chauvinist ex-revolutionaries in 1914 against Wilhelm II's "pangermanism"—is the great "world confrontation" with the *yanqui* plague.

The "Message to the Tricontinental" defines Che's goal, as inscribed in history and not in mythology: a mortal struggle, a war of extermination against a foreign enemy. This war is inspired by an ideal, of course, and by an ideology, but have there been any wars which did not proclaim some ideal or ideology?

Che believes he thinks as a revolutionary. He expresses himself as a soldier. "Since imperialists blackmail humanity by threatening it with war," he says, "the wise reaction is not to fear war." He speaks of the "tactical purpose" which consists of "getting the enemy out of its natural environment, forcing him to fight in regions where his own life and habits will clash with the existing reality." He sets forth the "strategic end" and its watchword: "Our every action is a battle cry against imperialism and a battle hymn for the people's unity against the great enemy of mankind: the United States of America."

We are much closer to the *Delenda Carthago* of Cato the Elder than to the *Proletarians of all countries, unite* of Marx and Engels.

The Message to the Tricontinental is not an appeal to end the war in Vietnam and its horrors. One cannot even state, from the text alone, that the message is really inspired by the Vietnam War, or that the Vietnam War is its central

---

* Official English text.

theme. Vietnam appears here as one demonstration, among others, of the evils of U.S. imperialism, and above all as a very good example, a very satisfying example, of the possibilities of resisting this imperialism. In the spirit of this "message," the United States remains the enemy that must be destroyed even if it withdraws from Vietnam. It is not the enemy because it is in Vietnam; it is in Vietnam because it is the enemy.

The United States, for Che, is the enemy always and everywhere. His approach takes in the entire world, and he does not miss a single Communist propaganda cliché. The message thus has something to say, naturally, about the "cold war between Israel, supported by the imperialists, and the progressive countries of the region." In the same way, it also retroactively touches on the war in Korea.

Many opponents of the Vietnam War, such as Dr. Benjamin Spock, respected leader of the American pacifist movement, have always stressed the distinction between the defense of South Korea in 1950 against clear aggression by North Korea, and the inadmissible war in Vietnam. This distinction does not exist for Che. For him the war in Korea is the one fabricated in the columns of *Pravda* or *l'Human-ité*, and he even justifies the ludicrous Paris demonstrations against "*Ridgway-la-Peste*," which proved somewhat embarrassing to the French Communist Party. On one side, "under the discredited flag of the United Nations," the imperialists. On the other, "the army and the people of Korea, and the volunteers from the People's Republic of China." The United States, Che admits, did not resort to nuclear weapons, but it "tested all sorts of weapons of destruction . . . including, on a limited scale, bacteriological and chemical warfare."

In December 1964, Che Guevara already had made a similar *tour d'horizon*, under the same "discredited" ° flag of

---

° The Spanish text says *fementida*, which means "treacherous"

the United Nations, in his speech to the Nineteenth General Assembly as head of the Cuban delegation. Denouncing the use of Puerto Rican soldiers as "cannon fodder in the wars of empire," he presented the resistance to the invasion of South Korea as an example of these wars of empire.

Che's address at the United Nations was the occasion of a little incident which offers both a typical instance of blind prejudice and a more unexpected demonstration of bad faith.

Citing North American aggressions in Latin America "in recent years," Che included "Colombia, whose capital was stormed soon after the rebellion provoked by the assassination of Gaitán." The Colombian representative, speaking in reply, let the Cuban delegate know that in 1948, during the civil war which broke out after the assassination of the liberal leader Jorge Eliécer Gaitán,* there had been no North American intervention in Colombia and, of course, no storming of the capital.

"We alluded in our speech," Che coolly answered, "to an earlier intervention which perhaps the *Señor Delegado* of Colombia has forgotten: the North American intervention at the time of the separation of Panamá."

It would have been better for Che's reputation if he had simply admitted a slip of the tongue. The United Nations transcript confirmed what all had heard: Guevara had mentioned not the "earlier intervention" in Panamá, in 1903, but a nonexistent one said to have followed Gaitán's assassination in 1948. The anthology compiled by Fernández Retamar (*Obra revolucionaria*) contains on page 483 the

---

or "perfidious" rather than "discredited," as the official English version translates the word.

* This was the *Bogotazo*, or "coup of Bogotá," which resulted in thousands of victims. A young Cuban named Fidel Castro was then in the Colombian capital at a student congress, and was involved in the first incidents.

reply to the Colombian delegate; the statement which Che denied having made appears on page 477.

The "anti-imperialism" of Che Guevara at the United Nations in December 1964 hardly departed from the Soviet line. Its leitmotif, in fact, was an appeal for support of this line, of the kind made by all the other "socialist bloc" speakers:

> In all parts of the world, imperialism attempts to impose its version of what coexistence should be. It is the oppressed peoples in alliance with the socialist camp which must show the meaning of true coexistence, and it is the obligation of the United Nations to support them.

Earlier in 1964, in a pure Stalinist *apparatchik* speech on the occasion of presenting "certificates of Communist labor" to the new Cuban Stakhanovists, Che followed a similar Stalinist orthodoxy on the international level. Since the end of the Second World War, he boasted, "the bloc of countries which form the camp of peace and socialism is very strong." Thanks to the "revolution of Lenin," there were "a billion men who direct history, who are building it, who are making it." He concluded that the duty of Cubans was not limited to the defense of Cuba: "Our duty lies equally in the unified defense of the great camp of socialist countries, in the contribution to their victorious advance." Any other party bureaucrat could have done as well with the themes and slogans selected, developed, programmed by the official "anti-imperialism" of Soviet propaganda.

At the beginning, Che's occasional irreverent remarks which might have sounded unpleasant to Russian ears, like some of Castro's remarks, did not bother the Kremlin very much: they served to emphasize the moderation of the USSR, and to remind the United States that the Kremlin too had to take into account the reactions of "socialist" public opinion. When the pranks became serious, directly challenging Soviet policy and thus violating the taboo which the orthodox notaries of "socialism" have made a codicil of the "Marxist-Leninist" legacy, the public life of Che Guevara would be promptly terminated. This is what happened after the Algiers speech in February 1965.

No taboo, certainly, had been broken by Che in his "educational talk" of March 20, 1960, when he explained that military aggression tended to be abandoned in favor of economic measures. "It has become very difficult to suppress the national political sovereignty of a country by means of pure and simple violence." In fact he knew of only two recent examples: "the ruthless and vicious attack by French and British colonialists on Port Said in Egypt, and the landing of North American troops in Lebanon."

Since he was going back to 1956 and the Suez affair, how did Che manage to avoid mentioning the Soviet tanks which were attacking Budapest at the same time?

The omission was significant, and Che himself added a cynical touch in writing soon afterward, to explain why there were so few cases he could mention: "It is difficult to invade a country which claims the right to exercise its sovereignty, in these times of the United Nations when the peoples want to have their voices heard and their votes counted."

It had been of little use to the Hungarian people to make their voices heard "in these times of the United Nations," but in the eyes of Guevara in 1960, as in the eyes of Khrushchev in 1956, a country's right to exercise its sovereignty could not be invoked against the USSR.

Certain intellectuals, trying to reconcile their "Guevaraism" if not their "Castroism" with their often belated renunciation of the beatitudes of Stalinism, have said that if Che had lived he would have condemned the invasion of

Czechoslovakia in 1968. It is hard to see why Che would have been moved any more by Prague than he had been by Budapest.

Castro's own speech of August 23, 1968, on the events in Czechoslovakia was viewed by the same intellectuals as a "somewhat ambiguous" approval of the Soviet actions. But there was absolutely no ambiguity in Castro's approval when he declared:* "We acknowledge the bitter necessity that called for the sending of those forces into Czechoslovakia; we do not condemn the socialist countries that made that decision." Only one "essential point" mattered, and this was "whether or not the socialist camp could allow a political situation to develop which would lead to the breaking away of a socialist country, to its falling into the arms of imperialism." And his answer to that question was clear and straightforward: "Our point of view is that it is not permissible and that the socialist camp has a right to prevent this in one way or another."

No, Castro had no reservations whatsoever, but he did have some criticism, of the "I told you so" variety. He criticized the Kremlin for having encouraged "revisionist" elements in Czechoslovakia by doing nothing about "the problem of Yugoslavia," for "the principal promoter of all that policy of bourgeois liberalism, its principal defender, was the organization of the so-called Yugoslav Communists." The welcome which Tito had received in Prague was proof enough, according to Castro, that it was high time for the "socialist" countries to intervene and bring Czechoslovakia back to reason: "How far can things go when this

---

* All quotations from this speech are taken from the English press release issued by the Cuban Mission to the United Nations, identified as "Translation of the transcript made by the Revolutionary government's Department of Stenographic Transcriptions."

well-known revisionist element historically denounced by
the revolutionary movement—a man who has served as an
agent of imperialism—could be received by a people
practically as a hero?"

In short, it was the Kremlin's own fault if it had suddenly
become "absolutely necessary, at all cost" to put an end to
such a situation. The Kremlin had waited too long; it should
have smashed Dubcek earlier, and it should now crack
down on all Dubceks, past, present, and future, before they
could lift up their heads.

Castro's "criticism" thus reinforced rather than weak-
ened his approval. It had a single aim: to demand *carte
blanche* for Cuba in Latin America. A "bitter reality" had
"persuaded" the Warsaw Pact countries "to send their
forces to crush the counterrevolution in Czechoslovakia
and, according to their statement, to back a minority in the
face of a majority with rightist positions." Castro now
wanted to know whether "in the light of the bitter reality,"
the countries which intervened "will also cease to support
these rightist, reformist, sold-out, submissive leaderships in
Latin America that are enemies of the armed revolutionary
struggle, that oppose the people's liberation struggle. . . ."

Fidel Castro spoke more than ever like Che Guevara
when he said he was "disturbed" because "neither the
Communist Party nor the government of the Soviet Union,
nor the governments of other countries that sent their
troops into Czechoslovakia, have made any direct accusation against Yankee imperialism for its responsibility in the
events in Czechoslovakia."

For Che also—for Che above all—every world-shaking
event, every crime committed anywhere and by anyone,
including the USSR, was to be used as a weapon against the
United States, "the great enemy of mankind."

On April 30, 1961, he had the excuse of the Bay of Pigs.
While informing the Cuban people about the ambitious

economic projects of the "socialist republic" which they, the Cuban people, were going to launch the next day, he suddenly pounced upon the "fascist pride" of President Kennedy, his "arrogance" and the danger that this represented for all. "The peace of the world," he shouted angrily if not hysterically, "depends on the anger, the hysteria of a fascist leader in a nation which is directly engaged in fascism."

He was calmer, but hardly more rational, on August 8, 1961, in his role as a "socialist camp" diplomat at the Punta del Este conference: "The Soviet Union," he quietly declared, "reaffirmed its decision to sign the peace at Berlin, and President Kennedy announced that he would go to the point of war for Berlin."

The chief of Cuba's delegation at Punta del Este did not explain why Kennedy would start a war in Berlin if the Soviet Union was ready to make peace there. But two weeks later Walter Ulbricht ordered the erection of the Berlin Wall, and Che Guevara no doubt believed, along with the then official Cuban organ *Revolución*, that the "world support" for this measure "probably had prevented the Western fascists from pushing the matter to dangerous limits."

In January 1964 the crazed hatred of Che exploded unexpectedly in the middle of the routine ceremony in honor of "deserving" workers. Bloody incidents had just broken out in the Panama Canal Zone, and *yanqui* soldiers were among the victims. Was this not "an indication, still only faint, of what is going to happen to imperialism in America?" Then Che starts ranting: *Yanqui* imperialism is "a rabid aggressor" seeking "new forms of aggression"; it reveals its "bestial nature," but it will not escape destruction.

Ah! What a dream:

The moment will come when the North American people also will feel in their own flesh what it means to have homes without fathers, without brothers, homes of orphans, homes of hunger because there will be no one to look after their wants.

Che's fever mounts. He imagines that the hoped for sufferings of the *yanqui* people are about to become reality:

This day, we see it, all of us; it is approaching, and it is not advancing cautiously anymore, over difficult mountain paths. It is heralded by the rolling of drums, it is constantly being talked about in Caracas, it has been going on continuously in Guatemala for nearly two years, it is everywhere in the Andes, the Sierra Maestra of America, as Fidel once called it.

Three years later Che was painfully making his way along the difficult mountain trails of Bolivia, painfully but not cautiously enough. And neither in Caracas nor in Guatemala did the rolling of drums signal the end of the United States.

Che's dream of blood and war was to reach its apotheosis in April 1967, with the "Message to the Tricontinental," marked more by hatred for one country than by brotherly love for the others:

How closely we could look into a bright future, should two, three, or many Vietnams flourish throughout the world with their share of deaths and their immense tragedies, their everyday heroism and their repeated blows against imperialism, compelled to disperse its forces under the sudden attack and the increasing hatred of all peoples of the world!

Che now was impatient with Soviet prudence in regard to

Vietnam, as he must have been two years earlier over Cuba's passive attitude toward the Dominican invasion. Lashing out at those for whom solidarity was only a matter of words, he drew his famous parallel to the gladiators of the Roman circus, with its unequivocal prescription: "It is not a matter of wishing success to the victim of aggression, but of sharing his fate; one must accompany him to his death or to victory."

Clearly, this was Che's implacable reply to Castro's furious indignation when, on January 15, 1966, he was trying to justify himself for having talked much but done nothing for the Dominicans in April 1965.

It was also meant for the Soviet Union and China, challenging them to enter the Vietnam War. Death, for himself or for others, did not frighten Che Guevara. Nor did destruction: It mattered little if nothing remained of Vietnam, or Cuba, or Bolivia, or other countries and peoples, if that could help bring the United States to its knees. In the "Message to the Tricontinental," this revered monument of "socialist idealism," Che did not even shrink from the prospect of a third world war:

> U.S. imperialism is guilty of aggression; its crimes are enormous and cover the whole world. We already know all that, gentlemen! But this guilt also applies to those who, when the time came for a definition, hesitated to make Vietnam an inviolable part of the socialist world; running, of course, the risks of a war on a global scale, but also forcing a decision upon imperialism.

Che believed he was passing on the torch of a revolution. He left only a war cry: war against the *yanqui*. In turning away from the struggle against national oligarchies, Che offered a new basis for the cleverest members of these oligarchies, those intelligent enough to see that the ground was slipping under their feet. No doubt many military men had already pondered over the example of "Nasserism" which had proved that a military caste could hold power, and the bourgeoisie retain its privileges, on condition only that there be an enemy to denounce in "progressive" terms. Che now placed at their disposal, as a posthumous gift, "the great enemy of mankind." Since the enemies of our enemies are our friends, weren't all enemies of the *yanquis* automatically defenders of mankind?

Early in 1970 I confronted post-Guevara Bolivia, with all of its surprises and paradoxes, at San Andrés University in La Paz, in a rear courtyard where a sign indicated the headquarters of the *Federación Universitaria Local* or FUL, the student organization of La Paz.

Inside I met a tall, gaunt man named Jaime Rubín de Celis, who was then *secretario de gobierno* or executive secretary of the Federation. On the wall opposite his desk was a portrait of Karl Marx; at the right, one of Che Guevara. But when I asked Jaime Rubín de Celis about the position of the Bolivian students toward the government of General Alfredo Ovando Candia, he tapped his hand on the desk and answered: "We judge him by his actions. He has taken a first step in the anti-imperialist struggle. We will remain on guard, ready to take up the battle if necessary. But we could not be hostile to a government which is opposed to imperialism."

I had just been given the latest issue of the FUL's official publication. Che's face filled the entire cover. The editorial was a solemn message: "Nancahuazú, the eye and soul of youth." Then came a long article translated from the French leftist magazine *Nouvel Observateur*: "The Challenge of Che Guevara." Right in the second line there was a mention of "the gorilla who rules Bolivia," but the reference applied to General Barrientos. As to General Ovando, who at the time of the capture and execution of Che Guevara was commander-in-chief of the Bolivian armed forces, Jaime Rubín de Celis and the revolutionary students of La Paz were waiting to "judge him by his actions."

The Bolivian example was by then illustrating in a striking manner how "anti-imperialism"—that is, concretely, the appeal to close ranks against the hereditary enemy represented by the United States—could push aside the now old-fashioned concept of "class struggle."

I tried to get the student leader, who called himself "Marxist but independent," to discuss this point, but the effort was futile. The government formed in the putsch of September 1969 had succeeded in neutralizing the "leftist" opposition, simply by expropriating a North American corporation, or seeming to do so. After having failed with his *socialismo* in Havana and his *foquismo* in Nancahuazú, Che Guevara had bequeathed to Latin America, under the name of *anti-imperialismo,* an immense confusion.

This could be seen on October 8, 1969, anniversary of Che's "last battle," the day chosen by Castro as *Día del Guerrillero Heroico* rather than October 9, anniversary of his execution. The students of La Paz celebrated Heroic Guerrilla Day with an "anti-imperialist march." Carrying portraits of Che, the anti-imperialist marchers booed the *yanquis* and threw stones at the U.S. Embassy. No one shouted anything against Che's Bolivian assassins, who had now become the "revolutionary government."

The confusion was even more evident in regard to the miners, whose misery and struggles had always held an important place not only in the manifestos of the Bolivian students but in their feelings of solidarity and their genuine revolts.

In September 1969, at the moment of receiving the reins of power from General Juan José Tórrez (who took them back a year later), General Ovando had promised the miners "prompt improvements." By October 31 he had returned to the Barrientos position, pointing to the low price of tin on the world market and asking the miners to be patient, because "improvised solutions could only make the situation more difficult."

With few exceptions, the La Paz students did nothing. Marching behind their portraits of Che, they asked only for "the intensification of anti-imperialist measures." Tin, unlike petroleum, had been nationalized for many years.

There was somewhat more emotion among the students in December 1969, when about 100 miners from Oruro began a hunger march of some 150 miles toward the capital. But neither the students nor the miners went very far. The miners halted after two days and 40 miles. The army did not intervene. The "revolutionary" government simply declared that it refused to negotiate "under pressure"; the "anti-imperialist" President added that the march was "subversive."

Why did the miners draw back before Ovando in 1969, when they were not intimidated by Ovando and Barrientos in 1965 and 1967?

The answer is found in *Jornada*, an evening newspaper financially linked to the extraordinary character to whom the next chapter is devoted: Antonio Arguedas Mendieta. The only Bolivian newspaper to immediately support the military putsch of September 1969, *Jornada* "revealed" on December 18 that the miners were victims of a CIA plot: this plot involved bringing the army into the mines to provoke "a split between the people in work clothes and the people in uniform."

Two days later Ovando himself took up the theme of a plot—not Communist, but *yanqui*—in Cochabamba, trying to rally against the miners the peasant masses his predecessor had so easily mobilized.

Ovando did not have the eloquence and popular appeal

of Barrientos, but his arguments, in all their tortuous demagoguery, were in the same vein. The "revolutionary" President was speaking of Washington, however, and not Moscow: "There are enemies outside and enemies inside," he said. "Those on the outside are extraordinarily powerful. Those on the inside operate in the shadows, in furtive and feline anonymity which proves that they realize the shame of their action. The revolutionary government is aware of their maneuvers. It knows which greedy hands are reaching out to receive payment for their treachery from sinister foreign agencies."

Imperialism does exist, and so does the CIA, but the Latin-American generals seem to have understood—well before the world's "leftist" intellectuals—how easy it was, with a little chauvinist demagoguery dressed as anti-imperialism, to make the Latin-American masses forget the role of the national oligarchy. Despite their own sinister and still recent past, which included the assassination of Che Guevara as well as the massacres of the miners, the Bolivian generals were now having a try at it.

One need not attach too much importance to the childish pseudo-doctrinaire tract, doubling as a pretentious anti-Trotskyite pamphlet, which Régis Debray called *Revolution in the Revolution*? But Debray was not only ridiculous; he was serving the Bolivian "ruling class" when he wrote, to explain the 1965 repression of the miners of Huanuni, Catavi, and Siglo Veinte, that "orders arrived from the United States to crush the worker movement." The Bolivian reactionaries, he implied, would have done nothing against the miners if the order had not come from the United States. Their principal fault was not in being reactionary but in being insufficiently anti-imperialist. So all they had to do to become acceptable to Régis Debray was to say "no" to Washington.

The Peruvian journalist Gonzalo Añi Castillo, using

information obtained indirectly from the imprisoned guerrillas of Perú, has cited in his book *Historia secreta de las guerrillas** an interesting example which proves that shouting "no" to Washington does not necessarily identify a certified "revolutionary."

The example is that of the "anti-imperialist front" which organized the 1958 demonstrations against Vice President Nixon in Perú, with the help, and the money, of local mining interests. The main organizers of the *Frente Anti-Imperialista* were Trotskyites, and most were no doubt sincere: After all, the money would be used to print anti-imperialist tracts. The mining companies obviously had not become pro-socialist. But the prices of lead and zinc had fallen. It was a matter of showing Washington that the economic difficulties were leading to discontent among the workers, which could harm the United States. The United States therefore would do well to help out the Peruvian mining companies.

Held in the prison of El Frontón by the "revolutionary" government of General Velasco Alvarado, the Peruvian guerrilla Hugo Blanco Galdoz, one of the most impressive figures in the history of Latin-American guerrilla movements, gave an interview to Marcel Niedergang which appeared on January 29, 1970, in *Le Monde*. What he had to say supported the revelations of Añi Castillo.

Blanco even adds details: namely, that local American-owned firms did not mind joining in the "anti-imperialism" of the national oligarchy: "Already in 1958, when Richard Nixon came to Perú, Cerro de Pasco, an American company, had sent its workers in trucks to the anti-imperialist meeting!"

The Peruvian guerrilla, who, unlike Che, knew how to get along with the Indian peasants of the Andes, also mentioned

* Lima: Ediciones "Mas Allá," 1967.

the dispute over fishing rights and the limits of territorial waters.

The generals in Lima had courted popular support for their putsch by confiscating properties of the *yanqui* petroleum firms, the most visible but not the largest of U.S. investments. They had later consolidated their power by sending warships to seize two "imperialist" tuna boats fishing some fifty miles from the Peruvian coast. In the *barriadas* (slums) of Lima, the people were incited to forget their misery and to share the national pride swelling under the bemedaled uniforms of their "anti-imperialist" generals.

"There are in Lima," Hugo Blanco recalled, "some big bosses of commercial fishing who are Americans, and who shout with the others: 'Down with imperialism!' " More lucid in his jail cell than those who were prisoners of their obsessions, the defeated guerrilla added finally, for his comrades on the outside: "Let us not be deceived by appearances."

Although the Peruvian generals had been adopted immediately as brothers in anti-imperialism by the Communists of Havana and the "progressives" everywhere, Bolivia's General Ovando soon had his problems. But it was not because he had been one of the men directly responsible for killing Che. Hadn't the Lima generals led the bloody repression of the Peruvian guerrillas, and weren't they keeping the survivors in prison? At the very moment, in fact, when the new President of Perú, General Juan Velasco Alvarado, was appealing to men of all political colors, including "bright red," his Prime Minister and Minister of War, General Ernesto Montagne Sánchez, was defending the *Junta Militar Revolucionaria* against the accusation of leftism. He did so by recalling that "its members took part in 1965 and 1966 in the preparation and execution of the operations against the guerrilla groups, and those groups have been annihilated by the armed forces."

Although he understood the new rules of the game perfectly well, General Alfredo Ovando Candia simply was too hardened in his ideas, too rooted in his attitudes, to make the difficult turn without accident. He skidded, and no doubt the CIA greased the track a bit to make sure he didn't get back on his feet. The CIA wanted a general more "to the right." It obtained one more "to the left": Juan José Tórrez Gonzales. General Tórrez, who had set up the junta of September 1969, took power himself on October 9, 1970.*

At a huge rally, Tórrez announced that his "revolutionary" government would rest on "four pillars": students, workers, peasants, and soldiers. Interviewed on October 18 by a *Pravda* reporter, he stated—and *Pravda* printed—that Bolivia was entering into "a stage of deepening of the revolutionary process" and that it was prepared to make "a great leap forward."

But what about the Americans, Nixon's Americans? The report of Governor Nelson Rockefeller published in August 1969, less than a year after the putsch of General Velasco Alvarado in Lima and less than a month before the putsch of General Ovando Candia in La Paz, abandoned all pretense of making the United States a champion of "democracy." Whether neo-Nasserism in Latin America was a stepson of Fidel or the bastard of Che was not Rockefeller's concern; he confined himself to verifying that it existed, and he considered it possible and even desirable to seek an accommodation.

First, Rockefeller's verification:

---

* Tórrez was overthrown in turn in August 1971 by Colonel Hugo Banzer Suárez, notably with the aid of that *Falange Socialista Boliviana* whose possible alliance with the peasants (see page 155) seemed so full of promise to Che Guevara on July 14, 1967.

In short, a new type of military man is coming to the fore and often becoming a major force for constructive social change in the American republics. Motivated by increasing impatience with corruption, inefficiency, and a stagnant political order, the new military man is prepared to adapt his authoritarian tradition to the goals of social and economic progress.

As to the consequences of this new role assumed by the new military, the Rockefeller report recognized that the situation was not "free from perils and dilemmas," but did not indicate any anxiety, even when noting "the appeal to the new military, on a theoretical level, of Marxism." He attributed this appeal to two factors not likely to frighten Washington:

> (1) It (Marxism) justifies, through its elitist-vanguard theories, government by a relatively small group or single institution (such as the army) and at the same time, (2) produces a rationale for State-enforced sacrifices to further economic development.

Thus, in Washington as in Havana, a sort of benevolent neutrality was the policy adopted toward those whom both Nelson Rockefeller and Fidel Castro termed "the new military."

By an extraordinary coincidence, the new military of General Tórrez took power on the day of the third anniversary of Che's execution in La Higuera by the old military of General Barrientos, the "new" and the "old" being the same. Tórrez, in his capacity as chief of staff, had led the special commission charged with getting rid of the remains of Che, and it was he who told Roberto Guevara in Vallegrande that his brother's body had been cremated.

In Havana, however, Fidel Castro said nothing. There is

not a word about the general's 1967 role in the issue of
Granma's weekly edition devoted to the third anniversary of
Che's death, though it was also the first issue published after
Tórrez' accession to power. The only contribution of
Granma on the events in Bolivia was the publication, on its
back page, of a long "Communiqué from the *Ejército de
Liberación Nacional.*"

This pathetic document notes that following the "ultrago-
rilla" coup of General Miranda, "a group of nationalist
revolutionaries, led by J. J. Tórrez, sought support in the
popular and progressive sectors." The authors seemed
happy that "thanks to popular support, the gorilla coup
failed, and Tórrez has assumed the presidency, promising a
people's revolution." But at the same time, they regret that
the new government had given birth to "illusions in some
progressive and popular sectors." The ELN communiqué
even recalled with apparent misgivings that "the nationalist
revolutionary military group led by Tórrez belongs to the
same trend which a year ago raised illusions in the more
naive sectors at the time of Ovando's accession to power."

The two sentences which follow would have been taken
as self-evident at the time of the Sierra, but were major
heresies in the columns of *Granma* now devoted to paying
respects to the Peruvian generals under the sign of Che's
"anti-imperialism." The first sentence stated that "we must
not expect revolution on the part of any savior general."
The second was even more explicit: "Revolutionary nationalism is basically a demagogic policy which tends to reduce
the people's will to struggle. . . ."

No one knew what this ELN amounted to on October 9,
1970, since its last active group, the one of Teoponte, had
just been wiped out. One year earlier, when a first group of
Trotskyite dissidents (it is difficult to know, from one year or
one month to the next, how many Trotskyite factions there
are in a given Latin-American country) published an appeal

for support of the "revolutionary government" of Ovando, it was reported in La Paz that a second group° was trying to put together the pieces of the ELN. Perhaps it was the latter Trotskyite influence which had slipped into the communiqué and which an inattentive anti-Trotskyite editor had allowed to be passed on to the Cuban readers on the back page of *Granma*.

I have called that document pathetic because the ELN at the same time tries to avoid burning any bridges to Tórrez, an attempt which leads the communiqué's authors into some painful twists and turns.

The general, savior or not, is not attacked for his past or for what he represents. Criticism is concentrated on his association with "anti-popular and totally disqualified elements." There is Colonel Villalpando, accused of being directly responsible for the massacre of the miners during the *noche de San Juan*. There is also the new commander-in-chief of the armed forces, General Reque Terán, branded as "one of the best known anti-guerrilla *gorilas*." And the communiqué expresses the fear that, "although he says that with him a representative of the people has entered into the Palacio Quemado," Tórrez might seek an accommodation with the right.

But while announcing that "our struggle continues in the mountains and in the cities until the final victory," the ELN leaves an opening for the general: "We are not inclined to have any illusions about a change of government resulting from a *coup d'état*, unless there is concrete proof that the government actually will do something to combat imperi-

---

° Both groups had been disavowed by the POR (*Partido Obrero Revolucionario*) led by Guillermo Lora. The day after the September 1969 putsch, Lora had categorically rejected "the idea that *gorilismo* can put into practice any revolutionary measures."

alism and eliminate the neo-colonial structure of our country."

The name of General Juan José Tórrez is mentioned only once again in this commemorative, and historic, issue of *Granma*. A short dispatch from *Prensa Latina*, at the bottom of a page, informs us that he has refused to grant a visa to a Bolivian refugee in Havana who, "persecuted by the repressive international apparatus of North American imperialism," wished to resume his place in the struggle of his country "for national independence and for the institution of a regime of pure socialist inspiration."

The request had been made by Antonio Arguedas Mendieta, former right-hand man of René Barrientos and great friend of Fidel Castro. It is time now to tell his incredible story.

IX

The Arguedas
Episode

Antonio Arguedas Mendieta stepped off the plane from
Mexico at Havana's José Martí International Airport
on Saturday afternoon, June 26, 1970.

As an official guest of the Cuban government, he was
welcomed by a large delegation headed by Foreign Minister
Raúl Roa and Manuel Piñeiro, chief of the secret service of
the Interior Ministry. The Cuban Foreign Minister was
there to greet a former member of the Bolivian government.
Piñeiro was welcoming a colleague, since Arguedas was, or
at least had been, a secret service agent—for Washington.

Others in the delegation included Mrs. Aleida March de
Guevara and Ernesto Guevara Lynch, Che's widow and his
father. They were on hand to remind Cubans that the guest
was the friend who had arranged for photocopies of the
Bolivian Diary to be sent to Havana.

In his "Necessary Introduction" to the Cuban edition
based on these photocopies, which came off the presses on
June 30, 1968, Castro had emphasized the anonymous
donor's altruism: "The manner in which this diary came into
our hands cannot yet be revealed; let it suffice to say that
this was done without the slightest financial remuneration."

On July 3, 1968, before the TV cameras where he was
scheduled "to reply to the Bolivian gorillas on the question

of the authenticity of the diary of Ernesto Che Guevara in Bolivia," Castro repeated that there had been "absolutely no financial compensation." Nor was it an espionage operation, he added: "To put it simply, every just cause has many sympathizers everywhere. . . ."

Arguedas himself, naturally, gave the same reason in his press conference at the José Martí airport on June 26, 1970: "I was inspired," the English edition of *Granma* quoted him, "by the example set by Major Ernesto Che Guevara and Major Fidel Castro, the comrades who began the epic movement for the second emancipation of Latin America."

A fugitive as of July 18, 1968, the former Bolivian minister had been officially identified on the 19th by President Barrientos as the man responsible for sending the diary to Cuba.

On July 24, 1968, on the occasion of a visit to a spaghetti factory in San José de las Lajas, Fidel Castro confirmed that "it was indeed the Minister of Interior of the Bolivian government who had photostatic copies of the diary of Che [ovation] put into the hands of persons connected with the Bolivian liberation army." This action had been "absolutely disinterested," Castro repeated, now attributing it to the indignation of Arguedas over "the manner in which the Bolivian regime had treated Che," as well as his opposition to "the general policies of the regime which tyrannizes Bolivia and which has shown itself to be tied, hands and feet, to *yanqui* imperialism."

Fidel Castro mixed his tribute to spaghetti with a tribute to Arguedas because this disinterested friend of Cuba, this enemy of the policies of the Bolivian government, apparently was on the point of being handed over by the CIA to his former protector, President Barrientos.

"After the arrival in Chile of the Bolivian ex-minister," said the Cuban Prime Minister, "the imperialist government of the United States and the CIA tried by every means to have him brought back to the Bolivian frontier, using all sorts of pressure. . . ." And for Castro, to have returned Arguedas to Bolivia would have been "to turn him over to the hatchet men of Barrientos and the CIA, so they could assassinate him. . . ." Renewing his offer of political asylum for Arguedas, already conveyed by Raúl Roa in the name of the Cuban government, Castro appealed to the Chilean people to resist "all the pressures of imperialism and of the CIA."

When the appeal of San José de las Lajas reached Santiago de Chile that day, Arguedas was holding a press conference, the first of a long series, replete with contradictions, which were to stake out his amazing geographic and political itinerary.

Proclaiming himself "Marxist-Leninist," the former Interior Minister and police chief of President Barrientos thanked Cuba for its "generous" offer, but added that when the time came for him to go to Cuba it would be "in the capacity of a fighter against an imperialist invasion." His intention now was to return to Bolivia "as quickly as possible" in order to take part in "the final battle against North American imperialism." In reply to a question, he said he admired and respected Fidel Castro, but did not wish "a solution of the same type" for his country.

On the next day, July 25, Antonio Arguedas went to the embassy of Argentina in Santiago and asked for a temporary residence visa in that country, then ruled by General Onganía. The latter had declared his full moral support of General Barrientos in the suppression of the guerrillas of Nancahuazú, and had let it be known that he was ready to give military support as well. Evidently Arguedas' unexpected request did not flatter Onganía, since his Foreign Minister announced the same night in Buenos Aires that the visa had been denied.

Also on the same night, through the correspondent of the

official Cuban news agency *Prensa Latina*, Arguedas sent a message to Havana expressing his "complete identification with the Cuban revolution" and signed: "Until victory or death."

On July 26, 1968, while the Cubans were reading his message in *Granma*, the Bolivian minister-turned-revolutionary took a plane to London, after stating in a radio broadcast that he intended to return to Bolivia to stand trial. At a stopover in Buenos Aires, he repeated this, specifying that he was going "to London and from there to New York"—all this in order "to return to my country." Asked by a reporter if the trip from Chile to Bolivia required routing through London and New York, he muttered something about the need to "make his gesture known" throughout the world.

For six days after that, reporters tried in vain to meet Arguedas in London. Was the CIA stronger there than it had been in Santiago, Buenos Aires, and also Madrid, where the ex-minister had not been kept from speaking to the press? In that case, we must suppose that the British authorities, before allowing Arguedas to continue his roundabout journey to La Paz via New York, prevented him from stopping off in Stockholm, Geneva, Algiers, or some other city where he might have had at least a chance of escaping from the CIA.

Even in London, however, Arguedas was free enough to meet Mrs. Alba Griñán Núñez, Cuban ambassador, who, as he admitted later, invited him for lunch, listened for two hours, "very moved," to the story of his life, and repeated Castro's offer of asylum. He also went to the Bolivian Embassy, apparently of his own free will. Bolivian Ambassador Roberto Querejazú Calvo informed the press that he had given Arguedas a message from President Barrientos, offering full guarantees if he returned to face the judicial processes of his country. According to Querejazú, Arguedas accepted the offer and promised to be in Bolivia "in a few days."

On the night of August 2, a laconic statement by the Home Office announced that Arguedas had departed from London Airport that afternoon.

Arguedas had indeed flown to New York, the better to escape from the CIA, it seems. As in London, no reporter was able to find him, but a State Department spokesman, Carl Bartch, confirmed on August 6 that the celebrated traveler had landed in New York on the 2nd, with a visitor's visa, "for a brief stay." Bartch said he knew nothing more about Arguedas or his plans.

The next public appearance of Arguedas came on the morning of August 8, in the press room of the Jorge Chávez Airport in Lima, Perú. He sought out the journalists immediately after getting off the plane, and his first statements were aimed at denying any connection whatsoever with the CIA. "This is the greatest infamy ever fabricated against me," he protested.

His stay in Lima, from August 8 to 17, was a busy time from the public relations standpoint. The CIA did not hamper him, though President Belaúnde Terry was not known as being particularly "resistant" to CIA pressure. Arguedas began by installing himself at the Hotel Bolívar, the best in town, and received all journalists who wanted to meet him. On the 9th he changed his hotel, supposedly to "escape from the press" and because he had "promised not to make any statements," but the same night he called in the reporters for another press conference at his new hotel. He was to give more press conferences on August 11, 14, and 17 before finally flying to La Paz.

The only "trouble" for him was a "warning," but no action, by Peruvian Minister of the Interior and Police, Carlos Velarde Cabello, to the effect that if Arguedas continued to make statements to the press, "he will have to leave the country." The *Prensa Latina* report appeared in *Granma* under the indignant headline: "Antonio Arguedas, former Bolivian Interior Minister, threatened with expulsion from Perú."

What did Arguedas actually say in Lima? Without alluding to the appeals and messages already addressed to him by Barrientos, he proclaimed: "I will return to my country when I am officially invited. . . . Even if they don't send me the ticket. No matter! I will return by foot, if necessary. . . ."

The air fare from Lima to La Paz was $70 at the time for a first-class ticket, or $51 for tourist class. According to Arguedas, he had left Bolivia carrying $1,800 and had not used any of it until he changed his first $100 bill in Lima. It was true that he was not accustomed to paying for his plane tickets; the one for the grand tour Santiago-Buenos Aires-Madrid-London-New York-Lima, worth $965 at the time (or $1,535 in first class), had been "sent to him," he said, in Santiago.

"I don't know who paid for it." he added casually, as if it mattered little to him and should matter little to others who the generous patron was.

The press conference of August 11 was reported in a long dispatch from *Prensa Latina* which appeared in the English edition of *Granma* under the headline: "IMPORTANT STATEMENTS BY ARGUEDAS TO BE PUBLISHED IN CASE ANYTHING HAPPENS TO HIM." The subtitle said: "REFUTES THE IMPERIALISTS' DASTARDLY ACCUSATIONS AGAINST TANIA THE GUERRILLA AND RÉGIS DEBRAY."

Arguedas announced on August 11 that he had given "revelations of the highest importance" to *Punto Final* and *Ramparts*, the pro-Castro magazines which printed the Cuban version of the *Bolivian Diary* in Chile and the United States. These revelations were not to be published unless he disappeared "forever," that is, as he made clear to Malcolm

W. Browne of the *New York Times*, "in case they (the CIA)
succeeded in silencing me by means of physical elimination."

Meanwhile, he tried to convince his listeners that he was
not a CIA agent and that this was "a vile accusation" made
possible by the fact that "some people are not accustomed
to seeing men act freely and on a strict basis of personal
conviction." To be still more convincing, he compared his
case to those of Tania and Régis Debray. According to
Prensa Latina, he said "a counterrevolutionary conspiracy
arranged by the CIA and the U.S. State Department is bent
on discrediting and dividing the revolutionaries of America
and the world." Before going after him, the plotters had
already tried to "have people believe" that Che's presence
in Bolivia had been revealed to the authorities by Debray,
and that Tania was "an agent who infiltrated Che Guevara's
guerrilla force."

The former Bolivian chief of police called all this "just
another dirty imperialist trick which proves to what extent
these figures, Debray and Tania, are considered dangerous
even after imprisonment or death."

As to the third figure, Arguedas himself, the Chilean
magazine *Punto Final* had just published in its July 30 issue
a long article on "the Arguedas Affair." It praised the
former Bolivian minister for passing on the diary to Castro,
thereby rendering "an inestimable service to the anti-imperialist struggle." But it revealed at the same time that before
Arguedas was given his high government post, he had to
"pass the admission test of the CIA." The "vile accusation"
he was so indignant about thus had already been admitted
by the Chilean magazine which was acting as his defender.

The article also contained the information that the CIA in
Santiago had offered to pay the expenses of Arguedas at the
beautiful Argentine mountain resort of Bariloche, if he

agreed to lay low and keep quiet. "Arguedas accepted," *Punto Final* added in the same unflinching matter-of-fact tone.

For *Punto Final*, "What counts is that armed confrontation with imperialism awakens consciences and creates friends." The article did not explain how this edifying conclusion applies to Arguedas' acceptance of a deal with the CIA, even if the deal was later called off. According to the Chilean magazine, it was the CIA which changed its mind. Arguedas, moreover, had not yet learned of Cuba's offer of asylum and the flattering words of Castro about him at the spaghetti plant of San José de las Lajas.

While continuing to deny that he had ever worked for the CIA, Arguedas himself confirmed at least part of the revelations of *Punto Final* in his last press conference in Lima on August 17, before his departure for La Paz.

His dilemma was clear. He had chosen to present himself as champion of the battle against the CIA; and to back up his claim of expertise about the agency, he had to admit that for some years he had played a part in the CIA's activities. But having done so did not amount to a favorable character reference for a man who wanted to be seen as champion of the struggle against the CIA.

He now admitted that when he joined the Interior Ministry in 1964 as undersecretary, the CIA tried to "blackmail" him into working for the agency. What made him susceptible to blackmail? He did not say, but he implied that he did not give in.

Questioned about the more recent past, he repeated that he had been a prisoner of the CIA during his stay in Santiago. A journalist asked him how, in that case, he had managed to hold a press conference. Arguedas replied that in order to do so, he had been required to promise "not to unmask the CIA." *Prensa Latina* quoted his double reason for agreeing to this: "I was threatened with a putsch in Bolivia and the death of my family if I revealed the secrets of the CIA."

His long transatlantic and transcontinental journey at CIA expense seems to have calmed his fears, both about his family and about the Bolivian government, since he ended this final press conference in Lima by announcing that he was returning to Bolivia precisely in order to "unmask the CIA which operates throughout the world and which, in particular, destroys the national independence of several Latin-American States."

A few hours later Arguedas arrived in Las Paz and held two more press conferences on the same day, August 17. The first, in an airport hangar, was interrupted after twenty minutes because the police feared there might be "some public disorder." The newsmen protested, and a second press conference was arranged for 5:00 P.M. in the city. It was held at the *ministerio de gobierno*, in Arguedas' former office.

The two main newspapers of La Paz, *Presencia* and *El Diario*, have published the verbatim transcript of these press conferences. The transcripts also appeared, in September 1968, in a compilation published by the FUL (students' organization) of Cochabamba, where it was placed a few pages after Che Guevara's Message to the Tricontinental.

The statements of Arguedas in La Paz on August 17 established once and for all that he had become a CIA agent in 1964. There is no way of knowing exactly when he ceased to be one.

He had been named undersecretary in the *ministerio de gobierno*, he said, soon after the putsch of Generals Barrientos and Ovando, which he called a "popular military uprising." Two months later, Colonel Edward Foggs of the U.S. Air Force let him know that if he did not quit his post "the U.S. would suspend economic aid to Bolivia and would adopt the most draconian sanctions and pressures against the government." But soon Colonel Foggs told him that something might be worked out, and introduced him to Larry Sterfield, then CIA chief in Bolivia. Sterfield suggested that he undergo interrogation by the CIA outside the country, in Lima. "Partly from opportunism and partly from curiosity, I accepted." They gave him "90 or 60 dollars, I believe," for the trip, and he went to Lima. The interrogation lasted four days and included, Arguedas said, the use of a lie detector as well as a truth serum. Arguedas passed the test. His services, both as undersecretary and as CIA agent, were satisfactory, since he was picked to become Interior Minister. The CIA gave him $6,500 and sent him to Washington where he received a number of briefings. On his return to La Paz, his nomination was confirmed.

There is no prime minister in Bolivia, but the Interior minister or *ministro de gobierno* is indeed a virtual prime minister on internal matters. And this key post of *ministro de gobierno* had now been filled by a CIA agent who carried out "numerous operations" on orders of the U.S. intelligence services, often forced upon him, he complained, "by means of blackmail."

One of the main "operations" was to bring into the ministry's intelligence department some of those Cuban refugees so dear to the CIA, who were to play an important role in the isolation and repression of the guerrillas: "I brought in Cuban agents such as Gabriel García García, Fernández, Mario González who was the interrogator of Régis Debray, and others whose names I don't remember right now."

Other operations: "Spreading of reports, often false, seeking to sabotage certain credit negotiations, for example with France. Later, infiltration of political agents, recruitment of local agents, support of certain personalities whose military or political careers were of interest to the CIA."

Arguedas also mentioned operations involving corruption or slander, but the way he selected "victims" or "benefici- aries," identifying them by name, suggests that his concern for the truth was somewhat influenced by his personal political strategy. One union leader, he said, replied with insults when Arguedas offered him $2,500 on behalf of the CIA. In another episode, the CIA had assigned him to frame a well-known journalist in a "petticoat scandal."

It was he, said Arguedas, who on orders of the CIA, leaked to *El Diario* false information presenting *Tania la guerrillera* as an agent of the East German secret service.°

At the same time, he did his best to involve Juan Lechín Oquendo, former Vice-President of Bolivia and leader of the miners, against whom he obviously pursued a personal vendetta. Juan Lechín had been in contact with Castro, had visited Havana, and once spoke of coming to reinforce Che's guerrillas.† Arguedas affirmed that the CIA asked him one day to provide a false passport for Lechín, because they "were interested in having Lechín travel abroad." In his view, this must have been more serious than giving *carte blanche* to the CIA Cubans in Bolivia or slandering "Tania the guerrilla," because this time he rebelled: "I told them that I was not accepting any transactions with Señor Juan Lechín Oquendo."

When did Arguedas cease to be a CIA agent? To the extent that there is any answer to this question, we have a choice among several, since in his August 17 press confer- ence in La Paz, Arguedas himself mentioned at least two different periods.

° This information, which came from Gunther Maennel (see page 54), had appeared on May 26, 1968, in *Welt am Sonntag* (Hamburg). It also was the subject of a dispatch by Benjamin Welles in the *New York Times* of July 15, 1968. Thus, if it was a CIA fabrication, the CIA could manage without Arguedas.

† See Chapter 5.

Did the break come at Santiago? He had just explicitly confirmed again the compromise he had reached with the CIA in the Chilean capital ("I was not to reveal the secrets, since if I did so, it would be the end of the government and the end of my family"). A reporter asked if his decision at that time to go to New York meant that he intended to maintain his CIA connections. "No," Arguedas replied. "I had already definitely broken with the CIA."

The journalist was not satisfied. "Señor Arguedas, I repeat: Why did you go to New York?" The answer given by Arguedas, *"por imposición,"* meant that the decision was "imposed" on him, although this time the blackmail did not involve a threat to the government or his family: "They said that no country in Latin America wanted to receive me, while it would be convenient for the CIA to take me to Paris, to abandon me in Paris. . . ."

Confronted with this "threat," Arguedas gave in and he did not regret it. He was even convinced that he didn't do badly, since "by the way I handled the problem, I ensured my return to my country. . . . If I had not agreed, it is very probable that right now I wouldn't be here but in Europe, looking for a way to come back to Latin America."

Unfortunately, no one at the press conference thought of asking him why, in his opinion, the CIA thought it convenient to take him to Paris, and why he himself was so worried about the prospect of being abandoned there.

A dialogue in Santiago between Arguedas and a CIA agent named Leondiris allows us to see, on the basis of his own account, that what Arguedas called *imposición* actually involved a proposal of his own and that the mysterious threat of Paris was no more than a simple (although curious) suggestion on the part of the CIA. "Why don't you go to France?" Leondiris asked. Arguedas quoted himself as replying: "I am not going to France. I would rather go, I told them, to New York." Leondiris: "And what are you going to do in New York?" Arguedas: "If you don't keep your word, I will go to the United Nations and I will denounce all this. . . ."

According to the verbatim text of the very pro-Castro FUL of Cochabamba, Arguedas added here that Leondiris seemed impressed by "this firm attitude." The no less pro-Castro, and pro-Arguedas, Chilean magazine *Punto Final*, no doubt embarrassed by having to tell its readers that the threat of complaining to U Thant could impress a CIA agent, gives a contrary version in its transcript: The agent's reaction, Arguedas said, was to laugh at him (*"Se rieron"*).

Whether the CIA "imposed" or Arguedas "proposed," Arguedas got his visa in Santiago permitting him to fly to the United States. And no matter what he had said earlier in the same press conference, Arguedas obviously had still not "definitively broken with the CIA."

He even admitted that in London, the CIA, gave him 500 English pounds and $1,000 in U.S. dollars, which explains how the "altruist" friend of Fidel Castro was able to arrive at the Hotel Bolívar in Lima with five suitcases, when he had not yet even dipped into the $1,800 he took with him from La Paz. He also said that the CIA in London asked him—he doesn't say whether it was before or after he received the money—for "a proof of loyalty." To pass this test, he gave the name of a Bolivian friend with whom he had left a tape-recorded statement by noncommissioned officer Jaime Terán, concerning the execution of Che.

He was still on excellent terms with the CIA in New York, since while he was there the agency gave him the telephone number of a contact in Lima, and Arguedas took it down.

In Lima he felt perfectly free, he said: The police of President Belaúnde Terry were "extremely courteous," he was surrounded by newsmen wherever he went, and some "lady journalists" even went so far as to "invite" (?) him. Dwelling on those pleasant impressions, he forgot that he had "definitively broken with the CIA," at least since his departure from Santiago if not before his departure from La Paz, and he suddenly proclaimed in that same third press conference of August 17: "Until Lima, I was an agent of the CIA, but as I saw that they were not keeping their promises, then: *Adelante no más!* From now on, no more! . . ."

What were these promises which the CIA did not keep? All one can infer from the perhaps deliberately incoherent statements of Arguedas is that he was expecting the CIA to "recall its men," or the United States government to recall its "specialized agencies," in order to deal henceforth with Bolivia only as "government to government." Besides, he added, "while they held me in London, in New York, these guys were weaving their intrigues in close contact with the Chilean government."

In any case, Antonio Arguedas Mendieta now, temporarily, had become the repentant sinner, eager to confess so that all would know "how North American imperialism corrupted me, how it debased me, and the way they trapped me in their net. . . ."

He had also become a great patriot who appealed for the union of all against "the common enemy." Since Bolivian nationalism had never gotten over the loss of Antofagasta in 1884, in the unhappy War of the Pacific, Arguedas took care to associate in the definition of the common enemy "the Chilean rabble and North American imperialism." To complete his story politically, he "revealed" that in Santiago (where he had already recovered his "dignity as a man" although continuing to be a CIA agent "until Lima") the CIA had vainly offered him money to "slander General Ovando by saying that it was Ovando who had sold Che's diary, to finance his election campaign."

The stay of Arguedas in Bolivia was marked first by

unexpected procedural disputes concerning what charges
were to be brought against him and which court had
jurisdiction over his case. In order to graduate as *capitán de
servicio* after serving for twelve years as a noncommissioned
aviation radioman, Arguedas had studied law; now he
defended himself brilliantly. His subtlest argument was as
follows: since one set of photocopies had been turned over
to him by the U.S. agent Hugh Murray, Che's diary had
ceased to be a Bolivian State secret, and there could be no
question of treason.

Usually, of course, under a military regime legal astute-
ness does not help an accused very much, but in this case
the accused was treated with kid gloves and on December
25, 1968, Arguedas was released in bail of 9,000 Bolivian
pesos, about $750.

On March 22, 1969, in a *Prensa Latina* dispatch datelined
La Paz, *Granma* reported that General Joaquín Zenteno
Anaya, who in 1967 led the troops against Che in the
Vallegrande region, had supported the argument of Arguedas in the Bolivian courts. According to the dispatch,
which alluded to "revelations of Zenteno Anaya, kept secret
until now," this "high Bolivian military officer" confirmed
that one of the Cuban agents of the CIA, Félix Ramos, had
photocopied the entire diary on the very day Che died.

Thus, *Prensa Latina* emphasized, quoting Zenteno Anaya,
"the State Department had knowledge of the diary well
before the Presidency of the Republic of Bolivia."

Granma, in publishing this story, seemed to have completely forgotten the "Necessary Introduction" to the
Cuban edition of that same *Diary*, in which Castro maintained, on the contrary, that "Che's diary fell into the hands
of Barrientos, who immediately delivered copies to the CIA,
the Pentagon, and the government of the United States."
Also ignoring Castro's speech of July 3, 1968,° *Granma*

° See page 230.

neglected to explain why the CIA, if it was first to obtain the diary, or Barrientos, if it was he who delivered it to the CIA, failed to destroy the manuscript when (if we are to believe Castro) there was such dread of its publication in Washington as well as in La Paz.

What mattered to *Granma* on March 22, 1969, was only the "image" of Arguedas, even if in order to polish it the Cuban paper had to rely on a Bolivian "gorilla"; for Zenteno had helped Arguedas to make his point, namely that the notes of Che "were neither military nor State secrets."

Free temporarily—and even permanently, from all appearances—Arguedas for many months moved about in La Paz without the slightest problem. He was seen taking his *cafecito*, like anyone else, on the terrace of the Hotel Copacabana. He had his office in the plant of the daily *Jornada*, which he owned at least partially, and where he received local personalities and foreign correspondents.

The calm was not disturbed until May 8, 1969, when a dynamite blast damaged his house. No one was hurt. Besides, Arguedas was getting a divorce and did not live there.

On June 6, while he was walking with a Spanish journalist not far from the Plaza Murillo and the Presidential palace, a burst of machine gun fire came from a passing car. The journalist was unhurt, but Arguedas was wounded in the left arm. After he left the hospital, he asked the *ministro de gobierno* of the moment, Colonel Eufronio Padilla, for a passport so he could leave the country. Colonel Padilla refused, and Arguedas took refuge in the Mexican Embassy that night, July 8. He had first sent a note to the press saying he would return soon to join the people of Bolivia in fighting "the colonialist power and its local hatchetmen."

Of all the depositions and official statements made by Arguedas before various judges in La Paz, the most striking were those in which he tried to erase his public confessions about his ties with the CIA.

"Tormented by a guilt complex and by the interference of the North American government in the internal affairs of Bolivia, and accustomed on the other hand to the language used by all groups of the left, I called myself an agent or member of the North American intelligence services . . . ," he explained to the military magistrate on October 23, 1968. He intended to "clearly establish" that "I have not been an agent of the North American intelligence services."

Arguedas repeated this on January 14, 1969, before the civil magistrate: "Tormented by a guilt complex and accustomed to using a revolutionary language, I called myself an agent of the CIA without, properly speaking, having exercised that role."

Properly speaking, he had not only "called" himself a CIA agent, he had described his "numerous operations" in this role. Nevertheless, interviewed by a UPI reporter in his *Jornada* office on April 22, 1969, he had the effrontery to proclaim again: "The most important thing that I want to make clear is that I have never been, am not, and will not be an agent of the CIA."

Antonio Arguedas Mendieta remained at the Mexican Embassy from July 8, 1969, to April 23, 1970. General Ovando, who had taken over the government on September 26, 1969, did not seem in a hurry to grant him safe conduct, even though the former minister had so courageously refused to "slander" him.

On the night of April 23, 1970, Arguedas arrived at the Mexico City airport and declared to the press that he planned to go on to "some socialist country." If he could help in "cutting cane in Cuba," he said, he would do so *de mil amores,* with all his heart. "Once I am in a socialist country," he added, "I shall unmask the colonial power of the U.S. and its efforts to justify *coups d'état* and interferences in Latin-American countries."

In Lima he had already announced he would do the same thing upon his arrival in Bolivia. Journalists who had attended his second La Paz press conference of August 17, 1968, knew that nobody had prevented him from "unmasking" anyone or anything. They were therefore somewhat skeptical.

But on the next day, interest in Arguedas was rekindled by sensational news: the Mexican paper *El Universal Gráfico* announced that the former minister had brought with him the hands of Che, amputated at Vallegrande for purposes of identification, and preserved in alcohol.* That night Arguedas held his twentieth or thirtieth press conference. He denied having brought the hands of Che, but made another revelation: "I hid them on a peak of the Cordillera of the Andes, where they will be recovered when it will be possible to get them to Señora Aleida March de Guevara." Then on May 4, in the Mexican magazine *Siempre*, José Natividad Rosales published a fantastic story told to him by Arguedas, which was reprinted throughout the world.

As Minister of Interior and chief of the national police, Arguedas had been in possession not only of Che's hands but his death mask, made at Vallegrande. He had asked President Barrientos what he should do with them. "Throw them into the garbage, we've had enough annoyances," Barrientos replied, according to Arguedas.

Up to this point, nothing unlikely. But then comes the rest of the tale.

Arguedas placed the hands in a larger jar, wrapped this jar "in the flags of Argentina, Cuba, and Bolivia," and

---

* See Chapter 1.

placed this "inside a *tihuanacota* chest lined with red velvet." On the outside he attached "a silver plaque with gold lettering," giving the name of *Comandante* Ernesto Guevara, with the dates of his birth and his death. The chest was placed in a tar-coated zinc container, and upon this Arguedas painted in red letters: "This chest contains the hands of *Comandante* Ernesto Guevara."

All this he had done by himself, according to Arguedas, *solito*, apparently even engraving the inscription in gold letters on the silver plaque.

Next he took the chest, which weighed "about ten kilos" (22 pounds) and drove to the Andean region known as Los Yuncas. He left the car and climbed up the peak with the chest, and there "I deposited my treasure." He took some photographs, he added, but "the secret of the exact location, I am the only one to have it."

The solitary climber of Los Yuncas* did not mention the hands of Che when he landed at Havana on June 26, 1970. Exactly one month later he was one of the honored guests at the July 26 commemoration in the Plaza de la Revolución. Castro presented him and had him applauded, as an extra added attraction, after having obtained the expected applause for the other special guests also linked, but in a different way, to the Bolivian guerrillas: Che's father, the mother of the Peredo brothers,† the parents of Tania, the mother and the wife of Régis Debray.

The main speech about the failure of the *zafra de los diez millones* was over, including the ritual "*Patria o Muerte! Venceremos!* [*Ovación*]" when Castro—perhaps someone

---

* A photo in *Siempre*, showing "Antonio Arguedas scaling the peak of Los Yuncas," also shows that he is roped to other mountaineers, not to mention the presence of a photographer.
† A brother of Inti and Coco—Osvaldo, called Chato—led the ELN group which was reconstituted in the Teoponte region. He was captured on the anniversary day of October 8, 1970.

had whispered a word into his ear—returned to the
rostrum: *

> We forgot something that we wanted to tell you on
> this occasion. We mentioned Dr. Arguedas who made
> it possible for Che's diary to reach our country
> [Applause]. . . . After his efforts in relation to the
> diary, Dr. Arguedas made every possible effort to have
> Che's death mask reach our country. This was the
> death mask made the day Che was murdered. In
> addition, Dr. Arguedas was able to save Che's hands
> and arrange for them to reach our country. [Applause]

The official transcript registers no movement of surprise
or emotion. Only applause. Then Castro, well-known for his
habit of democratically consulting his people before making
a decision, asked the crowd what should be done with the
hands of Che. And the crowd dutifully answered: "Shouts of
'Preserve them!' "

Where did the hands come from, these hands which
Arguedas did not mention on June 26 and which Castro
nearly forgot on July 26? Even if we could take seriously the
story of the *tihuanacota* chest, Arguedas had not had a
chance to make another climb to the peak of Los Yuncas.
But assuming that the hands *were* somewhere in La Paz, did
Arguedas carry around the alcohol-filled jar in his suitcase?
It would be a rather gratuitous insult to both the Mexican
police and the CIA to consider them so careless as not to
search Arguedas' belongings, and so incompetent as not to
find the jar.

It's a macabre story, and I have no taste—nor do I see
any necessity—for pursuing it. What we were told, of
course, is not true. We may even wonder whether Castro
does not regret having used the story, or having fallen for it.

---

* Official English text published by the Communist Party of
Cuba.

In his somewhat unconvinced and unconvincing postscript to the July 26, 1970, speech, he had announced that
Che's hands—"framed by the olive green sleeves of his
uniform and his major's stars and enclosed in a glass
urn"—would be placed inside or near the statue of José
Martí "in a special room." He even gave the impression that
this special room was to be inaugurated "the day of the
anniversary of his death." This would have meant October
9, 1970, or, if there was much work to be done, October 9,
1971, or, if the construction of "a special room" met with
really tremendous, unforeseen technical difficulties, October
9, 1972. As far as I know, all these dates have passed by
without the expected solemn announcement of the exhibition of "Che's hands."

The various stories told us about how Che's diary reached
Cuba are no less ludicrous than the episode of the hands.
But here we can, and therefore must, try and solve the
mystery.

In all his press conferences and in his statements to the
Bolivian magistrates, Arguedas, with rare consistency, had
maintained that he simply mailed it. In his deposition of
September 17, 1968, he said he mailed the manuscript on
June 14, at about 7:00 P.M., insisting that he had pasted on
the stamps himself and no one else had been involved. "I
repeat once more," he said in a deposition on January 14,
1969, "that to send Che Guevara's diary to Havana, I used a
European address, and that the method used was the mail."
This European address happened to be "an address in
Frankfurt," which he said he had kept under the glass top of
his desk.

On September 17, 1968, he provided an additional detail:
the address came from notebooks found on Coco Peredo
and shown to him by one of the Cuban CIA agents whom
Arguedas had brought into the ministry, Gabriel García
García. The minister had skimmed through the notebooks

"stained with blood and smelling strongly"; he had noticed the Frankfurt address and copied it before returning the notebooks to García.

This story was about as believable as the tale of the *tihuanacota* chest. To begin with, a letter from La Paz to Frankfurt would have been delivered only five or six days later, and to send it on from Frankfurt to Havana would take the same number of days, assuming that the addressee forwarded it immediately. If we add the time needed for the "minute examination" of the photocopies Castro had mentioned, and the time for deciphering the difficult handwriting of Che as well as for typing and rechecking it, the text placed in the mail on the evening of the 14th in La Paz could hardly have reached the printer in Havana before the 25th or 26th at the earliest. Yet the magazine *Bohemia* told us that the first copies came off the presses of the Osvaldo Sánchez Printing Unit on the 22nd.

Furthermore, there was the fact that the thick, mysterious package addressed abroad had to pass through postal censorship; Arguedas himself, in an earlier interview in *Siempre*, had eloquently described the "checking of correspondence" carried out by the CIA in Bolivia. There was finally the fact that the address had been found in Coco's notebooks, which were in the hands of the CIA. Even if the CIA considered the presence of such an address under the glass top of Arguedas' desk as the innocent whim of a collector, was it conceivable that the agency would have no interest in Coco's European contact? And wouldn't it have watched with special care the mail that contact received from La Paz, or sent to Havana?

It was only on July 22, 1970, while in Mexico, that Arguedas came up with a completely new story, which he gave to his friend Rosales for the magazine *Siempre*.

The diary, we now learned, did leave La Paz on June 14, 1968—not by mail but in the hands of a "representative" of

Arguedas who went to Havana via Lima and Mexico,
arriving there on the 17th. Except for the date of departure,
there was nothing in common between this new version and
the one he had insisted upon for nearly two years. There
was even a big difference in the description of his generosity: whereas in the first story he had to pay only for the
postage stamps, in the second version he "paid the entire
cost of the trip" of his envoy.

Who was this "representative" of whom no one had
spoken, and why was it that Castro, so full of tributes to the
former chief of the Bolivian police, never praised the virtues
of the heroic and unsung messenger? Was it to protect this
messenger, to allow him to continue his work in the service
of the revolution in Bolivia or elsewhere? This again would
deny to the omnipresent and omnipotent CIA the most
elementary professional competence. If the messenger existed, the CIA knew him for a long time. Nothing could
have been easier, in fact, than to identify a man, linked in
one way or another to Antonio Arguedas, who took a plane
from La Paz to Lima on a certain day, then flew to Mexico
and on to Havana.

The CIA may even have known the messenger without
having to look for him, but before going into this, we must
return to the reasons given by Arguedas, or attributed to
him, for his action.

José Natividad Rosales offers two reasons, blessing the
ex-minister—*Bendito sea Arguedas por todo eso*—for having
carried out "an intelligent and spectacular maneuver
against the CIA, a successful maneuver which prevented
both the adulteration of the historic document and a new
military invasion of Cuba." Fidel Castro prefers a third.
Thanks to the attitude of Arguedas, he explained to the
workers of San José de las Lajas, it had been possible to
"knock down the fabulous deals which were being con-
cocted around this document by corrupt elements of the

Bolivian government and by certain imperialist enterprises."

Several Bolivian generals and several capitalist firms, American and European, indeed tried to make money with the *Bolivian Diary*. But it is hard to picture Antonio Arguedas Mendieta sacrificing his career, and risking his life, merely for the satisfaction of blocking somebody else's possible profits. Besides, Castro himself, in his speech of July 3, 1968, had shown that any business deal could not have been as profitable as all that: with so many copies already in circulation, no one could be sure about any exclusive rights to the *Diary*.

By declaring that day that the Bolivian leaders "lie when they say that no copy of Che's diary got out of Bolivia," Castro undermined not only the third argument but the second as well. As to the first, there was nothing to be undermined since it really was nonexistent.

This first argument developed by Rosales, and apparently Arguedas' favorite, was that publication of the *Diary* in the United States would have provided the excuse for an immediate invasion, so Arguedas' action prevented this. But if Washington wanted a suitable "provocation," Havana's own publication of the *Diary* certainly provided an even better documentary proof of Cuban interference than a Bolivian or North American edition. And I recall only in passing Castro's statement in his "Necessary Introduction" to the effect that, in any case, "*yanqui* imperialism never needed pretexts."

The second argument—did Arguedas deserve the gratitude of Cuba and of the "progressive" world for having prevented the *yanqui* villains from falsifying Che's text?

No less unafraid of contradictions than his friend Arguedas, Castro had been the first to suggest also that the *yanquis* in fact had hoped to suppress the text. As he explained in his "Necessary Introduction," it was for this reason that the diary had not yet been published by June 1968, although it had been in the hands of the CIA since October 1967. And on July 3, 1968, he celebrated its publication in Havana because "in the first place, this ensures the distribution of a document whose circulation imperialism and the Bolivian gorillas were highly interested in preventing."

But it was in this same speech of July 3 that Castro had given the lie to those who wrongly affirmed that no copies had left Bolivia. It would seem that if the CIA wanted to prevent publication of the diary, it would have begun by making sure no copy of it got out of its hands.

The same precaution would have been taken, obviously, if the CIA intended to alter the text before publication. Castro mentioned a reporter "closely linked to the CIA" who had obtained a copy and was trying to place it with various publishing houses in the United States. Either the CIA was holding onto the diary in the hope of suppressing or at least "doctoring" it, or it was simply helping some "closely linked" newsman to make an extra buck. Castro cannot have it both ways, but he tries. In any case, as Castro had already mentioned in his *Introducción necesaria*, "newspapermen connected with the CIA had access to the document in Bolivia and made photostatic copies of it"; thus it had become practically impossible for the CIA to do any doctoring before publication, and the sacrifice made by Arguedas was useless.

Useless, it suddenly appeared, for everybody except Fidel Castro: if the Bolivian *ministro de gobierno*, agent of the CIA, was a double agent, he could have sent the diary to Cuba on orders of his second boss.

This is what I had believed at first. Precisely because so many pages of the diary were known to so many people through photocopies,° Castro had good reason to fear its

_____

° A photo shop in the center of La Paz had a display poster in publication: It would be a bomb, and not one that would damage Washington. Written on the run, pulling no punches, without regard for anything or anyone including himself, the observations, reflections, confessions, and illusions of Che amounted to a document tragically depressing for the faithful of the Castroite Church and horribly embarrassing for its hierarchy. There was no technical possibility of destroying the diary while accusing the CIA of having done it. But there remained the hope of being able to superimpose a fictitious interpretation over its real meaning, that is, to brainwash the reader by arranging for him to read Che's text only after putting on the rose-tinted glasses of a "Necessary Introduction." The scheme was not a bad one: Countless readers remain persuaded, since Fidel tells them in his preface, that the *Bolivian Diary* is "a model for guerrillas."

Then I started wondering again about Antonio Arguedas Mendieta. If he was a double agent, why is there no trace of any pro-Cuban action on his part before the diary affair? Was Castro more interested in prefacing the *Bolivian Diary* than in helping Che to survive?

Fidel, true enough, tried to present Arguedas as a sort of hero of the clandestine struggle. "For many months," he revealed in his speech at San José de las Lajas, "the former Minister of Interior of the government of Bolivia had an attitude of cooperation with the Bolivian revolutionary movement, running extraordinary risks to his life." Arguedas, naturally, was happy to embroider on this theme. Even while he still remained "under the control of the CIA," he declared on June 26, 1970, at Havana airport, he "was already engaged in the organization of a small force—though not linked with the National Liberation Army, it had

---

its window advertising photocopies of the diary "at reasonable rates."

the same aims as that body—called the Armed Forces of National Liberation."

Arguedas never supplied any details about his "Armed Forces of National Liberation," and Castro never gave any details as to how Arguedas showed his "attitude of cooperation with the Bolivian revolutionary movement." But we have a good deal of information concerning the activities of the *ministro de gobierno* while he was heading the repressive police apparatus in Bolivia.

Arguedas not only bore the overall responsibility for the massacres of the miners, culminating in the *noche de San Juan,* he was personally involved in the assassination of one of the union organizers, the Trotskyite Isaac Camacho Torrico. Arrested by Arguedas' men in July 1967 at Siglo Veinte, Camacho permanently disappeared after he was taken to Arguedas' ministry in La Paz. Arguedas himself announced on August 8 that Camacho had been "deported to Argentina," but searches carried out there and elsewhere have been in vain.*

The attitude of the minister toward Che's guerrillas was no less in conformity with the police tradition of Latin America, and his actions fail to indicate any "double" role.

It was Arguedas who destroyed the urban guerrilla organization, notably through the arrest of Loyola Guzmán and the efficient use of the information found on her. True, chasing the guerrillas in the mountains was the business of the military. But Arguedas assigned "between ten and twenty" of his agents to them, plus a dozen men with specially trained police dogs. He was also responsible for the activities of the various CIA Cubans he had hired, who were officially under his orders. As a double agent, Arguedas would have tried at least to obtain some useful information

---

* There is a disturbing analogy here with the case of Jorge Vázquez Viaña (Loro), mentioned in Chapter 7.

from them, in turn. At no time did Che Guevara draw any advantage from having such a highly placed "friend" in La Paz.

There is a mysterious postscript which forms part of the Arguedas episode, even though it is not easy even now to grasp its significance.

On October 24, 1970, a message bearing the initials ELN and the signature "*Comandante* Aníbal" circulated in La Paz. It announced that despite the defeat of the ELN reconstituted at Teoponte, and despite the capture of its leader Osvaldo Peredo (Chato), the guerrilla struggle was going on. New fronts would be opened up, it said, one of them under the command of Arguedas, "who redeemed himself by sending Che's diary to Fidel Castro."

On November 3, 1970, the bodies of two students, Ernesto Fajardo and Mario Saavedra, were found in the Sopocachi quarter of La Paz. That night a communiqué signed ELN announced to the press that they had been executed by the organization for having falsely issued the October 24 statement in the name of the ELN. The two students, according to this communiqué, belonged to a "group of *hampones* (thugs) who had deceived public opinion by usurping the prestige of our organization." The communiqué went on: "Neither these gentlemen nor Señor Arguedas, under whose orders they said they worked, have ever belonged to the ELN."

By a strange coincidence, in June 1968, a few weeks before his flight from La Paz, Arguedas had triumphantly exhibited to the press three young rightist terrorists of the Bolivian *Falange*, who had been arrested by his department. The main defendant proclaimed that the aim of the *Falangista* movement was to gain power through an urban guerrilla movement, but an official *Falange* statement affirmed that all this had been staged by Arguedas. This main defendant was none other than Ernesto Fajardo.

Nothing more was heard about him until his body was found in the Sopocachi quarter and identified as that of a member of the false ELN supposedly led by Arguedas.

Another incident, no less mysterious and still more difficult to interpret, also seems to be related to the Arguedas episode: the assassination in Hamburg on April 1, 1971, of the Bolivian consul, Roberto Quintanilla Pereira. Named to this post a year earlier by President Ovando, Consul Quintanilla had previously been Colonel Quintanilla, intelligence chief for Arguedas at the *ministerio de gobierno*.

The murder of Quintanilla was never explained, although his wife and his secretary had struggled with the killer, a woman wearing a wig, before she escaped. The murder weapon, left behind, was a Colt Cobra .38 Special, No. 212607. An investigation by INTERPOL established that this pistol had been sold in Milan on July 18, 1968, to the publisher Giangiacomo Feltrinelli.

A millionaire with a special taste for revolution, as Howard Hughes has a special fear of germs, Feltrinelli was the official Italian publisher of the *Diario del Che en Bolivia*, and was listed as such by Castro in his "Necessary Introduction." As widely reported by the press, the mangled body of Feltrinelli was found near Milan on March 16, 1972, next to a powerline pylon which he apparently was planning to blow up.

On the night of Quintanilla's murder, a communiqué signed by the ELN was distributed in La Paz, claiming responsibility for the assassination in the name of "revolutionary justice." According to this communiqué, Quintanilla had been executed for the murder of Inti—Guido Peredo— who had been slain in La Paz on September 9, 1969,° when Quintanilla was still chief of intelligence but Arguedas was

° See page 179.

no longer *ministro de gobierno*. The communiqué made no mention of the breakup of Che's urban organization in 1967, directed by the same Quintanilla under the supervision of Arguedas.

While some aspects of the Arguedas episode may remain mysterious, there can be no doubt as to why Che's diary was put into Castro's hands.

The explanation is there right under our nose; sometimes discussed in private conversations, it is rarely formulated in writing. To my knowledge only Gregorio Selser, an Argentine author who has written several books on the CIA, referred to it in the preface to his *La CIA en Bolivia.* Naturally it is impossible to prove, but it is the only logical explanation: knowingly or not, Antonio Arguedas sent Che's diary to Fidel Castro for the benefit and with the aid of the CIA.

Unlike Gregorio Selser and many others who attribute a sort of genius to the CIA, I myself have little admiration for the efficiency of this celebrated agency. In fact I know of very few instances when it lived up to its reputation, and many in which it showed total incompetence.

But in the case of Che's *Diary*, the solution was compelling as well as tempting. Obviously if such a text came out in La Paz or New York, the world would consider it a fake, although if an intelligent agent of the Central Intelligence Agency (there are some) had been assigned to concoct a fake diary of Che designed to discredit the guerrillas, he would not have gone as far as Che did in the genuine diary. Washington could only congratulate itself on having waited for Havana to be the first to confirm Che's death. There was one way to ensure that the diary's authenticity would be recognized by all, and that was to get Castro to publish it first.

* Buenos Aires: Hernández Editor, 1970.

In the past, even some of the CIA's technically successful operations—such as those against Mohammed Mossadegh in Iran in 1953, or against Jacobo Arbenz the year after in Guatemala—were carried out in a clumsy and noisy way, not exactly the mark of a good secret service. But leading Fidel Castro to launch the *Bolivian Diary* from Havana, by making him believe that he thus was pulling a trick on the *yanquis*—this must be considered as one of the few truly brilliant exploits of the CIA.

X

Myth and Reality

In the autumn of 1945 the English weekly *Tribune* was flooded by indignant letters after it published an unflattering report on the behavior of Soviet troops in occupied Austria. Some of these letters not only called the Vienna correspondent a fool and a liar or made "other charges of what one might call a routine nature," but carried "the very serious implication that he ought to have kept silent even if he knew that he was speaking the truth." This led George Orwell° to comment in his *Tribune* column:

> The whole argument that one mustn't speak plainly because it "plays into the hands of" this or that sinister influence is dishonest, in the sense that people only use it when it suits them. . . . Beneath this argument there always lies the intention to do propaganda for some single sectional interest, and to browbeat critics into silence by telling them they are "objectively" reactionary.

° Orwell quotations are taken from Sonia Orwell and Ian Angus, eds., *The Collected Essays, Journalism and Letters of George Orwell*, 4 volumes (New York: Harcourt, Brace & World, 1968).

This *Tribune* article appeared on November 23, 1945. Two months later the magazine *Polemic* published Orwell's major essay on *The Prevention of Literature*: "The enemies of intellectual liberty," Orwell insisted, "always try to present their case as a plea for discipline versus individualism. The issue truth-versus-untruth is as far as possible kept in the background."

Orwell died on January 21, 1950, at a time when Ernesto Guevara de la Serna, aged 21, was completing a journey of nearly 3,000 miles by motorcycle across Argentina. Guevara was still politically uninvolved except for a vague anti-Peronist sentiment inherited from his family. Orwell had been arrested during the Spanish civil war in Catalonia by the NKVD special units assigned to physically eliminate anti-Stalinist elements from within the anti-Franco forces. Before devoting the rest of his life to unmasking the false revolutionaries of the so-called "left", he had barely escaped from the true assassins of the same so-called "left".

The arrogant and inhuman totalitarianism which Orwell fought was the "socialism" advocated in *El socialismo y el hombre en Cuba*, and presented as the ideal of the "new man" under the signature, and in the myth, of Che Guevara. The fundamental postulate of that "socialism", as defined by Orwell, was that "freedom is undesirable and intellectual honesty is a form of antisocial selfishness." Che was no hypocrite; he defined his conception of "socialism" in practically the same terms.

Lenin once said that facts are stubborn. But so are lies. Orwell knew better than most that some lies last a long time: he was aware that because of the Russian *mythos*, "known facts are suppressed and distorted to such an extent as to make it doubtful whether a true history of our times can ever be written." The Russian myth eventually collapsed, but the Cuban myth took its place. Che's share in that myth is now larger than ever because more and more "intellectuals of the left" are wavering in their unconditional allegiance to Castro, and need a substitute.

On September 30, 1968, for example, eight French intellectuals led by Marguerite Duras protested Castro's approval of the invasion of Czechoslovakia. They were still careful, however, to stress that they viewed this as "the first serious error to our knowledge" in a revolution which they had "considered until now as exemplary." On May 21, 1971, sixty intellectuals from various countries, including Marguerite Duras together with Jean-Paul Sartre and Simone de Beauvoir, had given up the "revolutionary" niceties to react with "shame and anger" to the public confession made by the Cuban poet Heberto Padilla after five weeks in prison. This "pitiable parody of self-criticism," said their letter published first in *Le Monde* and later in the *New York Times*, was full of "absurd accusations and delirious assertions" recalling "the most sordid moments of the era of Stalinism."

Sartre and the others, who for so many years had been Castro's faithful servants, were now viewed by him as "miserable ones," and Padilla himself was assigned to denounce them as "cynical enemies of socialism." But contrary to Stalin, who remained jealous of Trotsky's shadow even though he might have done better at times to take shelter in it, Castro eagerly and constantly polishes Che's halo, in the hope that its gleam will reflect on him and that the myth of Che will help keep alive his own, the Cuban myth.

"A totalitarian State," Orwell observed, "is in effect a theocracy, and its ruling caste, in order to keep its position, has to be thought of as infallible. But since, in practice, no one is infallible, it is frequently necessary to rearrange past events in order to show that this or that mistake was not made, or that this or that imaginary triumph actually happened."

Example: Che, according to Castro's "Necessary Introduction," conducted himself in Bolivia "with the firmness, mastery, stoicism, and exemplary attitude that were proverbial in him."

So much for the myth. But let us remember, with Orwell, that "freedom of the intellect means the freedom to report what one has seen, heard, and felt, and not to be obliged to fabricate imaginary facts and feelings." What is the reality concerning Che's conduct in Bolivia? Proverbial or not, the only quality mentioned which Che actually demonstrated was stoicism; a sort of stubbornness as well, which could pass if necessary for firmness; but certainly no mastery, nor any exemplary attitude for future guerrilla movements.

Castro, however, was sure he could exorcise any evil thoughts about Che's adventures among the *animalitos*.

> Many were his contacts with the Bolivian peasants. The character of the peasants, who were extremely suspicious and on guard, was no surprise to Che who knew their mentality perfectly, having dealt with them in other circumstances. He knew that, to win them to his cause, a prolonged, arduous and patient effort was required, but he had no doubt that in the long run he would succeed.

Che expressed a slight hope of this kind in his summary of May 1967.* But in the June summary he implicitly admitted that the army was more persuasive than the guerrillas in dealing with the peasants, since it had succeeded in turning them into *chivatos* (informers), not only by frightening them but "by deceiving them about our objectives." The last monthly summary, for September 1967, is totally unreconcilable with Castro's statement: Guevara records with

---

* See Chapter 7.

resignation, as an unalterable fact, that "the peasant masses do not help us in any way."

The only author who has acknowledged this contradiction, so far as I am aware, is Richard Harris. In his *Death of a Revolutionary*° he writes:

> It is difficult to accept Fidel's assertion in this regard when one takes into consideration the fact that Che's diary is filled with bitter remarks about the indifference and suspicion that he and his men encountered in their contacts with the local peasantry.

As to the use of "systematic terror" envisaged by Che Guevara in his April 1967 summary, Harris comments, in an understatement which still compares favorably with the complete silence of so many other writers, that "this is surprising in view of Che's previous opposition to the use of terrorism as a tactic of revolutionary guerrilla warfare." Harris consoles himself with the thought that "at any rate, neither he nor his men subsequently committed any acts that could be considered as terrorism against the peasant population."

Obviously a rural guerrilla movement cannot possibly serve as an example when it is incapable of winning over the peasants of the region, and is not even able to obtain their neutrality.

A true revolutionary ought to concern himself less with protecting Che's myth than with studying how future guerrillas can learn from his mistakes, to avoid going the way of Nancahuazú. Che felt that he was a true revolutionary. If he had survived, would he have been more honest and perceptive than his incense-burners? Surely he would have been more honest. One might still wonder, however, about his ability to perceive things clearly.

° New York: W. W. Norton & Co., 1970.

Confronted with the obviously unexpected hostility of the peasants, he displayed a startling lack of both sensitivity and understanding. He drew no conclusions from the fact, admitted in his June summary, that the army's propaganda was more effective than his own. Perhaps Bertolt Brecht, in the period before he learned to keep quiet, would have found that the moment had come either to change guerrillas or to change peasants. But Che counted on terror, the terror inspired in the peasants by the guerrillas which might prove stronger than the terror instilled in them by the army.

In the May summary (the one in which he expresses some hope) Che reports that the army has arrested some peasants who had been in contact with him. He evidently considers this as some kind of progress: "Now comes a period when terror will be exercised on the peasants from both sides, though with different characteristics. . . ." He notes on July 3, without showing any particular concern, that since the guerrillas pay "high prices," the peasants provide goods out of a mixture of "fear and interest"; on the 6th, that the guerrillas are crossing "an inhabited area which received us with terror"; on the 7th, that "fear remains rooted in the people."

The *Diary's* page for July 4 did not appear in the first editions that came from Cuba, nor did I find it in the official American edition° which I bought in 1972 in New York. But the page was in the Daniel James version, and also appeared in the official Spanish text.† After having marched until 3:30 P.M. that day, Che writes on July 4 that his group encountered "a peasant named Manuel Carrillo who received us with panicky terror." The *Diary* then adds with a burst of uninhibited satisfaction: "*Comimos opiparamente*, we dined sumptuously."

° *Bolivian Diary*, Ramparts Edition (New York: Bantam, 1968).
† 3rd ed. (Mexico City: Siglo XXI Editores, 1968).

Like Che Guevara in Bolivia, Hugo Blanco failed in Perú, but his example proved that it was possible to approach the Indian masses without resigning, or condemning, oneself to treat them as *animalitos* whose support or submission could be obtained only by systematic terror.

Convinced that "Trotskyism at its ultimate point of degeneracy is a medieval metaphysic," Régis Debray shrugged off Hugo Blanco as an insignificant emissary of the Fourth International "from Argentina." In his *Le Monde* interview while he was in the prison of *El Frontón*, Hugo Blanco told Marcel Niedergang:

> I was not sent into La Convención° by the Fourth International as they said, as Régis Debray wrote. I discovered La Convención by chance. A spontaneous 'unionization' movement had already begun. I only followed the current set in motion by the peasants of the valley themselves. It was a matter of fighting blow by blow. I never pretended to be 'protector' of the Indians. I simply tried to show the value of mutual aid.

Hugo Blanco Galdoz came from Cuzco, Perú's ancient Inca capital, where his father had been a judge. He had studied agricultural engineering in Buenos Aires. He also worked there as a laborer in one of the meat-freezing plants, first joining a union (Peronist) and later a political party (Trotskyite). The "chance" which led him to the valley of La Convención was the fact that he was being detained in the Cuzco prison, together with some peasants of the region, on a charge of resisting the armed forces.

Considered by the Communists a "provocateur" and "adventurer," Hugo Blanco (known to the peasants by the name Condori) was also abandoned by the bureaucrats of

---

° A relatively fertile Andean valley in the Cuzco region.

the Fourth International. Captured on May 30, 1963, he
was sentenced on September 9, 1963, to twenty-five years in
prison. When General Velasco Alvarado took over Perú's
government in October 1968, he was in no hurry to grant
amnesty to this "leftist" who, unlike the others, refused to
recognize him as a revolutionary. Hugo Blanco was not
freed until Christmas 1970; the news was hardly noticed
under the headlines devoted to the freeing of Régis Debray.

I met Hugo Blanco early in 1972 in Mexico City, where
he had arrived a few months earlier. He was living in a new
house in the Navarte quarter. As instructed, I took the
stairway to the third floor and walked to the last door on the
right at the end of the corridor. Before me, two lovers
walked together arm in arm. Only when they arrived in
front of the last door on the right and turned toward me did
I recognize, under the student beard and youthful pink
cheeks, the former Peruvian guerrilla who had spent seven
of his thirty-seven years in prison.

What was he doing now? He glanced toward the young
woman busying herself in the kitchen: he was happy. He
had a temporary passport, valid for one year, and was
teaching Quechua language and culture at the University of
México's department of anthropology. He would have liked
to return to Perú if permitted to do so, and if he were also
permitted to resume his work among the peasant unions.°
He was not planning any secret operations, and he still
considered himself a labor organizer rather than a military
leader. Armed action could only be the final step in the
mobilization of the masses, and it was a fatal mistake to use

---

° At the time this was written, he still had not received
permission to return. He left Mexico on June 12, 1972, for
Buenos Aires, and was arrested a month later and served with
an expulsion order which he appealed. On October 26, 1972,
the Argentine authorities put him aboard a plane to Chile. It is
probable that his travels are not over.

it before the masses were ready. The first creations of the peasant unions of La Convención were not military camps or arsenals, but schools.

"No, the Indian peasants are not animals," he said. "They are suspicious, yes, but they have good reasons to be. You have to live among them, understand them, follow their way of reasoning and lead them to act according to their own logic. I myself prefer freedom to discipline. They do too. Life pleases me more than death. The same for them. They had the desire to defend their human rights before they had the slightest knowledge of the principle of class struggle. To fight for drinking water is a normal thing, and this normal thing can become a revolutionary act."

Hugo Blanco condemned the theory of the *foco*, but he admired Che—for his sincerity, his lack of opportunism, his "absolute internationalism, untouched by the Stalinist notion of socialism in a single country." Like Che, he failed; but despite all the mythologies, what he accomplished will prove to be infinitely more lasting, infinitely more significant than the imprint left behind by Che.

For of all the Latin-American guerrillas who believed that revolution in Latin America must begin with the peasants, he was one of the few who began at the beginning. Unlike Che, he tried to be one of the peasants before thinking of himself as their leader. The Indian peasants of the valleys of Lares and La Convención, at Hugo Blanco's side, organized unions, established schools, occupied the lands they were supposed to work as serfs for the feudal landowner or *gamonal;* they certainly took a bigger step forward than their brothers of southeastern Bolivia who trembled before Che Guevara.

Che Guevara's blindness in his Bolivian enterprise becomes more understandable when we see how in *Pasajes de la guerra revolucionaria*, his amended memoirs of the Sierra Maestra published in 1963, he was able to convince himself

that the urban fighters who did not accept the new Cuban
regime deserved none of the credit for the victory over
Batista.

There had been frequent disputes, during the struggle
against Batista, between the *sierra* and the *llano*, the
mountain and the plain, or more exactly between the rural
maquis and the urban resistance. By the start of 1960, a
large part of the anti-Batista urban resistance, thoroughly
anti-Communist, had gone over to active or passive resistance against Castro. Incapable of understanding this attitude, Che Guevara in 1963 retroactively resolved the
problem of the *llano* by discrediting its men and minimizing
the importance of its operations.

One of the accounts in *Pasajes* is titled "A Decisive
Meeting," and concerns the meeting held in the Sierra
Maestra on May 3, 1958, to analyze the strike of the
preceding April 9, sabotaged by the Communists. The
appeal for "total war" made by Castro on March 12, 1958,
had been premature, and so was the "revolutionary general
strike." But in 1963 Che was not writing to criticize Castro's
recklessness and the imprudent romanticism of the urban
fighters; his aim was to justify, under the name of "realism,"
the sabotage organized by the PSP Communists in 1958,
since these were the men who had become the cadres of the
administration in 1963.

The reason for the failure of the strike, Che explains, lay
in the "subjectivism," the "putschist conceptions," the
"adventurist policy" of the worker representatives of the
July 26 Movement, who "opposed all participation of the
Partido Socialista Popular in the organization of the struggle."

This is Che talking, not some veteran of the PSP. The
cadres of the PSP had been planted in the Batista unions
with the tacit, and shrewd, agreement of the regime. The
leaders of the workers' resistance mistrusted and despised

them. "Fundamentally," Che goes on to admit, "the party of the workers had not seen with sufficient clarity the role of the guerrilla and the personal role of Fidel in our revolutionary struggle." But he regrets even more the attitude of his own people toward the PSP. With regard to the "decisive meeting," he thus notes with belated dismay that the replacement of David Salvador with Nico Torres as "worker delegate" of the movement was hardly an improvement, since "Nico declared himself ready to collaborate in a disciplined manner with the *Stalinistas*, while adding that it would lead nowhere."

The Che of 1963, who was neither the Che of 1958 nor the Che of 1967, seemed particularly shocked by the fact that Nico Torres had used the term *Stalinistas* to designate the "comrades of the PSP."

Che's purpose obviously was not to show that the "socialism" installed in Havana had been opposed by the combatants. It was to establish that the *llano*, including the workers, lagged behind the *sierra*, which was more advanced from a revolutionary standpoint. And naturally, since the *sierra* was more mature, it followed that it must have been more effective, and therefore should get the credit for the victory.

All this was given a pseudo-dialectical coating in Che's preface (also written in 1963) to a pamphlet on "The Marxist-Leninist Party," a compilation of Castro speeches and of extracts from a manual written by an old Finnish Stalinist, Otto Kuusinen:°

The *sierra* was ready to strike at the army as often as necessary, to win battle after battle, take its weapons,

° The choice is quite representative of neo-Cuban "anti-imperialism," since Kuusinen was the Soviet-appointed quisling who headed the "government" of Terijoki after the Russians invaded Finland in 1939.

and arrive one day at the complete seizure of power by means of the rebel army. The *llano* was in favor of a general armed struggle in the whole country with, as a final stage, a revolutionary general strike. . . . These contradictions have roots going deeper than tactical disagreements: the rebel army already is ideologically proletarian, and thinks as a dispossessed class; the *llano* continues to be middle class, with future traitors in its leadership.

Che Guevara had tailored an orthodox "Marxist-Leninist" costume to fit the revolutionary movement, but it was a costume for a fancy-dress ball, not for history.

The *sierra* and the *llano* had at their core the same children of the bourgeoisie, and it was a joke to call one more "proletarian" than the other, even ideologically. Moreover, no matter how ready it was to "strike at the army as often as necessary," the *sierra* would not have been able to strike even once at the army of Batista, had the army not been already demoralized by its increasing isolation from the people.

Coming down from the mountains, the *barbudos* confronted only what was left of that army after the actions of the urban resistance had captured the imagination of the people, and after the barbaric repression of these actions had disgusted the bourgeoisie, so that officers as well as soldiers had lost all desire to fight for Batista. Yet Che somehow convinced himself that the few hundred guerrillas of the Sierra Maestra really had succeeded, on their own, in militarily defeating a regular army. What was more serious, and would prove fatal in Bolivia, was that he also persuaded himself that this was the norm—that from then on, anywhere in Latin America, any peasant guerrilla movement "ready to strike at the army as often as necessary" would be certain to prevail.

Even the rural combat force, to begin with, was essentially a product of the city. The Cuban peasants were friendlier to the young guerrillas than were the Indians of the Andes, but they did not join them in substantial numbers until the last months of 1958.

The *ejército rebelde* of Castro and Guevara became something to talk about only when the initial core built around the *Granma* survivors was augmented by a fifty-man detachment organized by Frank País, chief of the *llano* in Santiago de Cuba, and commanded by "future traitor" Jorge Sotús.° It first became a potential military threat when a planeload of weapons from Costa Rica arrived in the Sierra Maestra, along with a schoolteacher named Huber Matos. As head of the "Antonio Guiteras column," *Comandante* Matos received the surrender of Santiago de Cuba (with the famous Moncada barracks) and Castro named him its military governor at the same time he made it his provisional capital. In October 1959, when he was arrested, Matos was military governor of the central province of Camagüey. He offered no resistance and did not try to escape by using the plane which was at his disposal near his headquarters.

The "future traitor" Matos was sentenced to twenty years for having written a letter to Castro asking to be relieved of his command and to be allowed to return to private life and teaching. He could not approve, he said, the increasing role played by the Communists in the revolutionary regime, but since he did not want to oppose Castro, he thought "the honest thing to do was to go."

The "trial" of Matos took place in December 1959. The first and star witness for the prosecution was Fidel Castro.

° Condemned late in 1959 to a twenty-year prison term, Captain Sotús escaped, accompanied by his jail guard. He died in Miami in a rather mysterious accident.

He "testified" for more than seven hours, facing the audience, not the court, and then departed without waiting for any cross-examination. The second witness, Raúl Castro, also declined to be cross-examined. No charges were presented, no actions alleged, no documents produced. In fact, if there was an indictment, no one knew anything about it, and there was no mention of any evidence either before, during, or after the trial, which consisted of little more than Castro's speech. All we know for sure is that Huber Matos was convicted of "treason and sedition," that the sentence was twenty years, and that he is still in jail.

Castro himself had been sentenced to only a fifteen-year term under the Batista dictatorship, for his armed attack on a military installation in 1953. He was released on May 15, 1955, after less than two years in prison. Sentenced to thirty years for complicity in a rebel movement, Régis Debray was freed by the Bolivian "gorillas" after three years and eight months. As this book goes to press, Huber Matos will have been in prison fourteen years, but that does not appear to trouble anyone.

Che Guevara has only sarcastic words for Sotús and Matos in *Pasajes*, notably in the story called "Reinforcements." Matos here becomes an *arrocero*, a rice planter, who after having brought the Sotús group in his truck, was so "frightened" by the danger he had faced that he took refuge in an embassy, then in Costa Rica. He returned, Che adds, "transformed into a hero," aboard an airplane carrying "some weapons." Che does not explain why such a "frightened" man should have returned to the Sierra at the most crucial time for the guerrillas, nor when and by whom he was "transformed into a hero," nor how Castro could have made this "future traitor" one of his most trusted *comandantes*.

In Bolivia, Che continued to display the same theoretical

scorn for the cities which he had shown in Cuba when he tried to rewrite history in 1963. Yet in his June 1967 summary in the *Diary*, he is aware that "our most urgent task," besides reestablishing contact with La Paz and stocking up on military and medical supplies, is "the recruitment of about 50 to 100 men from the city." *From the city . . .*

Che's preface to "The Marxist-Leninist Party" should have been enough to squelch the notion of those visitors to Cuba, determined to love Castro's revolution but not Kuusinen's, who claimed to see in the realities of Cuba and in the ideas of Guevara an imaginary "Spanish-type anarcho-syndicalism."

Everything which in the Cuban civil war recalled the Spanish anarcho-syndicalist tradition—anti-authoritarian, anti-military, relying on armed militia and the revolutionary general strike—Che either scornfully dismissed or harshly condemned as being the work of the *llano* with its future traitors and its adventurist labor leaders. But the illusion that Che belongs to that Spanish tradition has survived, and continues to be part of his myth.

By setting up as a prototype of his "new man" the Stalinist Stakhanovist turned *guerrillero del trabajo*, did Che Guevara fulfill the dream of the Spanish anarchists who burned banknotes in the public squares?

Should the Cuban working class be thankful to Che, and should the workers of the rest of the world envy their Cuban counterparts, for enforced "voluntary labor", for increased work quotas with reduced pay, for substitution of medals, inscriptions on honor rolls, and certificates of Communist labor in place of wages? Were those the goals of Spanish anarcho-syndicalism?

The French author Daniel Guérin has written on social issues for more than half a century. In one of his most

important books* he defended "the necessity as well as the
feasibility of a synthesis between Marxism and anarchism."
Throughout 278 of its 296 pages, he does not forget
Bakunin's warning against the "doctrinaire socialists" who
aspired "to place the people in a new harness." Bakunin, he
explains, was right when he said that for the Marxists, "only
a dictatorship—their own dictatorship, of course—can
create the will of the people," and that for libertarians, "no
dictatorship can have any other purpose than to perpetuate
itself." But then come eighteen pages devoted to Cuba, and
Guérin loses his head.

He had been among the 470 Western intellectuals invited
to Havana by Castro, at the expense of the Cuban workers,
for the "Cultural Congress" which opened the "Year of the
Heroic Guerrilla" in January 1968. Three weeks later he
arrived at this conclusion:

> The Cuban revolution, seen at close range, shows
> itself to be so authentically socialist in spirit and in
> purpose, if not in all its forms, that the prospect of
> having to return to a capitalist country seemed a bitter
> one to more than one of the guests.

I doubt very much that even a single one of the 470
"intellectuals of the left," who for three weeks had been
"provided generously with butter, coffee, meat, and other
foods which are rare or severely rationed," actually considered sharing the life of the Cuban workers. Guérin, aware of
the severities of rationing which affected the nonguests, also
could have learned by reading Raúl Castro's May Day
speech that year in Camagüey, that the foreign delegates to
the Cultural Congress were able to enjoy a lot of ice cream

---

* *Pour un marxisme libertaire* (Paris: Editions Robert Laffont,
1969).

because the ninety-five workers of the Guarina factory worked Saturdays and Sundays to accumulate 1,758 "voluntary"—unpaid, that is—hours of production.

What did the "libertarian Marxist" see at close range in the Cuban revolution to justify his enthusiasm? He speaks of "trade unions" while admitting, in parentheses, that "there is no question in Cuba of trade unionism." He knows that these unions without unionism are "subordinated to the Communist Party, in the factory as well as on the natioanl level," and that this party "as a matter of fact" is directed by "a small hard core, a politico-military apparatus, which operates in a secret and hierarchical way." That isn't all:

> In Cuba the unions are somewhat like poor parents. Their field of action is limited, since there is hardly any possibility (or hardly any reason) for claims in view of the friendly relaxation which prevails in the place of work, and a strike is "unthinkable." However, the CTC, the Confederation of Cuban Workers, born well before the revolution, has recently been revived. It sets a framework for the workers and inspires them. It is based on the principles of worker democracy and proletarian internationalism inherited from Spanish anarcho-syndicalism.

Thus, where Cuba is concerned, Guérin is able to revive not only the CTC's governmental bureaucracy, but the worn sophisms of Stalinist "syndicalism" (no reason for claims) and of company "unionism" (the friendly relaxation which prevails in the place of work). He also tells us that "on the social level, the regime appeared to me as a kind of paternalism, in the best meaning of that word, organizing and active."

I didn't know there was a good meaning of the term "paternalism" to which "libertarian Marxism" could rally. "Its benefits are handed to the people from above," says

Guérin. In the key chapter of his book, titled "Lenin or Socialism from Above," he has just rejected such "concepts which socialism should get rid of if it wants to recover its libertarian authenticity."

As proof of Cuba's "best" kind of paternalism, Guérin points to "the work week reduced to 44 hours."

Obviously Guérin never burdened himself with the admittedly painful task of reading at least the weekly edition of *Granma*, which is published in three languages. Anyone who worked only a 44-hour week in Cuba in 1968, Year of the Heroic Guerrilla, who refused to work extra unpaid hours or to cut cane on Sundays, was denounced as an "antisocial" element. If he persisted, despite pep talks and harassment, he was labeled "counterrevolutionary." And counterrevolutionaries in Cuba were duly warned as to what awaited them.

The repression has not lessened since then. On October 4, 1970, for example, *Granma*'s front page carried the banner headline: "THE LOAFER STEALS FROM THE PEOPLE EVERY DAY AND AT ALL HOURS," in two lines of bold capitals ⅝ inches high. A third line, ⅜ inches high, added: "WE MUST TAKE MEASURES SO THAT THIS KIND OF THEFT WILL NOT GO UNPUNISHED." This was the theme of the speech delivered by the *jefe máximo* on September 28, 1970, on the occasion of the tenth anniversary of the CDR (Committees for the Defense of the Revolution).

The CDR's job is continuous surveillance of the population, section by section, street by street, house by house. CDR groups check on the movements of each person: the visitors he receives, the comments or swearwords he might let out, the hour he leaves for work and the hour he returns, and of course his zeal or lack of it in the rallies and other "voluntary activities" of the regime. Thanks to the CDR, the behavior of the entire Cuban population is on file.

Fidel Castro now directed the CDR to mobilize against

those who did not work hard enough, because "in a collectivist society, where man works for society, loafing must be considered a crime, just like robbery."

Everyone agrees, he said, that a man who breaks into a distribution center and "makes off with a sack of loot" must be punished. "In the same way, or worse, the loafer steals from the people." For "the water he drinks and the water he uses to take a bath; the light bulb which gives him light, if he has it; the clothes he wears; the food he eats, the shoes on his feet—all this is stolen, because it takes work to produce all that." When he announced next that "in the labor movement the struggle against loafers, absenteeism, and parasitism has reached tremendous proportions," the *Granma* account in English adds: "(Applause and shouts of: *Fidel, hit the lazy bums hard!*)"

While Daniel Guérin was deceiving himself and his readers with his report of a 44-hour work week, Susan Sontag wrote in the April 1969 *Ramparts*: "Some Thoughts on the Right Way (for us) to Love the Cuban Revolution." She knew very well, and wanted to explain away, the fact that "the Cuban revolution presents in part an extremely uncomfortable challenge to American radicals."

Many young American radicals, who proudly arrived in Havana in ritual dress and hairstyle of the hippie establishment, had already learned that unless they quickly identified themselves as members of a *Venceremos* Brigade, a team of voluntary workers, they were about as physically safe amid their "brothers" of the CDR as they were in the streets of downtown Manhattan amid the "hardhats" of Peter J. Brennan. Ms. Sontag tries to help them accept it:

> Although their awareness of underdevelopment inevitably leads to an increasing emphasis on discipline, the Cubans are devoting a great deal of effort to safeguarding the voluntary character of their institutions.

> . . . Nevertheless, the trend is, inevitably, and cor-
> rectly, given their problems, toward more discipline,
> more organization.

Aware that there may be some who have "at best, a very
ambivalent attitude" about this trend, Susan Sontag "inevitably" but not "correctly" contradicts herself from one page
of her article to the next. And at the same time she
contradicts *Granma*, Che, and Castro.

After an ecstatic tribute to Cuba's "extraordinary accom-
plishments of labor and productivity," she describes as
characteristic of the new working conditions the very
"unproductive" behavior Che and later Fidel tried so hard
to eradicate, denouncing it as criminal: *The Loafer Is a
Thief*. For Susan Sontag, Cubans have a way of "making
work seem like fun." Joyously she describes the way: "lots
of talking, joking, high noise level, lack of punctuality,
irregular hours, absence of hierarchy and deference, and
plenty of inefficiency."

It was Che Guevara who, condemning what Sontag
praises, imposed on the Cuban workers that "regimenta-
tion" she recognizes "in most countries belonging to the
'socialist camp,' " which "makes a mockery of the pretensions to revolutionary socialism."

The Russians, of course, had started it, and whether Che
copied them or reinvented the system, it was the same. Men
like Andreï Amalrik have been deported to Siberia for years
at hard labor under a 1961 decree by Nikita Khrushchev
which, translated into Spanish, sounds like genuine Che
Guevara. It concerns "the struggle against individuals
refusing to participate in the collective effort and leading an
antisocial and parasitic type of life."

As dictator of the Cuban economy, Che transferred the
Siberian "socialism" of the Soviet Union to a tropical island
known as "the pearl of the Antilles," and Castro was happy

to enforce it as "the socialism of Che." The system was eventually codified, amid what *Granma* termed "massive demonstrations of popular joy," in Law No. 1231, enacted on March 16, 1971.

This law is based on the principle that "the working class condemns all forms of idleness as an offense similar to theft." It postulates that an "antisocial attitude toward work" constitutes "an unhealthy example for the new generations."

Law No. 1231 applies to all men aged seventeen to sixty, and all women from seventeen to fifty-five. It establishes not only the "offense of idleness" (Article 8), but a "punishable state of pre-idleness" (Article 3). One has reached "that punishable state," under Article 3, when absent without reason for more than fifteen days, or after having been cited three times for shorter absences. The penalty is "internment in a reeducation establishment" for up to one year, with "productive activities." If the delinquent is not "reeducated," Article 8 applies. The penalty for the "offense of idleness" is "loss of liberty" for twelve to twenty-four months—always, naturally, with "productive activities," meaning hard labor.

Article 4, paragraph 2 of Law No. 1231 appears to have no Soviet precedent and is thus an authentic innovation of the Cuban "revolution." It provides, as a "mitigated" application of Article 3, "confinement to domicile with obligation of working under the surveillance of the working community and the organizations of the masses near the domicile." The law does not specify whether the guilty party may choose punishment in a labor camp rather than having to submit to the absolute rule of the CDR and their zealous informers.

Two years before that crowning achievement of Che's "socialism," on the occasion of the eighth anniversary of the

CDR, Castro had already announced an open hunting season on *vagos*.

Vagos, in 1968, Year of the Heroic Guerrilla, were all those who, rebelling against the "discipline of work," refused to be regimented in the factories and plantations or to be indoctrinated in the political centers. They were the nonconformist youth of Cuba, and therefore, in Castro's view, they were agents of the enemy:

> Little young men influenced by imperialist propaganda among other things. . . . Some of them are busy corrupting 14- or 15-year-old girls, and promoting prostitution with sailors from capitalist° countries. . . . They carry their little transistors to show off ostentatiously their addiction to imperialist propaganda. . . . They spend their time breaking telephones, the telephones which are free, which belong to the people, and which they did not break when it was a *yanqui* monopoly. . . . They destroy the portraits of Che. . . .

For such persons aged fifteen and over, there was henceforth a special military regime to "teach them to get in line with the community." The new Cuban "community" had no place for rebels: "What did they think?" Fidel thundered. "That we are living under a bourgeois liberal regime? No! There's nothing liberal in us. We are revolutionaries! We are socialists! We are collectivists! We are Communists! But they, what did they want? To bring in here a revived version of Prague?"

Che's example is indeed as incompatible with the Prague spring as it is with Spanish anarcho-syndicalism. But his example was useful to Raúl Castro, Minister of the Armed Forces, when he affirmed on May 1, 1968, that "we refuse

---

° Sailors from "socialist" countries, of course, do not patronize prostitutes.

to erect an altar to the god of Money and to humiliate at its feet the conscience of men." Raúl did not mean, of course, that men no longer had to work themselves to death for money. He meant that now they had to work themselves to death without money. And Che's example was useful to *Granma*, too, when in its special issue on the third anniversary of Che's death it boldly mistook Bolívar for Stakhanov under the title *Gloria eterna al Guerrillero Heroico.*

Like Bolívar, the editorial said, Che felt that "the fatherland is America," and he left for the Andes in 1966, as he had gone to Cuba in 1956, to struggle against "the common injustice of the continent, the daughter of a common exploiter, *yanqui* imperialism." But the main accent in its remembrance of Che's life and works concerns the impulse he gave to "the magnificent movement of voluntary labor," the role he played in "the constant raising of productivity," and his part in "the struggle against absenteeism," all of which for him represented "a vital task of the working class."

In short, Bolívar or not Bolívar, when *Granma* invokes "Che, Inti, Coco, Tania, and all the Latin-American combatants who fell on the same front," it is chiefly to recall that each of them showed "that firmness and combativity in work that characterized *el guerrillero heroico.*" Thus it is preferably through hard work that the people should imitate them.

Was Che an anarcho-syndicalist? That's what some "leftist" intellectuals wish to believe. For the Cuban workers, Che's "discipline of labor," like Trotsky's "Soviet Taylorism" in 1920 for the Russian workers, was not a myth. It was the bitter reality. And what Isaac Deutscher said of Leon Trotsky is more than ever true of Che Guevara:

> In his aberration, Trotsky remained intellectually honest, honest to the point of futility. He made no

attempt to conceal his policy. He called things by their
names, no matter how unpalatable. . . . He hoped to
persuade people that they needed no government by
persuasion. He told them that the workers' State had
the right to use forced labor; and he was sincerely
disappointed that they did not rush to enroll in the
labor camps. He behaved thus absurdly because before
his mind's eye he had no cold machine of coercion
slowly and remorselessly grinding its human material,
but the monumental and evanescent outlines of a
"Proletarian Sparta," the austere rigors of which were
part of the pioneering adventure in socialism. . . .

Che an anarcho-syndicalist? . . . As dictator of the
Cuban economy, he was like Trotsky after his belated
adhesion to Bolshevism, the most doctrinaire, the most
authoritarian, the most conventional of party men.

It was Che who told the workers of Havana in January
1964: "Marx, in his inspired vision of all that was going to
happen, spoke of labor in Communism as a moral necessity
of man, and this is incorporated in the program of the Soviet
Communist Party for the construction of Communism." In
October 1962, when he announced that the Union of Young
Communists was "organized with eyes upon the luminous
future of socialist society," he had already added another
"moral necessity of man": that of "liquidating without
compromise all who remain behind, who are not capable of
marching to the beat of the Cuban revolution."

Che a nonconformist, iconoclast, friend of heretics? . . .
Speaking in March 1963 of the "construction of the party,"
he claimed for it, in the name of the working class,
naturally, a "unique and controlling dictatorship." His
"Bolshevik" enthusiasm had not faded—quite the contrary
—when he frankly stated two years later in *El socialismo y
el hombre en Cuba* that the dictatorship of the proletariat

was exercised "not only over the defeated class but also, individually, over the victorious class."

In Bolivia, true, he sometimes felt "anti-establishment." On September 8, 1967, for example: "How I would like to gain power just to unmask the cowards and lackeys of every kind, and rub their snouts in their excrements!" The cowards and lackeys he was talking about were the leaders of the Hungarian Communist Party, but if Che expressed himself on that day in such an unorthodox style, it was precisely because he was no longer in power, and his vanity had been dealt a blow along with his Marxism: "A Budapest daily," he had just learned, "criticizes Che Guevara, a pathetic and, it seems, irresponsible figure, and praises the Marxist attitude of the Chilean party which adopts practical attitudes in practical situations."

For Che, although always unobtrusive and ready to stand aside for Fidel in Cuba, was not without self-esteem.

In the "analysis of the Cuban situation" which concludes his *Guerra de guerrillas*, Che discussed the possibility of an assassination attempt on Castro, and remarked that the assassins still would have to eliminate Raúl Castro and "the author of these lines." In October of the same year (1960) his article "Notes for the Study of the Ideology of the Cuban Revolution" spoke in the plural of "the thought of the military leaders of the revolution" and of the manner in which they trained themselves (still in the plural) as "political leaders."

In March 1964, Che was interviewed in Havana by Lisa Howard for ABC television. Is it true, she asked, as believed in the United States, that you exert the strongest revolutionary influence in Cuba?

Che smiles, takes his time, and his reply, expanding on the question, shows a satisfaction he can hardly contain: "For a long time, in the United States as in many other countries, I was given the honor of being considered the brains of the revolution, the cool intelligence in command, the power behind the throne. Well, speaking for myself, that hardly bothers me, but my revolutionary honesty, my innate modesty, obliges me to admit that the most important man in Cuba, the most serious danger for the United States, is Fidel Castro and not me."

Was Che a Don Quixote? . . . The opening of his farewell letter to his parents has often been quoted: "Once again, I feel under my heels the flanks of Rosinante; I am taking to the road again with my shield on my arm. . . ." Thus Che chose to see himself as Don Quixote.

This image has seduced all those who refused to see the Salem witch hunts in the Moscow trials, and who saw a tale of chivalry in the Chinese "cultural revolution." Jorge Semprún, screenwriter of such films as Z and *L'Aveu*, is not among them. In the message he sent to Havana on the occasion of Che's death, he vehemently protested against attempts to present his action as "an explosion of revolutionary romanticism, as beautiful as could be, but ineffective." Semprún seeks to defend Che against revolutionary romanticism; there may be a more urgent need to defend revolutionary romanticism against Che.

Che, Don Quixote? . . . In his *Examen del Quijotismo* written in 1950, the great Cuban essayist Jorge Mañach discussed Don Quixote's "illusion of power." Don Quixote "parades tirelessly the strength of his arms and his bravery," and Mañach sees in this "the psychological core of his arrogance, of his faith in himself, and of his optimistic presumption in every situation." Perhaps Che Guevara gave proof of this kind of *quijotismo* when, in the *Diary* summary for June 1967 he notes first the "total absence of contacts," second the "absence of peasant recruitment," then jumps suddenly to the conclusion: "The legend of the guerrilla is spreading like foam; we are already invincible supermen." Supermen for whom?

In his farewell letter to his parents there is also a passage where Che presents himself as "a little *condottiere* of the twentieth century."

Unlike those soldiers of fortune of the fifteenth century, Che Guevara obviously was not a hired adventurer, a professional fighter working for pay, a mercenary. If he felt something in common with them, it was the fact that he too was ready to go and fight wherever he was needed. As a *condottiere* of the twentieth century, Che did not rent out his sword to a prince; he offered it free of charge to a people. What is significant is that he considered himself a man of the sword.

Che was a warrior. A warrior, and not only a guerrilla. He loved the battle. He loved the sight of weapons. He loved the life of the soldier.

One can imagine how the eyes of the poorly armed guerrillas must have shone when they saw three machine guns with tripods, three light machine guns, nine M-1 carbines, ten Johnson automatic rifles. But the eyes of Che gleam too brightly when in *Pasajes* he recounts the arrival of these weapons in the Sierra Maestra, where he was still only the medic, nothing more. "For us, this was the most marvelous sight in the world. There, placed as in an exhibition under the envious eyes of all the fighting men, were the instruments of death. . . ."

Che Guevara loved not only weapons but everything that was part of the soldier's life in the field, including the dirtiness of it.

With the pleasure of an ex-city dweller who has never liked civilized, or civilian, life and who finally feels at home among the guerrillas who have returned to nature, he recalls in *Guerra de guerrillas*:

> Our bodies gave off a characteristic and overpowering odor which repelled any stranger who might have

approached. Our sense of smell was completely syn-
chronized with this way of life. One could recognize
the hammocks of the guerrillas by their individual
odor. . . .

Che had explained earlier that it was not always easy to
keep clean. But when he lists minutely the various articles
which are of prime necessity to every guerrilla, he does not
include soap. He adds only that it is practical to carry some,
"not so much for personal cleanliness as to wash the dishes."
As a physician, he explains that dirty dishes can lead to
intestinal infections. He mentions no inconvenience in dirty
bodies.

When we discover, seven years later in the *Bolivian
Diary*, Che's satisfaction in talking about anything dirty and
everything smelly in the life of the guerrilla, we cannot help
feeling that this must have some significance.

On May 13, 1967, the group has trouble digesting a pig
eaten the night before. "A day of belching, farting, vomit-
ing, and diarrhea, a true organ concert . . . ," Che
comments with apparent good humor. On the 16th he has a
severe attack of colic, and his men have to carry him in a
hammock. He wakes up "covered with shit like a baby,"
and he "stinks of shit from a mile away." That day there was
no water. But on September 10 he notes merrily: "I almost
forgot to report an event: today, after something like more
than six months, I took a bath; this is a record that several
others are about to reach."

During these six months, the guerrillas passed through
streams and stopped along river banks. They were not
always in a hurry or on the lookout. What kept Che from
taking a bath, or indeed from having all of them do so?

For those who love the life of the soldier, certain
drawbacks easily become the subject of jokes or even
boasting. But Che was indulging in filth, not joking about it.

Perhaps it gave him the feeling of an extra sacrifice for the cause, a privation voluntarily accepted in the obscure belief that external dirt helps to preserve internal purity.

An Agence France Presse dispatch reported that Régis Debray, in prison, told one of its reporters: "For me, the adventure of Guevara was a mystical adventure, and the last months of his life, a Passion, his revolutionary Passion. He brought to mind irresistibly the image of Christ. . . ."

The myth of Che thus was complete. For those more concerned with the facts than with the impressions of Mr. Régis Debray, the adventures of Che, however, suggest not Christ but the Church of witch-burners and conquering monks. Che Guevara was not afraid to kill. He said as much to the United Nations on December 11, 1964, in response to the Venezuelan representative whose government he had accused of genocide and who had reminded him of the ongoing executions in Cuba: "Yes, we have had executions. We are carrying out executions and we will continue to do so as long as that will be necessary. . . ."

Finally, in his "Message to the Tricontinental," Che leaves as his testament a hymn to hatred and death:

> Hatred as an element of the struggle; a relentless hatred of the enemy, impelling us over and beyond the natural limitations that man is heir to and transforming him into an effective, violent, selective, and cold killing machine. . . .

And this "Message," celebrated by Christians and pacifists as well as Maoists or Trotskyites, ends in a bellicose delirium, not unprecedented in the history of "war poetry" but which the deaths of two world wars would seem to have made impossible to such an unblushing degree:

> Wherever death may surprise us, let it be welcome, provided that this, our battle cry, may have reached

some receptive ear and another hand may be extended
to wield our weapons and other men be ready to intone
the funeral dirge with the staccato singing of the
machine guns and new battle cries of war and victory.

A revolution worthy of the name should be able to do
without such literature. It even seems that a literature
worthy of the name ought to do without this revolution.

Today there are all kinds of books about Che, and
countless articles in newspapers and magazines. Most of
them belong to the genre of hagiography, the literature
devoted to the lives of the saints. The model of this, no
doubt, is the brochure *Viva Che!* ° in which Marianne
Alexandre collected an assortment of "contributions in
tribute to Ernesto 'Che' Guevara." Many of these "contributions in tribute" had already appeared in various foreign
publications, notably in the special issue of the official
Cuban magazine *Casa de las Américas* early in 1968.

We find in this collection an excellent translation of the
beautiful ballad *Guitarra en duelo mayor*† by Nicolás
Guillén, the greatest Cuban poet, who politically, alas, has
always been an obedient Stalinist bureaucrat. We also find a
poem by the English professor Andrew Sinclair—who is no
Stalinist but who, alas, hasn't the talent of Guillén—with
this apotheosis:

After Zapata

Lumumba

GUEVARA

Viva la tierra

° New York: E. P. Dutton & Co., 1968. (London: Lorrimer
Publishing Ltd.)
† Published in *Casa de las Américas* (January–February 1968),
with music by Harold Gramatges. The word "duelo" in the title
means "mourning."

The same Professor Sinclair published, in the "Modern Masters" series edited by Frank Kermode, an entire book about Che*; its dedication pays tribute to "the extensive research and Cuban experience of Marianne Alexandre."

Sinclair's book has some relatively sacrilegious passages: comparing Che Guevara as a "symbol of revolution" to Fidel Castro, Ho Chi Minh and Mao Tse-tung, he thinks that Che's martyrdom set him above the others, "even though his talents as a guerrilla leader may have been inferior." But Sinclair's conclusion is that "history will probably treat Guevara as the Garibaldi of his age, the most admired and loved revolutionary of his time." (At least it is Garibaldi this time and not Bolívar.)

As for the "extensive research" of Marianne Alexandre, here is how she explains, in her "Notes on the Life of Ernesto 'Che' Guevara" which serve as an introduction to *Viva Che!*, why young Ernesto was not able to practice medicine in the jungle as he wanted to when he arrived in Guatemala in December 1953: "He made an application, but the Guatemalan authorities demanded that he renew his doctor's diploma first, which would have meant more years of study."

The real story, as confirmed by people who knew Guevara during his stay in Guatemala under the regime of President Jacobo Arbenz, is quite different. John Gerassi, no less a partisan of Che than Marianne Alexandre, tells it in his introduction to *Venceremos*:

> He went to the Ministry of Health and asked to become a staff member in a hospital in Totonicapan, but was told that permission would be granted only if he became a member of the Communist Party. He angrily told the official to go to hell and stalked out.

* New York: Viking Press, 1970.

Among those paying tribute to Che in the Marianne Alexandre collection was Stokely Carmichael, the champion of black power. For him, Che was not dead: "I do not wish to speak of Che as if he were dead. It would not make sense. His ideas are with us. . . ."

Two years later, in April 1970, Carmichael was a guest on David Frost's television show. Frost asked him to name "the white man and the black man you most admire in the world." The black man he most admired, Carmichael replied, was Kwame Nkrumah, the deposed "Redeemer" of Ghana whose five-year dictatorship produced more statues in his honor and other expressions of the "cult of personality" per capita than Stalin in his entire reign. And the white man he most admired? Carmichael had now forgotten Che Guevara. "I would think Adolf Hitler was the most. . . ." Interrupted, according to the *New York Times*, by "gasps, booing and jeering from the studio audience," he hastened to explain that this was not a moral judgment. "But if we're judging his genius objectively, we have to admit that the man was a genius."

It is impossible to list all the various and curious ways in which the myth of Che has been exploited on canvas, in posters, in music, in the performing arts. But some have to be mentioned because they are either amazingly, and unwittingly, truthful, or unbelievably grotesque, or fantastically shameless.

German avant-garde composer Hans Werner Henze told *Granma* in April 1969 that his latest opus was dedicated *al comandante Ernesto Che Guevara* and titled *Le Radeau de la Méduse*, explaining that this was because of "a perfect coincidence between the painting and Che's life." Géricault's famous painting at the Louvre Museum was inspired by a real-life drama of the time: the shipwreck of a boat called *La Méduse* in 1816 off the west coast of Africa. A total of 149 men had clung to a raft after the wreck; when the raft was spotted twelve days later, only fifteen remained, and they were dying.

Che Guevara's tragic adventure in Bolivia can indeed be compared to such a shipwreck, but it is difficult to imagine what positive element Henze and *Granma* found in the "perfect coincidence."

During the same year (1969), at the Holland Festival in Amsterdam, a team of composers and librettists presented an opera called *Reconstruction*. The idea, as summed up without any trace of irony in the French magazine *L'Express*, was a new conception of *Don Juan*: Don Juan represents American imperialism, and the women he rapes represent underdeveloped countries. Thus he violates Bolivia (upon a couch in the shape of South America) and kills her father the Commander, when he comes to defend her. The Commander is none other than Che Guevara, whose giant statue appears for the grand finale.

The most extraordinary product of the exploitation of Che's myth in "art" was a piece of pornographic trash shown in lower Manhattan's Free Store Theater and brazenly named *Che!*

Essentially it was an exhausting catalogue of sexual, and homosexual, practices. According to its author Lennox Raphael, a black "poet" from Trinidad, it "symbolizes the ideological struggle between American imperialism and the revolutionary movements." According to its producer-director Ed Wode, who raised the ticket price to $10, it quickly grossed $50,000 in the small off-off-Broadway theater. According to Martin Gottfried, drama critic of *Women's Wear Daily* who wrote a piece about it in the *New York Times*, "for all its clumsiness" it was, compared to other sex productions, "the only artistically interesting show in the lot." As for me, looking for an "ideological" meaning behind the sexual acrobatics, I could see only that Che was machine-gunned to death by the President of the United

States, before whom he kneeled when his act of fellatio
failed to satisfy the President. Is that what Che did wrong
and why he was killed?

Che Guevara certainly was above not only this type of
"homage" but many others which, although not so filthy,
were equally based on self-interest, distortion, or irresponsible fancy.

He was a complex person. I do not understand how a man
can at the same time hope that his children will refuse to
tolerate injustice and yet coldly plan to terrorize peasants
when he cannot convince them by other means. But his lack
of material interest was absolute; and his sense of equality,
contrary to his sense of justice, was unadulterated.

When I was in Havana in January 1959, speaking with
the *barbudos* who had been with Fidel in the Sierra and on
the long march with Che to Las Villas, I frequently heard
stories about the appetite of Fidel, who demanded triple
rations even when there was not enough to go around for
the other men. This always was told with good humor, with
sympathy, indeed with approval, to emphasize that Fidel
was built and worked like a horse—they called him *el
caballo*—and he of course had to eat accordingly. I never
heard anyone say that Che granted himself the slightest
material privilege or lived better than his men, but it was
quite noticeable that the *barbudos*, while devoted to Che,
were not at ease with him as they were with Fidel and, even
more, with Camilo Cienfuegos.

Che Guevara was not an ordinary man. He would have
pushed aside the tin crown imposed on him by so many
devout followers or cynical politicians, and the plastic
mythology erected around him by so many swindlers or
idiots, fakers, and demagogues. Che Guevara was not
always human. He was sometimes a tragic figure.

The most impressive page of the *Bolivian Diary* is that of
August 8, 1967. It sums up the entire guerrilla war of Che:

its grandeur, if there is a grandeur in such fanatical dedication; its pettiness, and there is pettiness in the greatest enterprises; its failure. Badly conceived, badly equipped, badly justified, spinning in the void, the Bolivian adventure was condemned from the start. Che Guevara, however, did not believe that just enterprises could fail or that sincere ideas could miscarry. He believed that if there was a setback, it was because the men were not equal to the idea or the enterprise.

On August 8, 1967, Che did not write at the top of the page, as he had on other pages: "A black day." There had been no military difficulties, none of his men had fallen uselessly. But Che realized that he had arrived at a turning point.

His asthma was crushing him. (What we know today about the origins and effects of chronic asthma, persisting into adulthood, should help to throw light on the personality and behavior of Che.) His tired mare was not moving fast enough, and Che became so angry that he jabbed his knife into the horse's neck. That night he gathers his men around him. He first says that he has become "a human rag" and that the episode of the horse proves that he sometimes loses his self-control. He does not doubt, however, that as far as he is concerned, "this will change." What he wants is that the burden of the situation be equally shared among all members of the group.

Then he states for one last time his unchanging truth: "This type of struggle gives us the chance to convert ourselves into revolutionaries, the highest level of the human race, but it also permits us to graduate as men; those who cannot attain either of these two stages must say so and abandon the struggle."

A fanatic as absolute as Che Guevara may inspire respect, fear, respect mixed with fear, aversion, disgust, resistance. He can be contagious, but only for other fanatics, or for weaklings. He cannot be considered "the most complete man of his time," as Jean-Paul Sartre proclaimed him. He cannot serve as an example for future generations, as Fidel Castro proposed when he shouted: "Let them be like Che!"

If the men of tomorrow are to be capable of feeling deep inside any injustice committed against anyone anywhere in the world, they cannot applaud Comrade Arnet for working like a slave 1,607 hours in six months; they cannot consider it normal that men should be sent to crush stones in the Guanahacabibes peninsula by decision of a ministry; they cannot accept as a democracy a regime in which the people's role is to vibrate like a tuning fork for the intuitive method of a *jefe máximo*.

They cannot believe that the true individual is the man who educates himself until he feels fully adequate to the new social power; that all individuals must form an immense column at the head of which marches the leader followed by the cadres of the party; and that those revolutionaries of the vanguard are too important to share a little dose of daily affection with ordinary men.

They cannot call peasants little animals because they do not know how to talk to them, or imagine that a massacre of miners can light up a panorama, or judge that the place of a Huber Matos is in prison. They cannot dream of massacres and destructions, either in the United States or elsewhere, and hope to be impelled beyond the natural limitations of man to become a cold killing machine.

If the men of tomorrow are to be capable of feeling deep inside any injustice committed against anyone, anywhere in the world, they cannot be like Che Guevara.

Paris, 1971
New York, 1973

Index